THE ASSET

The Asset is adapted, modified and up-dated from the novel *Den vidunderliga utsikten* (*An Amazing View,* originally published in Swedish), by the author.
It was translated to the English by Line Valen.

Cover design by
https://peggydesmons.wixsite.com/cekwasa

©**2019 by M Gustafsson**
ISBN 978-0-9899880-8-7
Published by Paperless Reads

M Gustafsson has three former books in Swedish in the Klara Andersson series.

Reviews in Swedish media:

This is intelligent entertainment, that is, both exciting and full of facts. MARI PETERSON, DAGENS NYHETER

A start with a bang... M Gustafsson has potential, so much is evident. ULF ÖRNKLOO, DEADLINE, SWEDISH PUBLIC RADIO

M Gustafsson's book is convincing and fast-paced and that is promising for future books. CRISTER ENANDER, HELSING-BORGS DAGBLAD

Impresses the reader being well informed, knowledgeable and credible. HELENA SIGANDER, DAST

THE ASSET
M GUSTAFSSON

This book is dedicated to my family. Thank you all for your patience, help and understanding.

CHAPTER ONE

Amsterdam

The acrid smell of burnt plastic forced her to open her eyes. She couldn't remember who she was... Everything was white. Someone was groaning. Her throat felt raspy and dry. It hurt with every sound. Then she realized that the moans were coming from her. Her head was throbbing so hard she was getting nauseous. She tried to focus, careful not to move, and saw that she was trapped in a narrow space.

The ability to think seemed to return in bursts. She was on the floor in an awkward position next to a toilet bowl. Several tiles had come off the wall and had broken on impact with the floor. The need to vomit forced her up.

As she steadied herself, other voices from outside the lavatory and distant shrill hysterical screams frightened her.

She had to pull herself together. Get out of there. Instinctively clutching her handbag, she pushed the door open. Outside the restroom a fog of fine gray dust suspended in the air made her cough. There were people on the floor, some unconscious and bleeding. The dust from the debris powdered everything gray. A woman with a gash on the back of her head was trying to get up from the floor.

As she kneeled to help the woman, someone shouted: "Everybody who can walk, get out of here *now!*"

Unable to think clearly, she got up and mechanically obeyed the command. The door at the end of the narrow hallway was bent and twisted, hanging from one hinge. On the threshold to the larger room, she froze. Her hand flew up to her mouth.

Dante's inferno, she thought. *Please, God, let me wake up.*

Pieces of furniture, shards of glass, and tattered remnants of clothes were mixed with severed limbs from an unknown number of bodies. A bloody slush covered the floor. There was an eerie sound: a chorus of crying men. High-pitched broken voices merged with wailing in darker tones. A hysterical scream suddenly stopped and turned into loud sobbing. Close to her there was a man on the floor cradling one of his arms as if it were a baby, rocking soundlessly back and forth. A bit further away another man, bleeding profusely from a wound in the chest, was just sitting there, staring, shocked beyond the limits of consciousness. A woman sat stroking a man's hand, but the arm ended at the elbow, in a sharp fragment of bone detached from the body. Their silence was so palpable that it emphasized the other sounds, making the room throb with grief and pain.

The large room, though unrecognizable, brought back her memory: She was Klara Andersson and she had been engaged as an interpreter at an extraordinary meeting of the North Atlantic Treaty Organization.

At one end of the room, there had been a glass wall. Only sharp shards remained around the edges, glittering in the sunshine. At the opposite end of the hall, a large piece of fabric had been hanging on the wall. You could still see the motif: the member states' flags surrounding NATO's own and today's date, though it was now burned and tattered, heavily stained with blood.

The interpreter booths flanking the other two walls had caved in like a house of cards. Where were her colleagues? Running from the door, she dropped to her knees and tore at the bits of paneling, trying to move them aside. A broken piece of a blister pack stung her palm. *Nico...* was printed on the metal foil. She dropped it and picked up a piece of a panel.

"Stop that immediately and get out of here," someone shouted, yanking her arm.

She let go of the piece of laminate as if it had burned her and looked up. A man in a dark suit looking incongruously clean nodded in the direction she had come from. "To the emergency exit," he commanded. "Now."

She joined a stunned stream of people looking like rag dolls limping out of the venue. At the bottom of the stairs, the doors were wide open.

Grateful for the fresh air, she sank down on the steps outside. The riot barriers had been pushed aside to make space for emergency vehicles and police cars with blue lights just arriving. An EMT running up the stairs made her move to one side. The first ambulance left. Camera flashes emanated from the crowd gathered by the fences.

She sat there, numb, still unable to grasp what had happened. Her head ached so badly it felt like it would explode, and the dizziness made her nauseous again.

Someone put a jacket over her shoulders, took hold of her arm and pulled her to her feet.

"Glad you made it, Klara," a remotely familiar voice said. She slowly managed to focus ... and burst into tears.

CHAPTER TWO

Stockholm, late summer, ten months earlier

Klara stepped out of the oversized, heavy duty elevator into the reception area of TV Plus, one of the larger commercial TV channels in Sweden. The old lightbulb factory had been tastefully restored, maintaining some of its original personality. High ceilings and an atrium made it light and airy. She glanced to her right, the executive area, but it was too early for any of the bosses to be around.

She turned left, towards the small office she shared with two of her colleagues. Her steps echoed as she crossed the large cubicle landscape where most of the other production teams shared space. After the summer vacation, she had received an offer to take over as production manager for Documentaries & Current Affairs, and her first week on the job had been all she had hoped for.

Klara unlocked the door and put her jacket on the back of the chair while powering up the computer. She seemed to be the only living soul there. There were four of them working full time on the project, but Nicklas, the producer, had an office of his own. That was just another detail that contributed to the feeling of being privileged within the company. The owner himself had approved their budget, and it was unusually generous for a private broadcaster mainly focused on entertainment. Her two colleagues' desks were placed perpendicular to the window, with the perk of a view of Hammarby Canal. On the left was Robert, a journalist, acting as both researcher and scriptwriter, and on the right Richard, the director. When she joined, they had just placed her desk at the short end of theirs. She wasn't crazy about sitting with her back to the door, but the room was small and it seemed the only way to fit the three of them in there.

The glossy black surface of the large monitor they shared for screening recordings reflected her image. Somewhat surprised, she saw that she was smiling. It had been a long time since she had felt that way.

Last fall, when she found out that Manuel, her husband, was having an affair with a younger woman, she fled Spain. Almost two decades of love, unreserved intimacy and loyalty had vanished in one devastating blow. She'd thought she would never get over the grief. It was so cliché she had never imagined that it could happen to her.

A job as a production manager with TV-Plus Entertainment had buried her in work and immersed her in another kind of daze. Seven days a week, live broadcast on Saturdays, reviewing costs and expenses on Sundays, only to start all over with preparations for the next show on Mondays. She had succeeded in forgetting all about herself.

Studying her reflection in the monitor again, she realized that the make-over she had done after the divorce wasn't bad at all. The mahogany-colored bob became her and was a break with her blond past. She was ready to get on with her life.

They were producing a documentary on intelligence services. A number of agents from the CIA and the former KGB, now called FSB, were lined up for interviews. Ex-agents rather, as only people who had left active service were allowed to talk to the media. Part of the program was already recorded; the team had traveled to Israel to interview a couple of agents from Mossad before she had joined them.

Once up to speed, she would be able to contribute to the production in more creative ways. The monitor was on, and she clicked on the folder with the recordings from Israel.

"Klara, I didn't expect you here so early."

Robert's voice startled her. She turned to face him. He was struggling to pull down his shirt over his still moist upper body. His hair was wet. "On nice mornings like this, I often run to the office and shower here," he explained while he finished dressing and sat down at his desk.

"I'm sorry," she mumbled, not quite sure what she was apologizing for. Robert was in his early thirties, bright and friendly, but the familiarity made her feel awkward. "I have a scheduled call with the Germans in ten," she said, changing the subject.

"That interview with Markus Wolf?" he asked and when she nodded he went on: "We're lucky you came with language skills. It would have taken us ages and cost fortunes to get the interviews translated from German, just to know which parts we wanted."

"This footage is great. He's quite outspoken about the interrogation methods he approved as head of STASI." She was proud to have contributed something useful already.

"What was the full name?"

"Of the STASI? The East German Ministry for State Security." she answered.

"Yes, that. It has to be right for the credits." He wrote it down on a notepad.

"Have you read Le Carré?" she asked. "Did you know Wolf is the character he calls Karla in his books?"

"Of course I do. How on earth would I have qualified to work on a program about intelligence services if I hadn't?"

Klara smiled.

"But did you know that the Swedish Secret Police had the only picture of Wolf that existed until the wall fell and he went public?" asked Robert.

"I had no idea. Maybe SÄPO is more efficient than they want us to know?" She was genuinely surprised.

"Maybe they are. Wolf was in Stockholm once, and they took the picture, though at first they didn't know who he was. There was no way to identify the man in the photo."

"Amazing."

"But you go on screening now. It doesn't bother me at all," Robert said, just as the telephone rang.

The stock-footage sales person from ZDF, one of the public TV channels, called with German punctuality. Klara managed to negotiate a good price in exchange for mentioning the company in the credits.

When she finished the call, Robert had gone into work mode, somehow managing to bolt down a sandwich while typing at great speed.

Klara decided to screen one of the interviews. At the briefing, Nicklas, the producer, had told her that the retired agent Reuven Levi had been candid and that it would make great television. Levi came to life on the screen. He seemed to be rather short, in his late 60s, stocky with almost no neck. Pale grayish brown crew cut and steel-gray, lively eyes. Like a vivacious grandfather. His smile promised a sense of humor. Levi was the only person appearing in this recording, but she could hear Robert's voice on the audio track.

She kept the sound low so as not to disturb him.

They were talking about the murder of Swedish Prime Minister Olof Palme, back in the mid-eighties, and what Mossad had done as soon as it became known.

Smart way to tie in Sweden, she thought.

Levi explained how they had compared notes with the other intelligence services, surprisingly even with the STA-SI... Klara had not expected the two agencies to be on speaking terms.

Klara's thoughts meandered. She remembered Palme's visit to Spain a few years before he was murdered. Felipe Gonzalez, the Spanish PM at the time, and his deputy Alfonso Guerra, both from the Spanish Socialist party, had spoken warmly and widely about having been welcomed by the Social Democrats in Sweden during the last few years of the Franco dictatorship, when the party was still illegal in Spain. Although she was just a teenager at the time, living with her parents on the Canary Islands, she had been proud to know that her country had been loyal to the Spanish Socialist Party in difficult times.

Lost in thought, she almost jumped when Robert stopped typing and shouted: "There it is! Rewind a little."

She realized she must have missed something important.

'... *peace conference...*' said Levi on the video.

"A bit farther back," he said, excited.

She found his question on the video:

'*... if you can tell us about some cooperation with the Swedish Intelligence Agencies?*'

'*I'm sure you understand that is impossible. But I can tell you something about a Swedish individual who actually made a well-planned mission of ours fail. That all started at the Madrid Peace Conference in October 1991, if you remember?*'

Klara perked up. *Wait, at my first international interpreting job?* She remembered the endless security procedures just to get in to the crowded room at the Royal Palace. She didn't have a lot of experience yet; it was only her third or fourth gig. The conference language was English. She only had to interpret about fifteen minutes in all when Spanish was spoken: the brief opening address by the Spanish Prime Minister, and some household information at some point during the day. She had been hired because she was in Madrid, and only for the first day of the five-day conference. The organization had not wanted to fork out for flying someone in from Sweden. She had doubted whether to take on the assignment, intimidated by the importance of the event, but in the end they had convinced her, playing on her sense of duty.

She hardly remembered anything of what had been discussed. When the brain is busy listening to the 'source language' and rendering what is said into the 'target language' with only a short delay, it doesn't quite have the capacity to retain much of the content.

'Can you elaborate on that, please?' Robert's voice asked on the video, returning Klara to the present.

'At the Peace Conference, one of the participants was Atef Bseiso. He was the top intelligence aide to Yasir Arafat. You remember Arafat, the chairman of the Palestine Liberation Organization,' explained Levi in the recording. *'We didn't know it at the time, but there, Bseiso established contact with a Swede from the Conference organization.'*

A Swede? Impossible. Levi was wrong. There had not been any Swedes within the organization, apart from herself. She was sure. She had attended several informational meetings and later been back to receive the draft of Gonzalez's welcome speech.

Apart from the guests, Palme, Sten Andersson, Minister of Foreign Affairs at the time but not for much longer, and Pierre Schori, the Secretary General of the Socialist Party, there had been no other Swedes present.

What was Levi talking about?

That was also why it had been weird that her voluminous Swedish-Spanish dictionary had been stolen. After the morning coffee break it was simply gone.

Klara was excited, it was like an ace up her sleeve that she had been present at that Peace Conference. She wanted to tell Robert and paused the video.

"You know, I was actually—"

"Oh, shit. I'm super late," he interrupted. "I booked a microfilm reader at the library." He nodded towards the monitor urging her on. "Try to finish screening the material. Ah, and I may not be back today."

"See you tomorrow then," she answered flatly, and feeling a little self-conscious she started the video again.

'Please tell us more.' She could hear Robert's excitement.

'About a year later, Bseiso arrived in Madrid from Washington. We had planned to take him in for interrogation, suspecting that he had been a part of Black September. If that was confirmed, we would have put him away for good. We informed The Spanish Intelligence Organization, CSID, because we wanted it to be a discreet affair. I am not at liberty to reveal the details, but this Swede helped him slip through our fingers and escape to Paris.' Levi paused as if recalling. *'We got Bseiso anyway. Only now it got messy because we had to improvise and ended up killing him. He was shot in the street outside his hotel. It was unfortunate, because it led to complications with the French, who were unhappy about the media repercussions, and the CIA, who was furious because Bseiso was their key contact with the PLO."* He paused again, and said: *'But, terrorists we kill, no doubt about that,'* as if showing off to the Swedish journalist asking the questions.

Klara shuddered. Levi sounded so matter of fact about killing someone. As if the problem was that they ended up all over the news.

It was strange, that something she had experienced so long ago, in another country and with a totally different job, suddenly appeared to be connected to her present life here, in Sweden.

She wanted to tell Robert about the Peace Conference first thing tomorrow, and decided to halt the recording at that point and instead view another. She checked her list. There was just one more video she hadn't yet seen. As far as they knew, nobody else had been allowed access to Mossad's terrorist database, much less record it. Well-edited, that piece might prove sensational.

The video buffered up and started showing a man in his forties, slender, with dark hair and bad skin, next to a computer talking about the database.

Ten minutes later Klara was sitting straight as a rod staring at the frozen image on the monitor.

There was a picture of her, taken some twenty years ago. The text *Al-Fatah Agent* was written in bold letters beside the photo, and a series of names and places she had never heard of. *Under deep cover. Believed to remain active,* the quote ended.

Reacting, she desperately pressed the button on the remote again and again. *Why isn't the damn thing working?* Looking over her shoulder, she saw that the other departments were full of people. The office was like an aquarium; three of the walls, including the window, were partially glass and the blinds were not drawn. They could see the screen, but for once, she was glad to be with her back to them, because she was sure they could have seen how scared she was.

When the screen finally went black—she had been turning it on and off all the time—she took a deep breath to compose herself. Tried to think, but the wheels of her mind seemed to turn in slow motion. Only someone who had known her back then could possibly see that she was the person in the picture. Then she had long, blonde hair and no bangs. Now her hair was mahogany red and cut in a short bob. The year of birth stated was incorrect, it made her ten years older, well over fifty—and she knew she looked younger than that. She recognized the photo, but was just too upset to remember where it was taken.

Why would she be in Mossad's terrorist database classified as a Palestine agent?

CHAPTER THREE

Klara could not fathom how her picture had ended up in the terrorist database. She had to find out where that photo had come from. She recognized it, but couldn't quite place it. At home she leafed through her old photo albums. It was not there, nor in the large envelopes with old stills that had never found their way into them.

Deep in the walk-in closet there was a plastic bin with some keepsakes. She found a small white plastic ID-card. That was it. The picture in Mossad's database was from her New York University student ID.

It was time to call Louis Hornett, her contact in New York. The man in the video said that Mossad shared their database with colleagues in the US, so he ought to know something about that.

"He retired, Ma'am," an impersonal female voice answered.

"He must have left a number, or a way to reach him," Klara said, trying to keep her voice under control. *How many years had it been since they last spoke? Five,* she thought. *Too long.*

"I am sorry, Miss Andersson, but I am not at liberty to forward that."

"You tell him to call me. Today." She was trembling inside. He had made her memorize this number and promised he would always respond if she needed him.

"I'll do that, but there is no guarantee as to when that may be, just so you know. Goodbye now." She hung up.

Speechless, Klara stared at the phone in her hand. She was scared and felt betrayed. The prospect of waiting days on end for him to get back to her felt unbearable.

Too nervous and upset to get any rest, she took a sleeping pill and went to bed. Of course she dreamed: crowds of people and interpreter booths. She woke up drenched in sweat from a nightmare: she was trying to escape through a crowd from a tangible but indeterminate threat.

Wide awake, she checked her cell phone.

Oh no, five-thirty. She was exhausted and had hoped for a few more hours sleep.

The sun shone right at her through the bedroom window. She loved the light of early summer mornings and could not bring herself to shut it out. This time of the year they still had fifteen hours of daylight and no real night, just twilight, from about 10:30 pm to 3:30 am. On sunny days like this, she had the energy to do things she otherwise found boring, like cleaning or ironing, but not now; she was too anxious.

Her efforts to go back to sleep were to no avail. Hoping it would help her relax, at least for a while, she picked up the newspaper. Having it delivered right to the door was an expensive luxury that would soon be gone, the newspapers had warned.

She went to work early again. While unlocking the office door she saw through the glass that there was a photocopy of a newspaper clipping on her desk. Robert must have put it there.

The clipping was from 1992, the New York Times. The headline read: OFFICIAL OF PLO IS KILLED IN PARIS. Holding her breath, she went on reading. *'The official, Atef Bseiso, 44 years old, top intelligence aide to the PLO chairman Yasir*

22

Arafat, was killed by shots fired by at least one gun equipped with a silencer, Palestinian and French officials declared. Two gunmen escaped after the killing.'

Her heart almost stopped when she looked at the picture. It was a headshot of a male somewhere between thirty and forty, round face with protruding ears disguised under long hair, dark, clean-shaven. She had a good photographic memory for faces, and she recognized the man. At first she couldn't remember the context, but she knew she had seen those eyes with the heavy lids, the large nose and the full lower lip before. But then he had a beard.

"What do you think of that?" Robert came in balancing a cup of coffee in one hand and a sandwich with cheese and Kalles, the creamed cod roe all Swedes love, in the other.

"I haven't had time to read it yet."

"It happened while you were living in Madrid. You must have read it in the papers."

Klara looked up from the clipping.

"I don't remember the attack in Paris. Maybe the Spanish press wasn't so interested."

"Well, you heard Levi. Now we can substantiate it, if we decide to use it. What do you think?"

"Makes good TV. He actually admits that they kill people," she answered.

Her eyes went back to the picture in the news article. As she thought of the man with a beard, a memory surfaced. There had been five interpreters' booths by the back wall, for German, English, Swedish, French, and Italian, at the Peace Conference. This dark, tall, powerful man had been walking about in front of the booths, looking out of place. He was dressed in fatigues, not the traditional long white shirt the other Arabs were wearing. She had noticed him because he had been standing for some time, and she remembered thinking that he might not have a seat. Everyone else had been assigned a chair. Afterwards, when she discovered that her dictionary had disappeared, the thought passed her mind that he had taken it. But that was absurd, he couldn't possibly have had any use for it.

So, it was true, she had been at the same event as Atef Bseiso, the man Mossad had killed in Paris and Levi claimed had met with some Swede at the Conference. A sudden whiff of cold air made her rub her upper arms with her palms. Now she debated whether to tell Robert about having been at the event or not. He was smart, and might crave more explanations than she was ready to give.

"Did you finish screening the material?" Robert asked, turning on the monitor. "Did you see the database?"

"Yes, yes, I finished that one," she lied. "Impressive. I have about ten minutes left of the interview with Levi."

The video caught Levi saying:

'It took us quite some time and effort to find out who had helped Bseiso to escape in Madrid.'

Klara held her breath again, hoping to learn something more.

'The fact that a Swede was involved was most unexpected and disturbing. But it was a long time ago, and by now I believe it is safe to reveal that it was a woman.'

It felt like the walls were closing in on her.

Does Levi believe that the Swede at the Conference was me?

She got up and went to the bathroom. There were paper cups by the sink and she helped herself to a glass of water. Closing the door to a stall, she put the lid down and sat there thinking while she sipped. The cold water cleared her mind. The first step, until she heard from Louis, was to gather more information about Mossad. Her presence at the conference could hardly be incriminating; she had not exchanged a single word with that man.

But she knew there were few things more lethal than to be considered a terrorist by an intelligence agency.

CHAPTER FOUR

Knowing more about Mossad might help Klara decide what to do about the picture. Robert's research before going to Israel was probably more extensive than anything she could find on her own.

Turning to him, she said, "I feel I need some background on Mossad. I hardly know anything apart from the name."

"Sure, I'll mail you the folder. I summarized what I could find, but they run a tight ship, so I guess nobody gets to know the really juicy stuff."

She learned that Mossad became known to the public when Black September, a Palestinian organization, kidnapped and murdered Israeli athletes and coaches at the Olympics in Munich in 1972. It was a blow to Israel's prestige. A small group within the government decided that Mossad should systematically pursue and eliminate all terrorists involved. Operation *Wrath of God*, aka *Operation Bayonet,* marked the start of Mossad's ever more professionally executed *wet jobs*.

The German police shot the perpetrators directly involved during the final stage of the drama, at the military airport Fürstenfeldbruck. But Mossad had orders to take out the others—those who had planned the attack and were safely hidden in Lebanon, Jordan, and other places around the world.

Klara shuddered, remembering Levi declaring with a smile: *'But, terrorists we kill, no doubt about that,'* on the video.

Time did not seem to matter, she learned. Well into the 1990's they were still pursuing Black September associates.

"I remember this," Klara said out loud. "This execution style hit in Madrid. But at the time, the media never mentioned Mossad."

"Which one was that?" Robert was instantly interested.

"I never knew the name, but here it says it was Zaki Helon. They mowed him down from a passing motorcycle while stuck in a traffic jam. Very close to downtown Madrid, by the Arch of Triumph at Moncloa. The passenger shot from the back seat. Both the driver and the shooter wore helmets with dark face-shields, and they disappeared from the scene before anybody knew what happened."

"That is a typical Mossad wet job. Not a trace of the perpetrators," Robert said. "They are out of the country before anyone has time to react." He paused, "Sometimes maybe the police get orders to not even look for them."

There was no suspicion of Mossad being involved in the murder of the Swedish PM Olof Palme, in spite of his sympathies for Arafat, Robert concluded in his research. Why kill Palme if they could kill Arafat himself? There was proof that they had Arafat in their cross hairs more than once during that period, but the order to kill was never given.

Robert had found a few particularly spectacular cases attributed to the Israeli Intelligence Service. One of them happened on Crete. The cleaning lady was bribed to call in sick and a bomb was planted under the bed by the person replacing her. When the terrorist was sound asleep, someone from Mossad called and the ring tone triggered the explosion.

Richard, the director, barged into the office. He was editing in another building and they hadn't seen him in a few days.

"How's it coming along?" Klara asked. She noticed that a couple of women outside the fishbowl were ogling him. Richard was good-looking. In fact, the women at TV Plus had elected him *Man of the Year* at the Christmas party.

He pretended to fall into his chair feigning extreme fatigue. "I'm exhausted. I see moving images even when I close my eyes," he complained. "No, seriously, I have run out of material. I have finished editing almost exactly 15 minutes of the material from Israel. I don't think we should give the Mossad more time."

"No, that's plenty," Robert said. "You have to leave room for the CIA and KGB or FBS. Plus something from that fantastic interview with Markus Wolf that Klara just bought."

"Yeah, true. So we got Wolf? Great. What else have you two been up to? I suppose Robert by now has taught you how to look busy doing nothing, just as he does."

"Klara is reading up on Mossad," Robert said, not taking offence. "Don't you think the most spectacular kill was the one with the cell phone?"

"Al-Hamid, was it? That guy who never spent two nights in the same place. Yea, that was really creepy."

"Tell me, then I don't have to read it." she said.

"Sometime in the late 1980s, Al-Fatah started using cell telephones for communications and coordination. And, of course, Mossad had the technology not only to listen in, but also to trace a call, geographically."

"Okay. So, then they could localize him?" she said.

"Not quite, but it was a step in the right direction," Richard added.

"After some time, they decided to produce a very special cell phone. It looked like any other; even if you took it apart, you wouldn't detect anything unusual. Until the right moment, it was just a regular mobile phone. And they managed to place it with Al-Hamid's people."

"Remember, we're talking about long before the 'burner phones' were invented. The problem was that Sidi Al-Hamid rarely picked up or made a call more than once from the same phone. So, Mossad had no option but to bide their time. It was like: *May Allah give you the patience to sit at your door until your enemy's funeral procession passes by,*" Richard dramatized.

"Oh, come on, what happened next?" she asked.

"You are not appreciating my storytelling talent?" Richard pouted. "Impatient, are you? Well then, let me tell you: One night, I think we are now in the middle of the nineties, the inevitable happened. The Mossad-device rang, and Sidi picked up the call. It lasted exactly 14 seconds, the Mossad people boast about this, then the telephone exploded in his ear and blew him away together with some of his bodyguards."

"This was still part of Operation *The Wrath of God*. There are rumors that it is still an active operation..." Robert clarified and continued. "Off the record they told us that operations like the one in Dubai when they entered with false British passports and killed that Hamas leader are over for now. The UK is a friendly nation, but they were not informed in advance, and were really pissed. So now they are concentrating on smart bombs. Small devices with a lot of power that they can plant and then detonate when they choose, from a distance. Like the one on Crete."

They remained silent for a beat. It seemed inappropriate to be joking about death and revenge.

Klara got up. "I'm going to the kitchen. Anyone want a coffee?"

She had to get out of there for a while. Mossad was clearly one of the most efficient and lethal secret services in the world, capable of keeping an operation alive for over 40 years. And she was in their database, classified as a Palestine terrorist. She was really scared, even if they had the name and the date of birth wrong.

CHAPTER FIVE

The next day Klara was composing a rather formal email in English, requesting meetings with a number of prominent politicians and heads of state for a future program. It was hard to find the right words to convince these high-ranking personalities to set aside time for a recorded interview with some un-known journalist from a small private Swedish TV-channel. And of course for the ratings, famous international politicians were "the more, the better."

She almost jumped when her private cell phone rang.

Please, let it be Louis, she prayed.

"Klara here," she answered.

"Hi, this is Helena from Polyglott. Is this a bad time?"

A little embarrassed for having sounded so curt addressing her agent, she changed tone.

"No, not at all. I was just concentrating on what I'm doing. How's life treating you?"

"Fine, thanks. I'm not going to take a lot of your time, but we just got a last-minute request. Some officers from Chile are visiting Karlskrona shipyard and it has only just occurred to them that their guests don't speak English. They hope to have help from tomorrow 9 a.m. for two days and promised to take a break every two hours. Are you interested?"

"Yes," Klara welcomed the opportunity to, for a couple of days, concentrate on something besides the picture in the database and the endless wait for Louis to get back to her. The extra income would also be welcome; 15, 000 Swedish krona for the two days would make a huge difference at the end of the month. "But I have to ask Nicklas, the producer, for permission. May I call you back in an hour?"

"As soon as possible, please. You know, if you can't make it, I have to step on it to find somebody else."

"Certainly, but you can count on me."

Nicklas had his own office and only came in for meetings. From her place she could see he wasn't there now. She pushed the papers aside and called his cell phone.

No answer.

Where the hell was he? Miffed that he had not told her where he was going or why he wouldn't be answering the phone, she locked the office and went to ask at the front desk. There was a large blackboard on the wall where everyone was supposed to write a number where they could be reached when they left the office, but since they all had a cellphone no one used it anymore.

The switchboard girl nodded towards the exec area. "He's in a meeting with Ubbe," she said.

Having spent half her life in Spain, Klara found the Swedish habit of abbreviating names—Nicke for Nicklas, Ubbe for Urban, and Robban for Robert—amusing, particularly for grown-ups. Here it was supposed to indicate a flat hierarchy.

"Thank you," she said and headed that way.

Ubbe was, among a number of other things, deputy CEO. His and Nicke's meetings could be about anything, because they were friends and often spent hours just talking. She knocked on the door.

"May I have a word, Nicke?"

Nicke looked irritated when she told him that she needed to take two days off. She didn't want to tell him the truth because she was afraid he might refuse.

"You know I just moved back to Sweden. Something has come up that I need to attend to. I'm sorry, but I really need these two days." Then she got an idea: "I can catch up during the weekend. I'll come in Saturday and Sunday and finish writing the letters and get some twenty-odd more mailed by Monday, I promise."

"Well, all right. If you promise it won't delay us," he said. "But please don't make this a habit."

It was humiliating to have to ask for permission from a guy younger than herself and with considerably less experience. She had been a producer herself for almost a decade, managed her professional life and produced more than a hundred broadcast hours. Of course she knew that time was of the essence to keep costs at a minimum. She had applied for the job as production manager at TV-Plus, far below her actual professional level, when she realized that merits from abroad did not count for much in Sweden. Fourteen years at Spanish Public TV, the last seven as executive producer, had only reluctantly been considered sufficient qualification by her present bosses.

She sighed and called Helena to confirm the job.

CHAPTER SIX

There were not a lot of people on the morning plane to Ronneby. Sleepy businessmen and some military officers in uniform. Klara used the time to prepare naval terminology, a field she had not come across before. She had searched on the Internet, read a few articles about the Swedish and Chilean navies, but without a clue as to what the meeting was about, that was hardly satisfactory. The glossary was just one and a half pages. Hopefully she would get a chance to talk to someone before the meeting started.

On arrival, a man approached her. He was in his forties, tall and fair-haired, wearing a suit and a trench-coat.

"Klara Andersson?" he asked, with a friendly smile. "Pär Westman. How fortunate that you could make it on such short notice. We usually get to borrow interpreters from the Armed Forces, but this time they couldn't help us."

Interpreters from the Armed Forces, she thought, *then they are used to getting the correct terminology.*

"I hope you can help me a little before we start, because I don't know much about ships in general and warships in particular," she said, hoping her smile would project all the confidence she was lacking.

"What do you mean?" he looked puzzled.

"Well, like the specific naval terminology."

He laughed.

"This is purely a courtesy call. The official handover of the ship. But the Karlskrona shipyard is almost legendary, it was there before the town, so they will do a walking tour, see the museum and eat well. I'm trying to arrange for the Navy to pick us up by submarine for a dinner out in the archipelago." He paused. "I'll join you then."

"Wait, wasn't there an incident with a Soviet submarine once?" she asked.

"Yes, a Soviet submarine carrying nuclear weapons was stranded here in '81. The official story doesn't tell whether the captain was drunk or tried to defect, but we had to let him go." Pär smiled. "The incident was called 'Whiskey on the rocks' because the submarine was of a type called 'Whiskey' and it ran aground on rocks in the shallows of the archipelago."

He had a charming smile and now that she knew this was just a courtesy visit, she relaxed.

"So, you aren't attending the meeting?"

"No, I have nothing at all to do with frigates. I'm working on the Visby project. But ask anything you want. I'll help you out if I can."

He seemed somehow low-key and intense at the same time, she thought. There was an air of discipline, a military bearing, in the way he held her arm to guide her to the car. She could smell his aftershave. Old Spice. A little old-fashioned, but it suited him.

She was sitting turned towards him on the passenger seat, and his hand brushed her knee when he changed gears.

"I'm sorry," he said, obviously embarrassed, pulling his hand away as if the touch had burned him.

Klara didn't know if she should apologize too, but she just shifted in her seat instead.

She took out the glossary she had prepared from her brown, soft-leather briefcase and started asking questions and taking notes. Pär gave her the words in Swedish so that she could look up the Spanish equivalents.

They drove along a road with water on both sides. Two large churches evoking a more grandiose past flanked an open square by the charming and picturesque city center. As they drove through a park with a yellow house on the right, Pär pointed to the Naval Officers' mess.

"That's where you'll have lunch," he said

"But I thought the shipyard didn't belong to the Navy anymore?"

"You're right, it doesn't. The German HDW let go of us some time ago, and Celsius Technology bought the shipyard. They are part of the Saab Group, so fortunately we're back in Swedish hands." He smiled and looked a little embarrassed. "Sorry for the TMI, that was probably much more than you wanted to know. As a matter of fact, we're not even called Karlskrona shipyard anymore. It's Kockums."

"I always thought Kockums was the shipyard in Malmö."

"We merged a long time ago and had to change the name."

"That doesn't sound like such a good idea. Karlskrona shipyard must be both senior to and more technically advanced than Kockums?"

"Right, Kockums in Malmö doesn't even exist anymore, but we never got our name back," he said.

Right past the officers' mess they came to a fence with surveillance cameras and a guard's hut. Pär went in and arranged for a visitor's pass for Klara.

Inside the shipyard, the old mast derrick dominated the area. They pulled up outside the tall building, its enormous wooden doors wide open. The second floor had been transformed into a conference room. Carefully restored, it had a low ceiling with dark, rough roof beams and walls in dark, old brick. It held all the equipment you would expect in a modern conference room.

After they entered the meeting room, Pär stood within her personal space. It felt awkward and too intimate. She took a step to the side, putting distance between them. Two men approached them, one average height and the other unusually tall even for a Swede. Both looked like they had forgotten how to laugh. There was something military about them as well, and Klara wondered if that was a requirement when you were contractors for the Armed Forces.

"Klara, this is Bengt Lindmark and Arne Berg. Klara Andersson." They shook hands. Berg was the tall one.

"Arne, plan for the meeting to be finished by two pm tomorrow," Pär said, as if giving an order. "I'm changing Klara's reservation so we can take the afternoon flight to Stockholm."

Berg nodded. "That won't be a problem," he promised. "You're coming to the dinner, I take it?"

Pär answered that he would be there, and they spoke about the planned submarine tour before he left.

Klara was as puzzled by his behaviour toward Berg and Lindmark as she was about his demeanor toward her.

Then she concentrated on the task at hand. Past the vast conference table of shiny worn wood, there were a couple of trays with coffee pumps, milk and sugar, and cookies. She feared the Chileans' reactions to the usually very weak Swedish filter coffee. In the interest of international relations somebody ought to issue a warning: never, ever, serve Scandinavian coffee to Latin Americans.

Three Chilean officers arrived, accompanied by a young Swede. The guests were dressed in dark uniforms with chalk-white shirts. She heard the young Swede click his heels before he turned and left.

The Chileans were heavy-set and not particularly tall, all three with mustaches of various types. They had the Latino twinkle in their eyes and expressed their appreciation of Klara's command of their language.

"Are you Spanish?" one of them asked, hinting at her accent.

"No, I'm Swedish, but I lived in Madrid for twenty years."

"You must have moved there as a baby," another one joked gallantly.

They sat down at the table. Mr Berg gave a formal welcome speech and Klara took notes while he talked. It took up several pages of her steno pad. She then leafed back and rendered, supported by her scribbles, what he had said into Spanish.

In response, the highest-ranking Chilean officer thanked the Swedes for receiving them and handed over an antique spyglass as a gift. It was much appreciated, as was the story about the old Spanish shipwreck it had been recovered from.

Before she knew it, it was time for a quick lunch. After dessert, the visitors were taken for a tour of the shipyard. They walked past the composite workshop, where *Smyge*, an ugly, angular boat that hardly looked seaworthy, was moored.

"What on earth is that?" one of the Admirals asked. Klara was as curious as he was.

"That is the pilot project for the shipyard's pride and joy, the YS 2000 also called the Visby-type corvette." Yet another serious and dogged-looking middle-aged man had joined the group and answered the question. "It is built of carbon fiber, in sections, in the composite workshop and then joined on-site." The guests were invited to take a look at the work in progress.

Klara couldn't help feeling pride in the ultra-modern, high-tech and obviously unique ship that Pär Westman, her new acquaintance, was working on. Something like this should be the object of much stricter security, she thought.

The navy did not pick them up in the submarine, instead dinner took place at the Naval Museum. There, Pär joined the group again. He immediately approached her.

"Did it go well?" he asked bending over and kissing her on the cheek, dangerously close to her mouth.

"I... I think so," she answered, bewildered.

Why is he behaving like this? Did my position in the car, when he brushed against my knee, invite this? After she had come back to Sweden a year ago, she had kept her distance from men. Nursing the wounds from the divorce, she had tried to find a way back to her own self. She had felt like a complete stranger to the social conventions and dating codes in her home country.

"I just want you to know how grateful we are." He smiled broadly and hooked his arm in hers. "You certainly have a way with the guys. Is the Spanish much different?"

"No, there isn't a big a difference, linguistically," she answered, "just some words that have a different meaning." She unhooked his arm, pretending to search for something in her handbag.

There was an uncomfortable pause and she was grateful when one of the Chilean officers called on her for help before Pär had a chance to say anything more.

CHAPTER SEVEN

Madrid, mid 1990s

The only thing Klara wanted when she graduated from high school was an economy ticket to the Canary Islands. And she knew she would not be using the return.

Her family had spent a few years there, and she had been home schooled, returning to Sweden only for the required exams. She was shocked when her parents decided to move back to their hometown of Boden, in the north. She made up her mind: as soon as she graduated, she was going to live in Spain.

Back in Sweden, home schooling was not an option. In order to benefit from her acquired language skills, Klara would have to relocate to one of the only two places offering Spanish studies:

Umeå, in the north, or Stockholm, the capital. That choice was easy. In Stockholm there would always be a movie she hadn't yet seen. The move also effectively marked her emancipation.

It turned out to be impossible to make friends; everybody had their own from the preceding terms. Stockholmers were snobs, and she was a hick with a northern accent. Having lived a few years in a "Third World" country like Spain didn't make her any more exotic. The Canary Islands were just a cheap vacation destination others visited only to sunbathe and get drunk on sangria, oblivious of the local culture she had taken part of. There, on the other hand, Klara had always felt special.

She got her one-week vacation in Gran Canaria for a graduation present. Before it was over, she took a boat to Malaga. It was much cheaper than flying, and that would make her money last longer. At a petrol station in the outskirts of the city she scrutinized the cars pulling in, looking for license plates from Madrid. As she spotted one, she studied the people inside. *Shady, I'll pass*, she thought. After a while, a white Mercedes driven by a man in his fifties, with a woman about Klara's own age in the passenger seat, stopped to fill up. She watched them for a few minutes before approaching them to ask if they would give her a ride to Madrid. They sized her up, and, a little reluctantly, said yes.

Fernando and Margarita were friendly, took her to lunch along the way, and quite naturally the conversation came to be about how she was planning to make a living. She answered honestly that she only had two thousand Swedish kronor and was looking for a job. Fernando thought they might be able to help her. They would introduce her to some people at a café the next day.

Cafeteria Fontana was located in the modern part of Madrid, facing the southeast entrance to Santiago Bernabéu, the famous soccer stadium of Real Madrid. There, Fernando and Margarita were sitting at a square table, accompanied by a fat, short, authoritarian-looking man in his 60s. A cane was leaning on the table by his side. Klara sat facing the woman, with the newly introduced man, Don Epifanio, to her left.

"You will not want for anything," Don Epifanio said.

It took Klara a minute to understand that the job they were talking about was becoming Don Epifanio's mistress. In spite of the surprise, she couldn't help playing with the idea. Fernando and Margarita were not married, they explained, and she was the living advertisement for life as a mistress. She was well-dressed, wore elegant jewelry, and had a stylish haircut.

Plenty of time to take acting classes, audition or do whatever I want, Klara thought. The only thing wrong with the arrangement was that she would have to sleep with Don Epifanio.

"You only need to be nice to me," he said, while he casually pressed his walking stick in between Klara's feet.

The cane moved almost imperceptibly upward. When it reached the hem of her dress, he lifted it and with an unexpectedly quick move, he put his large and slightly moist hand on her thigh.

She clumsily pushed his hand away.

"Don't worry," he said. "I am never violent. Are you a virgin?"

Klara looked at Fernando and Margarita. How could they have misjudged her so totally? Fernando was staring at her and Margarita's smile was condescending.

"Fernando has known Don Epifanio for a long time, he is kind and generous," Margarita said, sensing Klara's reaction.

"No, thank you," she said, and left the café with as much dignity as she could muster. Her sexual experience was not extensive, but the uninvited touch of a stranger had convinced her that sex and love belonged together, and she could not offer the one without the other.

She just wanted a job. A real job. She could never make a living as a prostitute and held desperately on to the thought that she possessed other qualifications for earning her livelihood.

A mixture of humiliation and disappointment flowed through her. The shame burned in her soul as well as on her cheeks. The glittering wide world she had set out to conquer had suddenly turned scary and ugly.

Casa Paco, a famous restaurant specializing in chicken, was not far from Cafeteria Fontana and not too expensive. Partly in defiance and partly for comfort, she decided to go there. While she was having her meal, a young man walked over to her. He introduced himself as the assistant to a photographer, indicating a man sitting at another table. The photographer gave her a friendly nod. They were looking for a pair of hands for a photo advertising a washing machine, he explained, and offered her the job on the spot. Klara silently thanked the Lord for her long, well-manicured nails. The shoot was scheduled for just a few days later.

A kind of justice, she thought.

This coincidence ended up providing her a living for the next year. She got addresses for various modeling agencies. Fortunately, she had done a photo shoot for a tourist brochure during her time on the Canary Islands and could show it. Her "book", the large-size pictures all models had to show, was in the mail, she lied. She got to do commercials and photo shoots, some fashion gigs and even a few assignments as a catwalk model. No fantastic fees or top-model status—that was unheard of in Spain—but she managed. Like so many girls her age, she nurtured a secret dream of a career as an actress, but she had little or no idea of how to get there. This felt like a step in the right direction.

She knew it was not a "proper" job, nothing to ground a future on. She decided to continue modeling while she figured out what to study at university. It was fun, and she was young. Her earnings were meager and depended on the number of jobs she did. There was no guaranteed minimum from the agencies, no fixed monthly income, no money from home—her parents would just tell her to come back. Her survival depended entirely on her determination to appear at every casting in town and look her best.

After a month she left the cheap pension and rented a small studio apartment. Her diet wasn't particularly healthy, a bread filled with calamari and a coffee with milk was often all she ate on any given day. In the small cafés around Plaza de la Opera that was the cheapest you could buy, and it was filling.

In commercial shoots she often had to wear her own clothes. Directors and Art Directors, sometimes even Directors of Photography, would pick and choose from her wardrobe, as if they thought she had an unending supply. Soon she learned that models would borrow from each other, to show a wider variety. Most of the time she also had to do her own hair and make-up. Only on certain fancy jobs, like fashion shoots and fashion shows, would there be a makeup artist and wardrobe staff. So, she had to spend a big chunk of her income on clothes and cosmetics.

The biggest hurdle to her success, photographers told her, was her northern snub nose that demanded complicated lighting and corrective makeup. They urged her to get a nose job if she wanted to advance in the business.

At castings and gigs Klara got to know other models, most of them French. Babette was a little older, close to thirty; at the decline of her career and desperately hunting for a man who could support her lifestyle. When they worked on location together for a travel brochure, Klara was surprised that the French photographer obviously preferred herself to Babette, but she eventually understood why. Babette was there for other reasons. She was having an affair with the owner of the travel agency and was given time off to spend with him.

Anne Marie was another French girl. She used to ask Klara to come along apartment hunting in the posh neighborhood Marqués de Salamanca. That was where her fiancé wanted to live, and as soon as they found a suitable flat, they would get married... It didn't take long for Klara to realize that Anne Marie would never find an apartment that suited her fiancé. What Klara never figured out was whether Anne Marie was aware of the situation or if she actually believed that they were going to get married.

Klara became aware of how different life was on mainland Spain. The Canary Islands were remote and a little old-fashioned, and because Klara had been living with her parents she had been accepted as part of the community. She was not at all prepared for what it entailed to be a "Sueca" on the mainland. The expression didn't necessarily refer to "a Swedish girl" but stood for all young emancipated women traveling from northern Europe to sun and beach destinations, ready for a vacation romance. Young Madrid men heard magnified stories told by their friends living by the beach and marveled at their opportunities to have sex, no strings attached. So of course, being a real "Sueca" in Madrid became a problem.

At one of her gigs she had to cover her front with a towel while a male hand was holding a stethoscope to her bare back. When the session was over, the photographer asked if she was a virgin.

"It's none of your business," she answered, feeling vulnerable. The question reminded her of the situation at the cafeteria that first day in Madrid, and sent a shiver down her spine.

"Well, I suppose you aren't, so why don't you sleep with me?"

Keeping her voice under control, she said. "I don't sleep with people I work with." Then she hurried to get out of there before the male model left, just in case.

At another job she was offered a double fee under the table if she would take off all her clothes. Afterwards, the agent asked her: "Did you?"

"I didn't. Why don't you warn us?"

"It is totally up to the model. It has nothing to do with *my* business," the agent answered. "But just so you know: if you didn't, he'll never work with you again."

Klara suspected that the agent got a kickback from the photographer each time a girl decided to do the nude pictures. The double standards were present everywhere, and it was evident that the macho view of women had not disappeared with the death of Franco.

The men Klara met at discos and parties were young and rich. They pretended to study at the university, though their grades usually stood in direct proportion to their parents' Christmas gifts to the teachers. For most of them, knowledge was unimportant; they just needed a title. They were going to inherit family businesses and fortunes without any effort or qualification. Her mother would have called them good-for-nothings. But they were entertaining and had plenty of time and money.

As a model Klara would average six, seven days of work in a month, the same as most of the other girls, so it was fun to have something to do while not working. Visits to their country houses when the parents were back in the city, lunches at the very exclusive Club de Campo, sports cars, polo, tennis, and golf—all this became part of her daily life. Klara and her girlfriends were very popular.

A typical evening would start sometime after nine with a nice dinner at a restaurant. Then they would drift on to some disco at midnight or later. They would dance until about four in the morning when the small cafés around the San Miguel market by Plaza Mayor opened. There they would drink thick hot chocolate with churros before going home.

The men always paid. At that time, no Latin man would take a woman on a date if he couldn't pay for it. Entertainment didn't cost anything when you were young and beautiful. On the few evenings that she didn't have a date, Klara would go straight to the night clubs. The doormen always let her in for free, as models lent glamor to the places and attracted customers.

None of those young men would dream of a life with the foreign girls. Introducing them to their parents was unthinkable. It was all right playing around, but once they tired of it, they were going to marry their *novia*, the fiancée from the same social circles, often the daughter of some suitable business acquaintance of their fathers. There was nothing contemptuous about the way they treated the models, as long as the girls didn't sleep around. They simply belonged to a different planet and nobody seemed to think that those two worlds could ever come together.

August in Madrid came as a shock to Klara. Its inhabitants abandoned the city. Those who did not have country houses visited relatives in the mountains or on the beach. There was little work and thus hardly any money coming in. She needed two full-day assignments a month to pay the rent, otherwise she had to sell or pawn something, and one more day to be able to afford to eat. She started to do odd jobs for TV. They were less well-paid and not considered as glamorous as modeling, but she couldn't afford to be choosy.

It was at one of the jobs as a walk-on in a TV program that her new type of work emerged. A production assistant inquired about her written English.

"Excellent," Klara said.

"Do you write Spanish as well as you speak it?" he asked.

"Sure. No problem," she lied, fully aware that she didn't always get the accents right, but she knew that her written Spanish was as good as many native speakers'.

"We need a translator for big job. Probably months. Not just scripts, also research and other documents. What do you say? Are you interested?" he asked.

And that was the beginning of a career change that would end up with her as a terrorist in Mossad's database.

CHAPTER EIGHT

For the first time since Klara came to Madrid she had secured her livelihood for the next several months. Her neat translations, written on a second-hand "Amstrad", a word processor with printer that she had bought cheap at the flea market, were well received. The occasional spelling error was excused, attributed to her not being native. She worked hard to maintain a high level of proficiency. The fact that she was working for TVE, the public Spanish Television, was a feather in her hat. It was *the* communication medium and kept people home at night, giving them something to comment on at work the next day.

Her spoken Spanish was by now impeccable, and before long she was asked to interpret between English-speaking parties and directors from TVE at business meetings. Klara had found her profession. This job she would not grow too old for; to the contrary, she would just get better with time.

She had been interpreting for three days during the negotiations for a large co-production of an innovative children's program between TVE and the North American enterprise Children's Television Company, known as CTC. It turned out to be interesting and exciting, and she felt like an important part of the project.

Everybody, especially the Americans, had joked about the power held by the interpreter, as neither party understood a word of what the other was saying. She was the only one who knew everything.

TVE was ruled by the political party in power, and they were fairly suspicious of the Americans. Mostly, it was just a question of smoothing over cultural differences, expressions that might be perceived as insensitive or downright insulting to the Spanish party. Technically, the project was complicated too. It was one of the largest co-productions TVE had ever undertaken, spending hundreds of millions of pesetas.

On behalf of TVE, the main negotiators were Carlos Alvarez, head of the Children's Program Department, and Blanca González, a legendary widow and mother of seven, the project manager. Negotiators on behalf of Children's Television Company, were Louis Hornett, executive producer, and the VP Pete Horton. Once they ironed out the agreement, the director general of TVE would come in for a couple of hours and sign the contract.

Klara was aware that the Americans were comfortable with the fact that she herself was not Spanish, and trusted her to be impartial.

After the third day of endless discussions about the puppets CTC was going to create for the show, Louis Hornett and Pete Horton invited her to dinner at Hotel Melia. Businessmen favored the hotel because it was close to Plaza España in the very heart of Madrid. Louis Hornett always stayed there on his frequent visits to Madrid. Klara had noticed that he was always in room 612 when she had picked him up to take him to TVE.

The interior of the elegant restaurant on the first floor of the hotel was decorated in white and dark blue. An array of candles made the atmosphere warm and intimate. The restaurant was almost full, but all you could hear was a soft murmur and the occasional chime of silverware against porcelain.

"What would you like to eat?" Louis asked.

There would only be the three of them, so she would not have to interpret, and both men seemed to enjoy entertaining her.

Klara couldn't make up her mind about what to choose from the restaurant's extensive French menu and left it to the men to decide. They started with Russian caviar. It came served in a small silver bowl between the half-raised wings of a swan of ice. The arrangement was at least two feet high. The candle light made the ice swan sparkle, attracting the light and then reflecting it, while it floated through the darkish room. She was impressed. She had never had Russian caviar before. The vodka came in foggy small cone-shaped glasses, pressed into bowls of crushed ice.

"Vodka that cold is like silk on the tongue and in your throat. It's only when it reaches the stomach that it flares up," Louis said.

The talk flowed around neutral subjects. Louis was African American, in his forties. He was fit, not very tall, about 5'10" Klara guessed, with an exquisite and discreet taste in clothes and elegant table manners. Pete was British, mid-thirties, the archetype of the aggressive media careerist married to a wife with a castle in Scotland and a yacht on the Riviera.

Louis was very interested in race issues and believed this kind of children's programming could prevent prejudice in children. There were several features in the planned co-production that had been designed specifically to obtain such an educational effect.

"Will you continue working with us?" Pete asked, as the waiter removed the plates after an equally exquisite main course.

"I don't know. I'm not an employee with TVE, but if everybody is happy with my work, it seems likely that they will extend my contract," answered Klara.

"We could make that happen," said Louis.

"I'm not sure that would be a good idea," Klara said, thinking as fast as the vodka and wine permitted. "That could be construed as pressure and at the present stage of the negotiations, it would give TVE a reason to ask for something in return."

The men exchanged a long, loaded glance, before Louis smiled and nodded.

Suddenly, the atmosphere around the table changed. The air conditioning was too strong, and she rubbed her arms. Louis noticed and offered his jacket.

"We'll think of a smart way to make the suggestion," Pete said.

"But it's important to us," Louis added. "We're prepared to pay you to keep you on the project, whatever your agreement with TVE is."

She picked up on Pete looking a bit surprised.

Her first reaction was joy. She wasn't exactly rolling in money. But a moment later it felt wrong, somehow.

Would it be wrong? she pondered. *I would work for both parties, so it's only right that both should pay...*

Pete was staying at the very expensive and elegant Hotel Palace, probably in order to mark his position as VP. He left soon after dinner.

The evening ended, not surprisingly, in Louis's bed. He showed more tenderness than she had expected and the sex was good, but not amazing. When the first gray light of dawn filtered through the shades, Klara saw that Louis had a tattoo high on his left upper arm.

How strange, she thought, while she studied the pale green omega sign. It was not very discreet, a couple of inches high and about one inch wide. A little later she noticed the alpha sign in the same place on his other arm. It clashed with Louis's suave style.

The telephone rang. It was four-thirty in the morning.

"It's 10.30 pm in New York," Louis apologized.

He held the conversation at a neutral level and it was impossible to tell whether it was work or private.

Klara felt uncomfortable. This should not have happened. It was a work relationship.

He kept the call short and returned to bed. When he started caressing her, she excused herself, picked up her clothes, and went to the bathroom. After a long shower she came back out fully dressed. Louis had ordered breakfast: a large table on wheels with anything you could possibly want.

"I took for granted that you drink coffee," he said and smiled. "We have some talking to do, you and I."

Now he's going to say that what has happened will not have any consequences work-wise. She wasn't so sure that would be true.

But she was wrong. That was not what he wanted to talk about.

"You have heard about the GAL?" he asked.

Klara was puzzled. "What does GAL have to do with anything?"

She knew that GAL, *Grupos Antiterroristas de Liberación*, had been a secret organization staffed by policemen acting under cover to fight ETA, the Basque terrorist group, in the 80s. The suspicion that the mysterious Mr. X, who gave the orders to kill, was the Prime Minister himself, had been a shock to the whole country, unthinkable in a democracy. In spite of the allegations, the same Prime Minister was still in charge.

"The former Minister of the Interior is indicted, but it's still a secret what for," Louis explained. "It worries us. As a company promoting equal rights and democratic values, we don't want to be associated with a country that doesn't share our respect for those values. Keeping in mind how politically dominated public television is, we would have to pull out of the cooperation if something like the GAL is brewing again. We want you to keep your eyes open and report anything you see or hear. Even if it is only a rumor."

"But I don't have access to anything more than what is on the news or published in the newspapers," Klara protested.

"On the contrary," Louis explained. "We think you are in a perfect spot at the heart of the public service TV. This is where the information is managed and decisions made whether to publish or keep it under the lid. We know that TVE is ruled iron-handedly by the party in power. The very party that allowed the GAL to happen, well—actually is behind it. I'm talking about reporting what you hear in the cafeteria, by the water cooler, or the vending machines. What media professionals discuss among themselves."

Louis was adept at trivializing her half-hearted objections. The arrangement consisted of receiving two thousand dollars a month for relaying overheard conversations and summaries of what she read in the newspapers. Almost too good to be true. Despite her reservations, she accepted.

A couple of months later, she realized that she was pregnant.

CHAPTER NINE

New York - two months later

Klara was quite nervous when she called Louis to tell him she was expecting his child. Would he be upset? Deny that he was the father? Strangely, he did not sound surprised. "Come to New York and let's discuss the situation. It might be a good idea not to tell anyone that you are pregnant, at least for now. Officially you'll be attending a training session here at CTC."

She relaxed, feeling taken care of, for once. He had gracefully accepted his part of responsibility and she was not alone in this mess.

At Barajas, Madrid's airport, she picked up a first-class ticket, arranged by Louis. She had never flown anything but economy before. It was a Friday, but the plane wasn't full, at least not in her class. Klara was served appetizing small, open sandwiches and champagne in proper glasses while the passengers in tourist class were being seated. The air company's colours, black with red details, were tastefully stated in the aircraft's interior. The leather chairs were spacious and had foot rests.

The only thing noticeable, now in the ninth week of pregnancy, was that her breasts were getting fuller. Some people had complimented her, saying that she looked beautiful, serene. She had no morning sickness. Actually, she felt better than ever, and strangely peaceful.

I am probably born to have babies, she thought happily, and allowed herself to enjoy the feeling for the first time. She fell asleep and dreamed that she was the mother of a multi-colored flock of children, all of them by different fathers. She woke up just as they started serving lunch, but didn't want to let go of the dream.

When the air hostess brought her the tea she had ordered, her mood changed. She was embarrassed realizing how much time and trouble her request had caused. She should obviously just have ordered a drink...

Reality intruded. She was all alone and she did not have a regular job. The child's father was married, and she didn't love him. She herself was just barely grown-up, she hadn't really had time to live yet. She had still not experienced love, not seriously. The difficulties of being a single mother in Spain were, objectively speaking, insurmountable. No paid maternity leave. A tiny living space, a two-room with a pantry six floors up, with an ancient elevator not big enough for prams. No child support. Middle class people in Spain had maids and poor people were helped by their families if they had to work while the children were small. She wouldn't be able to afford a maid and she had no family. In Catholic Spain it was still considered a great shame to be a single mother. Maybe she would be pardoned to a certain extent, because she was a foreigner. But could she live with being the mother of a child who would never meet his father, maybe not even be allowed to know who he was? A child with origins in the African-American middle-class and growing up...

Yes, well, where?

Louis wasn't at the airport. It hurt and concerned her, made her doubt his commitment. Instead, a young African-American woman walked up to her and asked if she was Klara. The woman's name was Tippy. She informed Klara that they didn't expect her at CTC until Monday, but if she wanted company during the weekend, she could call her on her home number. They exchanged cards.

Tippy took her to a small apartment on West 84th Street, on the first block off Central Park and only a few streets north of New York's famous Museum of Natural History. It was a smartly decorated but impersonal one-bedroom apartment on the first floor of a classical New York brownstone. CTC's office at One Lincoln Plaza was practically within walking distance, but there were also convenient bus and metro stops on Central Park West that would take her there. Tippy left her to unpack and freshen up. Louis would pick her up for dinner.

Both of the apartment's windows faced the street, a big one in the living room and a smaller one in the bedroom. You walked right into a large room, with the kitchen to the left and a dining corner to the right. Beyond it, the door to the bathroom. The living room spread out straight ahead. Beneath the window there was a burgundy plush sofa and a low table with a bronze table-top. Quite pretty and a little exotic. There were bookcases in dark wood along the walls. They were practically empty. Some paperbacks, a few decorations and a rather ugly vase. Only the lower shelves were filled. A quick look at the CD collection revealed music of good quality and a good sound system. In the bedroom there was a queen size bed, a bedside table, a hat-and-coat stand and the door to a spacious walk-in closet.

Klara put her suitcase in the closet and unpacked only the most important things. She took out clean underwear and went into the bathroom.

Long, sharp chimes from the doorbell forced her out of the shower with dripping wet hair. She found a lovely em-

57

erald green bathrobe on a hook and put it on, on her way to open the door. After a look through the peephole to make sure Louis came alone, she opened the door.

"I'm not ready yet," she said, and with a gesture she asked him to wait on the sofa, turning to go back to the bathroom.

He didn't try to kiss or embrace her, just said: "Don't take too long."

She heard him play music while she dried her hair. The chorus part of Carmina Burana was on full blast while she got dressed. As she entered the living room he turned the volume down.

"We need to talk. Sit down."

"I'm not asking you to get a divorce," interrupted Klara. He looked so uncomfortable that she felt sorry for him. It was embarrassing, but just as well to clear things up.

"That would be unthinkable," he said, almost irritated. "Nobody can expect me to give up two children because a third is on the way, I know you understand that. But that's not the issue."

Klara stared at him in surprise. What could be more important than the fact that she was expecting?

"I have something very important to tell you: with the TV productions as a cover, I can travel quite freely. I can stay for long periods of time in countries of interest..."

"As a cover?"

"I manage my own travel arrangements. At the moment, I am often in Kuwait and the Middle East," he continued as if he hadn't heard her. "CTC is a completely legit company that we use for my cover. I work for the CIA."

A thousand thoughts whirled through Klara's mind.

There was a long silence. The warm sunshine of the late afternoon fell on the wall behind him, shining on the glass of the framed poster from an art exhibit. His skin looked even darker in contrast with the background. It was hard to see his facial expression, but the tension in his voice mirrored the seriousness of the revelation. The importance of his confession was gradually sinking in.

Louis waited.

"Why are you telling me this?"

"Your reports are of no interest to CTC. You're reporting to the CIA. And you're being paid by the CIA."

Her head felt empty. Crossing her arms over her chest, she mechanically rubbed her palms along her sleeves, looking at him in silence. It was one thing to secretly watch out for threats to the democracy of the country, and quite another to be cooperating with the CIA.

"You're my asset and the arrangement is only between the two of us. Nobody knows who my source is."

The shock slowly eased its grip on her and the lump in her throat dissolved. She felt that they now shared a dangerous secret. Assisting a foreign power was exciting—but another feeling was emerging: the realization that she had been tricked.

They were sitting at opposite ends of the plush sofa. He took her hands in his and looked into her eyes.

"I wouldn't be a good father. The decision is yours, of course, but I hope that you decide to have an abortion," Louis said.

She pulled her hands back. How stupid she had been. So naïve. He had misled her. The deception hurt.

The slap sounded like a shot.

Heat pulsed in her hand as he raised his own to his left cheek.

"Get out of here. Leave. I never want to see you again."

He left without another word.

Later that night she heard him come back, but she refused to open the door. As the evening turned into night, she began to suspect that the apartment was bugged. Louis didn't seem to worry that she would do anything dramatic. Klara was torn between common sense and irrational emotions. Deep down she knew that she was not a victim. She had been as responsible as he for their ending up in bed. It was hard to accept that she had nobody to blame.

When she heard steps on the staircase the next morning, she opened the door and asked him to come in.

"I don't see that I have an alternative," she said, and swallowed.

He nodded. After a few seconds he said, "I've taken the liberty to contact the German Hospital in Madrid, in case you decided to go with that option," he said.

"In Madrid? But abortions are unlawful there... Over here it's legal. Why Madrid?"

"I thought you would feel more comfortable there. I can arrange for it to be done in Spain discreetly. You've heard of Dr. Hasselberger's German Clinic?"

She had. The German Clinic was famous for their outstanding cosmetic surgery, only a smidge under the legendary Pignatari from Brazil.

"But he's not an obstetrician..."

"I know, but I thought you might do that nose job you've mentioned at the same time. That would make an excellent alibi."

As she had stopped working in front of the cameras, she had forgotten about that. The typically north Scandinavian "potato nose" was no longer a problem, but she must have mentioned it to Louis at some point.

"How long would that keep me from working?" she asked.

"Not a day longer than your planned training session here at CTC. Though if someone asks, you might have to confess that you got a nose job done while you were here."

She took the next flight to Madrid and went directly from the airport to the Clinic. Dr Hasselberger met with her on arrival to discuss her nose job at length. He took some pictures, explained the procedure and the expected outcome. Her nose would be just the same, without the inconvenient bulge at the end. It was a weird conversation because he did not address the abortion and Klara couldn't concentrate on her nose.

Then the anesthetist came to see her. He measured her blood pressure, listened to her heart and lungs, and said: "You're young and healthy. We don't expect any complications. We're going to do that other thing, while you are sedated. You will not feel a thing."

It was close to four am when Klara woke up. She was about to ring the bell for the nurse when she realized that she didn't need to. There was a glass of water by the bed and she felt no pain, only a stinging sensation on her left butt cheek. She found a gauze covering the place where a fairly large birthmark used to be. They had not discussed taking it away, but perhaps the doctor had found it visually offensive and decided to remove it. *Three for the price of one*, she mocked herself.

The hospital was extremely silent, almost spooky. She got out of bed and walked to the window, mainly to fight the childish feeling that she was alone in the whole world. After a while she saw an ambulance pulling up to the emergency entrance. The sirens and the lights were off. She watched as two men exited the vehicle and opened the back. Seeing other humans soothed her loneliness. They entered the clinic. Klara waited. She wondered how long it would take them to come back out. After a little while she got cold and turned to go back to bed, when something caught her eye.

The two men came back into view, carrying a large black bag. It looked like the body bags she had seen on TV shows. Klara shuddered. That couldn't be. She knew that dead people do not get moved in ambulances.

CHAPTER TEN

Stockholm, Present time

The assignment at the shipyard had been easy and yet she had felt useful and appreciated. It had been perfect to keep her mind off the picture in Mossad's database for a little while.

She wanted to try to hold on to that positive feeling and was going to pamper herself with a glass of wine and some aged manchego cheese, play Bebo Valdes and enjoy the *Vogue* magazine that should be waiting for her on the door mat.

As she was about to turn the key in the lock, a strong feeling that something was wrong came over her. She paused. Gritting her teeth so hard it almost hurt to clamp down, the adrenaline racing through her veins, she forced herself to fling the door open.

Someone was standing by the window with his back to her, apparently admiring the view. The room was dark—only the floor lamp by the couch was lit—and at first she couldn't see who it was. Fear turned to surprise in a kind of anti-climax.

"What the hell?" Klara said, in command of her voice again.

"Not what you'd call arms wide open," Louis said, turning around to face her. "Close the door."

A tumbler with a pale-yellow liquid stood on the coffee table by the couch. The bottle of the 18-year-old Glenmorangie next to it indicated that he had brought his favorite drink. As the ice cube he normally put in it had melted, she concluded that he had waited a while.

"Why didn't you return my call?" Klara's voice quivered with rage.

Her new home, her haven, had been violated. Someone had entered uninvited and made himself at home. He was like something from another life, a ghost she had assumed lost as he hadn't answered her call when she needed him.

"Klara, this is not a social visit," he said.

It had been five years since she saw him last, and he had aged. His hair was grizzled and his skin had acquired a grayish tone. *How far into his sixties?* she wondered. She had never known his exact age. He wore a brown camel hair blazer and his light blue shirt was open at the neck. A mistake. His neck was wrinkled and sagged a little. Klara had to fight off a hint of tenderness brought on by his new frailty.

On the way to the kitchen she realized that the conversation ahead needed food as well as alcohol. His mere presence used to make her feel less vulnerable, and seeing him now produced that same effect.

"I guess you're here to talk about the picture of me in Mossad's database?"

Louis came into the kitchen. He sat down at the small drop table she had bought second-hand and cleaned of old paint, watching her as she sliced the cold cuts and cheeses.

"You never told me you were retiring." She slammed the knife on the counter. "I felt betrayed. While I was active I could always reach you on that number you made me memorize. I freaked when I discovered that Mossad believes I'm an Al-Fatah agent, and when I called you, you weren't there." As she heard herself speaking it occurred to her: "It was *your* doing? For sure they wouldn't have included anything that absurd in their records by themselves."

"I'm afraid we have a few things to discuss, Klara," Louis said. "I never planned to get you involved."

She shuddered.

"Remember that I was active in the Middle East? It's got to do with that…. But come sit down, I need to see you while we talk."

She carried the tray into the living room and sat down in her grandmother's armchair, pulling the woolen shawl Grandma had woven around her shoulders. The two items somehow anchored her to reality. Louis sat on the couch, across from her.

"We have problems with a powerful Saudi extremist group, and we think you can help."

"We had agreed that operation *Absinth Angel* was going to be my last mission," she reminded him. The operation was named after a figure in a painting at Café Slavia, in Prague.

"Klara, there's no way to un-recruit an agent, you know that." He paused to let his words sink in. They had discussed this before, when she thought it was safe to get married and distance herself from the Agency.

"Working for the CIA here in Sweden is out of the question, Louis. That would not only be unethical, but also high treason. Moreover, I don't speak Arabic, nor do I have any contacts that could be useful. What on earth do you think I could do?"

It was her TV work that had made her an asset to Louis— and by extension to the CIA. Both in Spain and in Czechoslovakia those many years ago.

"We'll get to that. How many people do you socialize with here in Sweden that know you from before?" he asked.

"Nobody. Apart from the cousins you know about."

"That's okay. We've taken that into account. No old admirers or friends from school?"

She shook her head.

"We planted that old photograph of you with a fake identity within reach of Mossad, as a way to make Fatima credible to the Arab organizations."

Klara got goosebumps. *So, it was planted.* "Fatima?" That was the name printed beside the picture. "But Al-Fatah must know that is not true? I don't get it."

"Important matters are prepared well in advance, no detail overlooked."

"You mean Mossad actually believes that Fatima is an Al-Fatah agent? If that photograph is tracked back to me, the mere suspicion means my life is at risk." She paused and then added: "And the Palestinians, why would they play along?"

"For now, it's only a file in Mossad's archives. They know no more than what you yourself have seen and have absolutely no idea of who that agent is today and where they can find her." His hand was up in the air, a stop sign pleading she would let him finish. "I have personally handled all contacts with Al-Fatah in this context. You are safe. *Nobody* but me knows where to find you. I did not expect you to stumble across that piece of disinformation in your present job. It speeded things up. When you called, I was discussing a joint operation with the Swedish authorities. I'll come back to that later. It took some time to organize my visit, mainly because I didn't want to risk compromising you."

Her vocal cords felt like they were tied in a knot and she had difficulty breathing. She drew the shawl more tightly around her shoulders.

"In the story I created, you are Fatima, with a past that suits the name and fits circumstances that occurred a long time ago. The most recent lead is that she cooperated with the ETA in Spain for some time, then went underground."

In Klara's cooperation with the CIA there had never before been any reason to pretend to be anyone but herself. This was something entirely different.

"And now I'm asking you to play that role," he said.

"And if I don't, what? Are you going to kill me yourself, or are you leaving the wet job to Mossad?" She knew she was being ridiculous, but she was angry.

"Nobody is getting killed." Louis' voice was hard.

"You should have informed me. Hell, you should have asked me if I even wanted to be a part of this. I had a right to know. You should have checked whether I had any objections."

He continued: "I have protected you all these years, Klara. And we will continue doing so, but we need your help. When this is over, we will reveal the truth to Mossad, that's a promise. You will be free and unsullied by suspicions. I know that you're able to handle this. And I'm sure that you won't have any objections when you understand what the mission is about."

She knew he was manipulating her.

"But what if I don't want to?" she asked, still reluctant to let him gain the upper hand. "You retired and fell off the grid, I moved on. I want to be a normal Swedish woman, work and have a life, maybe meet a man who's the right age and can vacuum and clean windows and irons his own shirts."

He didn't respond.

"Because men like that actually exist," she continued, staring Louis right in the eyes. "That's my dream of the future, my dream for the rest of my life."

"I wasn't aware there was someone particular in your life?" Louis asked, with a small smile.

"That's none of your business." It came out like a hiss. She didn't want him to know how lonely she felt and didn't like what he was implying. But now she realized he had been keeping tabs on her even after she moved back to Sweden, almost a year ago.

"You can get that idyllic life later, if that's what you really want. But I can't quite picture you in a suburban villa with a Volvo and a dog. You and I both know that you demand other things from life, the same way I do."

She felt the figurative knife go straight in and twist. He knew which buttons to push.

They fell silent. At a distance she heard an old subway train pass; the new trains were less noisy. They had finished the food and Louis got up, walking over to the glass cabinet. From a silver tray he chose a bottle of Torres 10 Gran Reserva and poured the brandy into a balloon glass. He warmed the golden-brown liquid between the palms of his hands, letting it rotate slowly in the glass. She watched—the slow and gentle movement was almost hypnotic. Then he handed it to her. She brought it to her lips. The aroma rose through her nostrils and spread out like a spider web behind her forehead before it ebbed away. She took a small sip of the velvety drink. She relaxed. He knew her so well.

They sat for a long time without talking. It was the calm before the storm, and they both treasured the moment.

"Certain technology developed here in Sweden is of interest to foreign powers," Louis finally said. "If the Sunni extremists get their hands on it, that would create a very serious problem for all western countries."

"Hard to believe that little Sweden has something that could be a menace to the world," she said.

"The Karlskrona shipyard." Louis pronounced it with an American accent.

Klara smiled. "YS 2000?" she asked.

"Your interpreting assignment was no coincidence. A ship like that would give our enemies the ability to get close enough to our aircraft carriers to sink them, or to get to a major coastal city without being discovered in time by either submarines or surface vessels. Even equipped with conventional EXOCET missiles, the YS 2000 in the wrong hands constitutes a serious threat to the world."

Before she had time to take in what he was saying, her thoughts raced down another track.

"Pär Westman? Is he involved in this?

"He assessed you and is ready to work with you on this."

"His assessments are certainly one of a kind. He was hitting on me." Klara answered, taunting him. Louis had more than once shown a bizarre ability to dispose of the men that appeared in her life. She went on.

"Why don't the Swedish authorities handle this themselves? It's got to be first and foremost their problem. Are they on board, or is it just you people at the CIA being paranoid?" she asked.

"Let me put it like this: we have mutual interests, and our chances to succeed are objectively a lot better than theirs. Therefore, we agreed that there are advantages in having us handle the operation. We were studying different possibilities and decided that the Chilean visit was the best option to bring you in. The pieces just fell into place."

"Your word is not enough, Louis, not for me to work for the CIA in Sweden. I need guarantees from Swedish authorities. And won't the Palestinians object?"

"As I said, I have personally, for quite some time now, handled all the details around your cover as Fatima. An old Arab in Israeli captivity confirmed, before he died, that Fatima Habib-Sjögren was his granddaughter. I have since been turning over information about sensitive matters to the Palestinians from time to time, in Fatima's name, in order to convince them that she is still their spy. "

It was his tone of voice, tired and tense, rather than what he said that made Klara stop and think. What he really meant was that the only way was forward. She had no choice.

"While you were at the shipyard, we flagged that Fatima could gain access to the blueprints of the ship. Al Fatah has no need for it, but needs money. We knew the Saudi group were ready to pay, but they refuse to accept any middle men. They don't want to expose their agent, so Fatima herself has to deliver. Therefore, you and I have to agree now. This will not work without you."

He reached into the inner pocket of his sports coat and fished out an air ticket along with a strange-looking key.

"This is a ticket to Zürich. Banks are open tomorrow. In a safe deposit box in Züricher Bank you will find background material on Fatima, some passports she would have from different countries and in different names, her driving license and fifty thousand dollars. The guarantee you're demanding is a document signed by the undersecretary of the Ministry of Defense, confirming that they are informed about, and consent to, your involvement in the assignment. Change the safe deposit box and leave what you don't need immediately in your new one. You need to start leaving a trail out of Switzerland as Klara, so open a bank account and get a credit card in your own name. Take a look at it all and get in touch afterwards. You can reach me at the Radisson Blu tomorrow afternoon. I'm meeting with old acquaintances from Swedish public television. I, or somebody I assign, will stay close to you at all times." He emphasized: "You will be protected."

"I haven't shot a weapon in years."

"Why don't you go to that shooting range at Fridhemsplan and get up to speed again? You used to be a good markswoman, you even have a Swedish license to own a firearm."

"I don't own a weapon anymore."

"You do now. Take a look in the closet."

She did, and there was a brand-new floor-anchored 12" by 8"safe in the right corner. The door was open and a Glock 17 was inside.

Louis stood right beside her when she turned around.

"The Glock 17's nozzle and internal mechanics are massive steel, but 17 percent of the weapon is plastic, making it considerably lighter than most comparable firearms. It is a precision weapon weighing just under two pounds and has a cartridge clip holding 17 bullets," he explained.

She tested the weight in her hand and nodded.

"Have you quit stuffing bills in your bra and keeping a stiletto strapped to your thigh?" he joked, and then added more seriously: "Speaking of stilettos, Fatima's signature weapon is a very special knife. You'll find it in the safe deposit in Zürich. You'll need to learn to master that knife."

It was early morning, though daylight was still many hours away by the time Louis had explained all the details. What she was being asked to do did not require any extraordinary talent. She didn't have to run faster, to hit harder or possess any other special skill, apart from learning how to handle Fatima's knife. She could basically be herself, with a different name.

She was excited about the operation. And also proud that Sweden had something that others coveted—even feared.

The plane for Zürich was leaving at 8:15 a.m.

CHAPTER ELEVEN

Klara worked during the weekend to keep Nicklas happy. Following Louis's instructions, she also started to explore the pub-bar scene, where the forty-somethings would go to dance. Or to look for a partner. "Krogen" the Swedes called it, a word that, to her, only evoked the smell of stale alcohol and cigarettes.

The first place on her list was Long Play, on Birger Jarlsgatan, in the heart of downtown Stockholm. At nine thirty she nodded to the bouncer who opened the door to the club to let her in. She took a narrow staircase down to the basement. It was quite dark and there were not many people, but the few upholstered benches along the walls were already taken.

What did people do in places like this, hang around standing at the bar? She felt uncomfortable. The place had a bar at each end of the small dance floor, but there were no stools. No one was dancing.

She looked around. The women were dressed up, some looking quite provocative. Obviously, that was the way you were supposed to look, not like you just dropped in after work. She noticed glances at her straight skirt, shirt and jacket, which made her feel even more out of place. She wanted to turn around and go home, but braced herself. It was part of the job. In the ladies' room, she applied lipstick, glad she

71

always kept one in her bag, though not normally a part of her make-up, and unbuttoned another button on her blouse.

On the way back to the dance floor she discovered another room, with comfortable leather armchairs and yet another bar. There, the sound level was considerably lower and all the tables were empty. She ordered a glass of wine and sat down by the door. The place started filling up after ten thirty, and for a second she worried that she might miss Pär in the crowd.

She watched as women asked men to dance, but she didn't want to do that. She wanted to feel chosen. When she saw a guy stumble toward her, she looked away and sipped her drink, hoping he would get the hint. He didn't. Bumping into her table, he asked her to dance. He must have started drinking at home, considering the price of alcohol in this place, because he was quite drunk. She wanted to say no, but didn't dare. When a guy invited you to dance, you couldn't refuse. That had been the biggest taboo when she was young, back in Boden. If you said no, in solidarity with the shunned guy, *nobody* would ask you to the floor anymore.

Pär was nowhere to be found and to make time pass she tried to figure out how this all worked. It was amusing. Some women were obviously hunting for a partner, maybe just for the night. Men seemed more laid back, kind of adopting the role of the prey. Having the women compete for them.

A *generational phenomenon?* she wondered. *More single women than men available?*

A less tipsy and well-dressed man asked her to dance. After a little while he said: "This music is awful. Why don't we go back to my place and listen to something good?"

But she was there on a mission waiting for Pär to appear.

"You mean to see your etchings? No, I don't think so," she smiled. The invitation to see the etchings used to mean "do you want to sleep with me," and as this guy was approximately the same age, he would be familiar with the expression.

"Wow, I haven't heard that in a long time." He laughed, introducing himself as Kjell, journalist at SR, the public radio network.

They went back to her table and talked for a while. Kjell seemed to be impressed by her job with the production company, obviously interested, and asked to see her again. She gave him her phone number but didn't really expect him to call.

To go out dancing was a way to feel appreciated, even desirable, albeit in a superficial, slightly anonymous way, Klara decided.

By now, the place was packed, and a lot of people seemed to be quite drunk. A strategy? Something to blame for going home with somebody they did not really want? Around midnight she gave up. Pär would have appeared by now, if he intended to come, and she had to catch the last subway.

After her return to Sweden she had been more fortunate than she had realized at the time, miraculously securing a first-hand contract for a flat. The official waiting list for a rental in the capital was eight years. Hers was a one-bedroom apartment on the top floor of a three-story building, close to the Traneberg bridge with an amazing view of the Stockholm skyline.

Each time she came home she would walk up to the large living room window and look out. The green area spreading out towards the bridge, the urban presence of light but constant traffic, and the occasional airplane from the nearby Bromma airport took the edge off her loneliness and filled her with a sense of belonging. Once she got a load of furniture from the storage in Madrid it had become *home.*

Even the weather had been merciful this last year, and she was welcomed by the best summer of the century. She came to love summer in Stockholm, the light, the water and the boats.

This time of the year though, she only had daylight at lunch-time. The darkness grew by half an hour every week, and even her amazing view was turning gray and unappealing.

CHAPTER TWELVE

Next Thursday morning, her telephone rang right at seven am. Her social life was still far from busy and she seldom got a call.

"Klara," she said, picking up.

There was a moment of silence at the other end.

"Hi, this is Pär Westman. Do you remember me? From the Karlskrona shipyard?"

He sounded nervous. A good actor, she thought, the telephone line was not secure, and in case somebody was listening she tried to play along with the charade, recreating the feeling she had when she believed he was interested in her.

"Of course I remember you." She was hoping things would start to move along and the operation would enter another stage once they started to meet.

"I didn't see you at Operabaren last Friday and didn't know how to reach you. Finally I got your phone number from the interpreting agency," he said. "Not easy at all."

"Then you must have given very powerful reasons, because I know that they don't normally give people our private numbers. How are you doing?"

Louis would have provided Pär with all her contact details and anything else he needed, but he would have gone through the motions and called Helena at Polyglott, to pretend to get Klara's number, anyway. Klara knew that every detail counted, in case the foreign courier was checking up on them. The honey trap had to look watertight

"It's a long story which I'd like to tell you over dinner, if you're available."

"When were you thinking of?"

"Tonight would be great, but you're probably busy. That's why I'm calling so early. I will be in Stockholm until tomorrow. The flight to Ronneby was fully booked." After a pause, "Sorry, I'm not very good at this. You must think I'm a complete idiot."

"Not at all. I'd love to have dinner tonight. When and where?"

She tried to sound flattered.

"Let's say Tranan. Six thirty?"

Tranan was a classic old beer house turned into a fashionable restaurant. It was crowded and loud; the acoustics were a problem for those engaged in conversation. A good choice for their purpose.

"Seven thirty would suit me better." She wanted some time to freshen up after work.

"Then seven thirty it is."

Finally, the zombie-like state she'd been living in was fading away. Manuel's children, Serena and Marcos, were grown up, had their own lives and didn't need her at close range any more. It was a luxury to have nobody but herself to care for, now that Louis once more had added a dimension to her existence. It was time to shred the cocoon she had surrounded herself with after the divorce.

Giving vent to her hedonism, Klara decided to pretend that this was a real date and thoroughly enjoyed getting ready. Her apartment offered yet another bonus: no close neighbors who could peep in through her windows. This allowed her to walk about and dry naturally, with oil on her well-tended skin after the rub in the shower. She chose underwear carefully. Stockings and garter belt instead of boring tights. Smiling, she thought about how exciting men seemed to find the mark of the button, outlined like a nipple against the fabric of a dress, or the glimpse of a lace bra.

Pär waited for her by the entrance to the restaurant.

"Wow, you look fantastic," Pär greeted her.

Dinner was quite pleasant. They maintained a lively conversation about anything and everything, just like any two people exploring each other on a first date. Walking back to his hotel, about half an hour from the restaurant, things got more awkward. They held hands, and he stopped once on the sidewalk to kiss her, but the conversation no longer seemed to flow.

Once in his room, Pär grew tense and silent. All business. She was getting to know the real Pär.

He placed his briefcase on a small desk along one of the walls and switched on the desk lamp. It was an attaché case in black leather with a combination lock on each side and it was unusually heavy.

"When I travel, I handcuff myself to it. I hate it, but it's part of the show. It attracts attention."

"I take it no important information is inside?"

"Both yes and no. If someone would take the trouble to steal it, I carry real but incomplete documents on each trip. It's a precaution."

They were taking no chances, she realized. As she didn't move, he nodded towards the briefcase.

"Why don't you make sure you know how to open it," he said. "Someone might ask you about it. There is a stethoscope in the drawer. You will need it. I'll read over there for a while." He sat down in the armchair in the opposite corner of the room and opened a hardcover book. She couldn't see the title, but the outside was a discreet beige and looked boring.

In character, she thought. *Not many people travel with hardcover books any more.*

Klara pulled the chair close to the table and studied the metal locks. They were unusual in the sense that they had four disks with numbers from zero to nine. Almost infinite possibilities. She had only seen this type of lock with three-number combinations before. The bolts were much too sturdy to attempt to open them with a pick lock or tool of any kind, keeping in mind that she mustn't scratch or harm them. Pär was not supposed to discover that she'd opened it.

She plugged the stethoscope into her ears and spun the first wheel on the left lock. It rotated freely, not revealing anything. Then she turned it slowly number by number. She thought she heard a faint snap on three, but wasn't sure and started over again. Yes, there was a difference in the sound on three.

Now that she knew what to listen for, she did the same with the other three wheels, writing down each number that made the mechanism click. When, after what seemed like a lifetime, she thought she had the correct combination of numbers on the left side, she used her notes to check and lined up the mechanism on the other side.

The briefcase did not open.

"I give up," she said, leaning back in the chair. "I would never qualify as a real spy."

Pär looked amused. "I'm proud the code is that difficult to break," he said.

"Give me a clue," she asked. "I think I got it right on the left lock, but the right one seem to respond to another set of numbers."

"OK," he said, putting aside his book. "As you don't seem to have noticed, I'll tell you: It's the date you came to Karlskrona shipyard. I thought I'd be a tad romantic, you know, maybe a man in love would hint that 'important date' to his lover.

Only on the left, it's day and month; on the right it's month and day."

That date had not occurred to her, not even remotely. She had turned the mechanisms methodically one number at a time until she'd heard the almost inaudible tick, and not thought of a combination of numbers.

Laying down the briefcase flat on the desk, she entered the numbers on the right side in the order he had indicated. Nothing happened.

"Sorry, the locks have a time limit too. You have 30 seconds to enter the correct combination on both sides, otherwise it will remain locked," Pär explained.

Klara sighed and once more entered the combination, reversing the numbers on the other side. It immediately snapped open with a metallic sound. The edges revealed that the briefcase was metal lined, but the inside was in soft brown suede.

There were blue folders with a few pages in each. Klara spread them out and was about to photograph them when he stopped her.

"Don't use that phone," he said and handed her another, identical telephone. "This was stolen from a big electronics store a few days ago. No surveillance camera got a clear enough picture to identify the thief."

Klara was impressed.

"Keep it with you at all times. Now it's connected to the hotel WiFi, but it doesn't have a sim card, so you won't confuse it with your own, not even by mistake."

Pär's meetings with FMV, the Defense Procurement Office, were at this stage mostly about equipping the ship, where and how weapons were going to be lodged and how that would affect the construction in terms of necessary reinforcements of the carbon fiber structure. He carried the blueprints in order to make a first assessment of the timeframe for completion.

From that point on, every evening he was in town, Klara had dinner with him and afterwards they spent a couple of hours at that same small hotel near Kungsträdgården. It had few rooms and marine officers were their priority clients, but it was still always miraculously available for Pär. And always the same room.

It was safe, she knew, swept for microphones and hidden cameras before his arrival on each occasion. Their time together in private was excruciatingly boring. They had already talked about everything they had to say while in public.

Thank God for the solitaire games on the cell phone, she thought.

He always carried the heavy briefcase, and every evening before she left, Klara would open it and take pictures of the blue-prints in there with the telephone he had given her. When the cell phone was connected to the hotel Wi-Fi, it would register the date and place where the pictures were made.

It was important to *walk the walk and talk the talk*.

CHAPTER THIRTEEN

The Baltic sea, outside Sandhammaren

Fahrid was both excited and relieved when the ice-cold water engulfed him. He carried the key on a chain around his neck, under the wetsuit. His clothes were carefully folded in a bundle and tied together by a string. In the middle of the parcel he had placed a spanner from the machine room, to ensure that it wouldn't float too soon and be washed ashore on some beach. He jumped clutching the bundle and a pair of fins. No one had seen him and it would be hours before anyone missed him. That was enough. Under water, he slipped his feet into the fins and headed toward the surface.

The sea was high, millions of microscopic drops of water broke away from the crests of the waves creating a dense, foggy curtain between himself and the sky. Still, he could see dawn breaking in the east. He heard nothing but the sea, not even the engine of the ship he had just left. The water temperature was only in the mid-forties but the wet suit kept away the cold. He felt a charge of energy and adrenalin. Every time a wave lifted him, he looked for lights, but the visibility was poor. In this harsh sea, it would take a couple of hours to reach the Swedish coast. Fortunately, the wind was blowing towards land; otherwise, it might have proved an impossible mission. With a simple sleight of hand, his watch changed into a compass. He checked his bearings and started swimming.

He changed his watch back to measure time. It was almost seven thirty. The swim had taken two hours and twenty-three minutes. He was in a hurry. His hands and feet had grown numb in the cold water, but now he stood on the shore and started walking towards the parking lot. The sand was covered by a layer of salt and crunched like thin ice with each step. It was warmer underneath. While he walked he fished out the key from the chain around his neck. There was the Volvo, the only vehicle in sight. In the summertime the place would be jam-packed with cars. He unlocked the door and got in.

The car had been there for some time, and inside it was so cold he could see his own breath. The windows misted over before he got the engine started. Turning the heat on, he cursed his superior's extreme precautions. Usually he travelled with regular flights and false papers, but this time they had insisted that his entry into the country must be completely untraceable. He had suggested half a dozen better solutions than swimming for hours in ice-cold water, but no one had cared to listen.

He opened the glove compartment. The passport, the driving license and the Beretta were all there, as agreed. And a small bottle, which on closer inspection turned out to contain much-needed vodka. He took a drink knowing that those like himself, who from time to time risked their life for Allah and the cause, had exemption from the prohibition to drink alcohol.

After he had warmed up a little, he got out of the car and pulled off the wet-suit. Quickly returning to the warmth inside he changed to the clothes left for him on the backseat.

Fahrid had flown to Odessa via Moscow, where he had picked up the bona fide documents identifying him as Ivan Antonovich, a Russian sailor. The contacts, both personal and official from his training period with the Russian Military Secret Service, provided many advantages. But these documents were no longer usable and had been disposed of, together with his work clothes.

In Odessa he had found a suitable ship and signed on. He had been part of the crew for what seemed like ages, waiting for further instructions. He kept to himself on the cargo ship. As his Russian was good, he stood little risk of being found out, as long as he played the part of a reclusive, taciturn Cossack of few words, taking care to keep his gaze empty, thus giving the impression of being a little "slow". Every time they called at a port, he had met with someone and been updated on the plan.

When the ship arrived in Helsinki, he was informed that the deal he'd been waiting for had been struck.

Strange, thought Fahrid, that Sweden, such a small country, not only builds its own combat airplanes, but also the world's most modern warships. Jas was a good plane, but not unique in its class. The ship, on the other hand, the YS 2000 Visby-class corvette, certainly was just that—unique. The pilot project had jokingly been called *Smyge*, Sneaky in Swedish. You couldn't see it, hear it or detect it. It was built on the same principle as the stealth airplanes, with flat-planed surfaces and sharp edges to avoid being discovered by radar, as well as its perhaps most unique feature: total isolation of both sound and heat.

The strict Swedish rules for export of arms and defense-related merchandise made it impossible to purchase the vessel in an official way. His mission was to supply his organization with what was currently on top of the Leader's wish-list: the blueprints to YS 2000. They would build a copy of the ship on a slightly smaller scale. Maybe 1:2 or 1:4, Fahrid speculated. Just enough to carry the necessary missiles. Then they would be able to place themselves strategically and attack without warning. With a little luck they might even manage to get away undetected, something nobody else could dream of, least of all the enemy.

He had studied at Embry Riddle in Daytona Beach, Florida, probably the best U.S. university in the field of aeronautical engineering. There he had maintained a different identity, the spoiled son of a lesser known branch of the Saudi royal family. Later that identity had been discarded forever. Only what he had learned mattered; he was never going to have to look for a job based on those merits.

To fit the role, he had to be very grand. A Ferrari, a luxurious apartment with a view of the beach, and lots of cash. But money didn't mean anything to him. His personal needs were modest and he had never experienced a shortage of anything important. The investment in his education had served its purpose in many ways, and the only thing that mattered right now was that, thanks to his training, he was capable of judging whether the documents he was going to pick up were complete and as sensational as his superiors were hoping. Fahrid was looking forward to studying the blueprints. If they turned out to be sufficiently extensive, all the hardship he had been through would be worth it.

He put the car into gear and started rolling out from the parking lot, looking for a road sign indicating *Simrishamn*. It was not far away. There, most of the houses looked like they were uninhabited. To Fahrid the architecture was very foreign: small, detached houses, often only one story high with steep roofs. Picturesque, like something he'd seen in books. Farther inland, the countryside reminded him of Yankee-land. A little like along Interstate 19 on the stretch between Daytona and Miami.

He stopped just north of Jönköping. On the other side of the highway, there was an old building in ruins beside a vast lake. There, on his side of the road, was a rest area providing all kinds of services. That would do.

Inside the low, light building, he first visited the restroom. Then, he looked for a payphone, only to become annoyed when the one he found didn't take coins. He didn't have a card and was reluctant to switch on the cell phone left for him in the car. It was important to leave the least possible electronic footprint. At a table close to the slot machines he discovered an old-fashioned brown phone with a coin-intake attached. Now, he just needed change.

He studied the restaurant. It was a buffet, which was good, as he didn't want to show that he didn't speak a word of the language. It was important to remain as invisible as possible, because he knew that he didn't look like a tourist. He was rarely hungry when he was tense and high on adrenaline like now, but he knew that after the long freezing swim he needed something of substance. After having made sure that the cash register had a digital display, he took a tray, picked a cheese sandwich and took a tea bag.

"That will be 84 kronor," the woman at the register said, her voice tired already at nine in the morning.

Fahrid stole a glance at the green digits. He gave her a 100-kronor note, got his change, and sat down by the window.

What an enormous expanse of freshwater, he thought. Lakes had always fascinated him, probably due to the lack of them at home.

The sandwich was stale but he ate it anyway. When he had finished the tea, he went over to the phone and put the 5-kronor coin in the slot, dialing the number. Relieved, he heard it ringing. At the third ring, someone picked up.

"Hamid," answered a deep male voice.

The call was cut off. No more was needed to communicate that he was on his way.

In the shop he found a map of Sweden and this time he paid with a 500 kronor-note. He then went back to the car and studied the map before resuming the drive. The traffic flowed smoothly, in less than four hours he was entering Stockholm.

The map was open on the passenger seat and from time to time he glanced at it to check how to get to Rinkeby. When the road signs for Bromma airport appeared, he followed these for a while. He drove past an enormous construction on the right-hand side, a wave-shaped white building that had to be an office complex. At the OKQ8 gas station, he turned in to Rinkeby. After getting lost a couple of times, he finally parked outside a reddish-brown block of rental flats with outdoor access corridors, and looked up at the second floor. He honked the horn a couple of times and saw people look out from behind the curtains in several windows. One of them opened and an elderly man stuck his head out.

"My son!" the man called in Arabic. "Welcome!"

Fahrid knit his brows, irritated. He did not like being reminded of his childhood. There had never been a father in his life. His very first memory, from when he was three or four years of age, was a resounding slap to his face. The disgusting infidel who slapped him alleged that she had found him in the street. He lived with her a few years in a small windowless room with a hotplate in the basement of the large shopping mall she cleaned. She'd kept him as a slave, to do the dirtiest work. But then she found out that she might be rewarded if she enrolled him in a religious school. That became the turning point. Her power over him waned and bit by bit he turned her into a subservient creature who waited on him and was forced to cater to his every whim.

Years later, when he finished his training as an operative and before he was allowed to leave the Kingdom, his superiors demanded a major gesture of loyalty. Fahrid knew they believed she had been like a mother to him, and he decided to strangle her with his bare hands. A bit like a game, a way of outwitting his superiors and proving to himself that he was a step ahead of them. It had been a stimulating challenge to turn a task into a personal deed —and she was an infidel, after all.

A moment later, the elderly man stood before him and he reluctantly let himself be embraced. Fahrid let him handle the bags from the trunk. As soon as the door to the apartment closed behind them, the man started apologizing. He expressed himself very respectfully and looked genuinely anxious about having taken the liberty of calling him his son.

"I have been living here for so long that I was forced to give the neighbors some kind of explanation to your arrival. I've told them that you're my son and that you've finally been allowed to come. Around here, that's a perfectly credible explanation."

Hamid had brewed strong tea, and on the table there was a plate of dried mutton with dates and another with cheese and bread. Fahrid ate, now with a healthy appetite, while Hamid contentedly watched him.

"There was an update on the radio that the Swedish sea rescue had been searching for five hours, in hard weather, for the sailor that was presumed to have fallen overboard from a Russian freight ship between Bornholm and the Swedish coast. They had to give up, finally. Just so you know," Hamid said.

"Good of them to try, but they will never find him." Fahrid said, amused.

Changing the subject, the old man said, "I know who she is... Where she works and lives. I followed her one night, but I didn't dare do it again. She might have noticed."

"You were right not to," said Fahrid.

"If you want to see her, the best thing is to take the subway at Hässelby, the one at 7:48 am. The front car. She gets on at Alvik. You can't miss her. She's the only one who gets on there with hair like that. Artificial red. Not henna."

Not a bad idea, thought Fahrid. He would be anonymous among the mass of people on their way to work. If he got the subway from the terminal, he wouldn't risk her noticing him getting on. If she was as good as he'd been told, she would be vigilant. He would scrutinize her at his own pace, be certain of all details before he contacted her.

"She doesn't look like an Arab woman at all," Hamid went on. "Is she really?"

"Don't worry about that. The less you know, the less you can tell," answered Fahrid, once more irritated. The comment put an end to all attempts at keeping the conversation going.

Hamid had made up a bed for him in the larger bedroom, which had a bedside table, a lamp, a radio, and an armchair, with a wardrobe covering all of one wall.

"How can you afford to live like this?" Fahrid asked, aware of the good quality of both the apartment and the furniture. He was suddenly conscious of how little he knew about life in Sweden.

"I have been given everything by the Swedish authorities," said Hamid with pride. "It has not cost the Kingdom a penny. I am a legal immigrant and I'm pretty old. They're tolerant about my not having learned the language. But I have to go to school every day, or the benefits are cut."

Fahrid did not like the sound of that arrangement. It made him suspicious.

"What do you mean? Why does the Swedish state keep you?"

"In this country it's like this, when you get a residence permit, you are kept. I speak Swedish better than they think, but if they knew, I might be forced to take a job and that's not what I'm here for. And if I didn't accept the benefits, everybody, especially the authorities, would snoop into why and where I get my money, and well, you know... that could be dangerous. So the best thing to do is to be like everybody else."

Fahrid was far from convinced, but he wouldn't have to worry about Hamid for much longer. "Go," he said. "It's going to be an early morning if I want to catch the 7:48 at Hässelby."

There was a worn Quran on the bedside table. This simple gesture reconciled him with the old man, in spite of his previous behaviors.

For the first time ever on a mission, Fahrid did not have a clear identity, a role to play. Normally, the efforts to take on a role amused him and kept him busy. During the often long periods of waiting he would create a background, find the right clothes, gestures, posture, and general look that suited the character. But this time was different. He had to keep his head down, take care not to be noticed, just melt into the scenery and try to be invisible until the documents were in his possession. A lot harder than playing a part. It made him restless. He had no idea how long it would take for the woman to gather the coveted information.

CHAPTER FOURTEEN

It was only five thirty when a gentle knock on the door woke him up. Still pitch-black outside. Fahrid made no attempt to hide the Beretta on his bedside table when Hamid came in with a pot of hot tea. The old man avoided looking at the weapon.

Let him be a little frightened.

After an invigorating shower and a careful shave, he was ready to start the day. In the living room he saw that Hamid was getting ready to leave.

"You're not coming with me," he said, irritated that Hamid was taking things for granted.

"No, no, no," Hamid answered. "I am getting ready for school. If I fail to turn up, I have to give an explanation, so it's better to just follow the rules."

The idea struck Fahrid as quite comical, such an old man at school, and again he felt he needed to learn more about this country.

He took the subway to Fridhemsplan and walked the long underground passage to the green line. There he left the station and took a walk. He didn't want anyone seeing him to wonder why he travelled back in the same direction he'd come from. A few minutes before the 7:48 train was to leave, he was back on the platform. Inside the train, he looked at the subway map. There were many stops on the way to Alvik. He sat farthest back in the first car, not caring that those seats were reserved for the handicapped. Most passengers were reading on their phones or the Metro newspaper, and he was a little annoyed at himself for not having picked it up for free at the entrance, just like everyone else. The stations flashed by and he felt his anxiety rise. Abrahamsberg, Stora Mossen and then, finally, Alvik. The subway had filled up and there were no longer seats for everyone.

If for some reason she didn't get on, he would wait at the following station, to see if she came on the next train.

As soon as she entered the car, he understood what Hamid meant. She had a completely unnatural, dark cherry red hair color, a color never granted by Mother Nature. She was taller than average and slim in a Western way. Nothing, neither clothing nor manner, revealed her origins. The old man was right, it was difficult to imagine that this was an Arab woman. Fahrid felt a grudging admiration. She was better than him, in that respect, better at fitting in. He had read her file. There wasn't a lot, and the photo he had seen must be at least twenty years old. She had disappeared and changed identity, and the Palestinians had doubted her loyalty after that. This was the big test. If the documents about the ship turned out to be as extensive as they expected, there would no longer be any doubt. But until that was confirmed, there were still certain questions. If she didn't deliver, he would have to eliminate her.

A mild warmth started to spread around his crotch and he felt his muscles tighten. He always got a hard-on when he thought of killing. The fact that it was a woman, a woman who probably wouldn't give up without a fight, made it even more exciting.

Fahrid got off at the metro stop T-Centralen. He had done what he had set out to do—identify her. It was unnecessary to do any more today.

91

Instead, he spent time getting to know the city. Hamid had shown him several Shi'ite mosques on the map. He would go there for prayers, to lend credibility to his role. It was an advantage to have more than one to choose from, then no one could keep track of the prayers he attended. Hamid had sought refuge in Sweden as a Kurd of the Shia minority, in part to distract from his true Saudi Arabian and Sunni origins, which hardly would have gained him a residence permit; Fahrid, playing the part of Hamid's son, would have to pretend to be Shia, too. As a Wahabbist, only the importance of his mission would justify such a violation of his true faith, and Fahrid was not comfortable with the situation.

Many Swedish women looked at him openly and he could see that they appreciated what they saw. It was even more obvious here than in the U.S. That disturbed him.

Shameless Western whores.

In order not to attract attention, he decided he would have to change his looks, fill his cheeks with latex and let the stubble on his face grow. He should also get clothes that didn't reveal the fitness of his body. There was a price on his head due to former missions, though only a handful of people could identify him. His success depended largely on no one noticing him.

The next day he whiled away wandering about the city and visiting different mosques at prayer times. Walking along Götgatan he discovered a second-hand clothes shop. A nice Hugo Boss suit was hanging in the shop window. He admired it for a few seconds and decided to check it out. There might be a future use for it. He went in and pointed at it. It fit him perfectly.

Carrying the clothes in a bag, he went to the Old Town to look at the historical architecture. He moved purposefully and walked at a fast pace, as if he was on his way somewhere to avoid anyone addressing him. First he walked in the direction of the Royal Palace, then over the bridge to Kung-strädgården and from there to Sergels Torg.

At Hötorget he turned right and went down the stairs to the subway. When he saw a dry cleaner's, he turned in the suit.

"But it's clean," the man behind the counter said.

Fahrid just shook his head and gave him a bored look. He got a yellow slip of paper in exchange for the suit.

After that he took the subway back to Alvik. Riding in the rear of the train he got off and went out, up a small hill. At Tranebergsvägen there was a bus stop that was a perfect place to watch her come and go. He would also come back during working hours to have a look at the gate to her building. Knowing the kinds of locks on the front and apartment doors, he would know what he needed to get in, if he ever needed to.

From his point of view the worst thing about this mission was the time it might take.

CHAPTER FIFTEEN

Cuba

Klara's life turned hectic that late autumn. The "grand finale" of the season's current affairs program was in the making. Interviews with the presidents of the U.S.A. and Russia and some other highlights had been recorded, and they were in a hurry to finish the episode.

She had never dreamed that she would do any of the interviews, but because of time pressure and efforts to limit expenditures, she was going to double as a journalist for two Latin-American politicians. She could travel alone and hire technical assistance on location, just a cameraman who would take care of the lighting and a sound technician. And she didn't even need an interpreter for the interviews.

Pär wasn't supportive, it meant suspending their smoke screen project for ten days. Klara argued that it added credibility to the role she was playing: she had a real job to take care of, and Pär didn't have much to say regarding how she saw fit to manage her cover.

The true reason was that she had made plans to meet with Serena in Dallas over the weekend, before returning to Stockholm. Fortunately the divorce from Manuel had not affected her close relation to his two children, Serena and Marcos. Serena was close to finishing flight school, and with another student, she had arranged to fly to DFW. He would take the plane back to Daytona Beach and on Sunday, he would return and pick her up and she would fly back. To hire the plane over the weekend was impossible—it would be far too expensive—but this way they could both add cross-country flight hours. This was going to be the first time Serena and Klara had met in more than a year.

Klara couldn't wait to see her and talk, drink lattes, and go shopping at some outlet during the forty-eight-hour visit.

It was interesting to moonlight as a journalist. On her way to Cuba, the first stop was Lima, Peru. There she interviewed a former Secretary General of the UN. Everything worked out really well, apart from the fact that her suitcase was lost. And as she was only staying 48 hours, there was little hope it would arrive before she left for Cuba.

There were two reasons to go to Cuba. The first was that Nicaragua's president was there at the moment. He had had a thrombosis some years earlier, and did regular check-ups with Cuba's best medical team. The other reason was to try to get an interview with Raoul Castro. In spite of being retired, his participation would make the program more significant.

He had not replied to her letter, but the fact that she'd been granted a journalist visa was interpreted as a ray of hope. Klara doubted very much it would happen; in countries with totalitarian regimes, whether you succeeded or not would depend on the whims of the powers that be. She knew that very famous journalists had often sat around for weeks in Cuba, waiting for an interview, only to be forced to return home with unfinished business. But at least the interview with Ortega was secured.

Coming to Havana by plane was like riding a time machine backwards. Everything had come to a stand-still after the rev-

95

olution. The airport, the terminal, even the airplane seemed to be reminiscent of the 1950's. The government employees had all the power—the tourists and citizens, no rights. You had to be flexible without being subservient in order to be treated with respect. Carefully measured doses of flattery used to work. People's fears were so tangible that they actually smelled, an acrid, sour smell, like old sweat. Still, on the surface, nothing was different here than at any other airport. Long queues formed at passport control. It seemed to take the controllers ages to decide whether each traveler's reason to visit the country was valid or not.

She had imagined that the journalist visa would grant her special treatment, that the very sight of it would speed up the airport bureaucracy, that they'd want to make sure she got a good start to her visit. That did not happen.

When she had called earlier that day from Caracas and tried to get hold of Ortega's press manager Carlos Cabeza, it was his wife who picked up: "My husband said you should take a taxi. We understand that you have a reservation at Hotel Paraiso. Please call again after checking in."

Klara got a little nervous. What if she wasn't important enough to get time with Ortega, even if the interview had been granted? To go home without the piece would be an embarrassing failure.

The taxi, a blue-green Chevrolet from the 1950's, had patched seats and a bumper from a different brand; no original spare parts were available in Cuba. The driver was big and tall, a fit man somewhere in his 30's. He was probably connected to the police, a snitch or paid informer. The drive was going to take about half an hour and she would pay the fee in American dollars; the amount was agreed before he started the car.

It was night and dark outside. She could not see a lot of the city. Along the road, there were lighted billboards, but not ads for Coke or new cars. Instead, they portrayed slogans in Spanish saying *Fight for the Revolution! Long live Che! Communist Youth fights the American oppressors!*

They came to an area where beautiful villas in colonial style were surrounded by gardens. The street lights were almost non-existent, and the few lighted windows had no curtains and almost all of them revealed naked lightbulbs. Klara concluded that the villas now served other purposes than that for which they had been built. Strange how all dictatorships were similar, no matter the ideology. In Spain also, during the Franco era, the most beautiful buildings had been seized by the police and the military. Architectural gems were often transformed into barracks or storage spaces or dedicated to dreary office functions.

Hotel Paraiso was not very different from the airport terminal. Also here, nothing seemed to have changed since the revolution. A driveway which probably once had been grand, with a fountain and a dying palm tree in the middle, was the turnaround for cars. Unfortunately, the hotel was pretty far to the south of the city center, and she wouldn't be able to go anywhere unless she managed to hail a cab.

The building was a concrete-gray shoe box placed on one short end, ten floors high, with an annex for the lobby, in glass and light blue. The color had flaked off in large patches and no one had bothered to repaint.

It was late, and the night staff was on duty.

"Cash or credit card?" asked the young, surly receptionist.

She wore her uniform in a way that you could tell that she was the commanding officer.

"It's prepaid," said Klara.

"There is nothing about that in my papers. If you don't have cash or a credit card, you can't stay here," said the woman, looking Klara right in the eyes.

Klara knew there was no use arguing. She handed over her personal credit card. She might need the cash. *You never know...* She tried to hide her frustration: you couldn't get a visa to travel to Cuba if you did not have a prepaid hotel room for the full period of your stay, and of course the receptionist knew that as well.

The room was large, sparsely furnished, with a narrow plastic table close to the wall, a mirror fastened to it, and two beds with bedspreads the same color as a couch that had seen better days. Something ethnic-looking hung on the wall in a cheap frame and there were heavy gray plastic drapes, their seams torn, behind the curtains, instead of blinds or shutters. The bathroom, with pale turquoise tiles, some of them cracked, had humidity damage on the ceiling.

She walked over to look out the window while she called Carlos again. She wouldn't be able to relax before she knew that the interview was secured. She did not have a room with a view of the sea. Instead, half of her field of vision was the gray concrete roof of the lobby, and beyond that a construction site, where rather nice terracotta-colored bungalows were almost completed.

"Good evening, Klara, I hope you had a good flight." Carlos had a beautiful velvet voice and spoke calmly with a soft Latin-American accent.

"It was fine, thank you."

"All is set for tomorrow. We'll pick you up at eight o'clock."

"Good. Did you find a camera crew for me?"

"Tomás Medina from Reuters will assist you, camera and sound."

Klara sighed, relieved that everything was OK. "Thank you so much. That's great."

While they talked, Klara tried to picture Carlos. She was ready for a one-night stand in Cuba. Was the platonic relationship with Pär, faking love in public, wearing on her? Now and again she wished she would meet someone, but she'd been too busy lately to give her love life any serious thought.

"Good night, see you tomorrow."

Klara slept well and got up at six to wash her hair and put on makeup. She was on camera again. That had not happened since she was in her twenties hosting a popular TV show for a couple of seasons. She had downloaded the videos from Lima to her computer, checked them thoroughly and felt surprisingly OK with how she looked and behaved in front of the camera.

Carlos turned up at 8 am sharp. He immediately picked her out from the crowd in the foyer and came straight up to her, his hand outstretched and a big smile saying:

"*Compañera!* Comrade. Welcome to Cuba."

When she had received the reply from Ortega's staff the first words were *Cro. Andersson,* and she had been confused by the abbreviation. In European Spanish Cro. would stand for "Caballero", something like gentleman, and historically, a knight. Now she understood that here, it meant *compañero,* comrade. Mistaking her for a man had added to the mystery. Had they addressed her Cra. instead of Cro. she would have gotten it sooner. In Cuba and Nicaragua, you were *comrade* with everyone: waiters, taxi drivers, cleaners, and, obviously, also journalists.

Carlos was ordinary-looking and efficient, short, rather chubby, a fatherly type in late middle age. Not one ounce of sexiness apart from his voice.

A car with diplomatic plates took them to Ortega's residence. It was a large villa in natural stone, with a big garden and shadowy terraces, protected by a high fence and armed guards. Right in the middle was a small lake, home to a flock of beautiful black swans. Klara had never seen black swans before. Inside the villa, they were received by a woman who acted the part of hostess. She was dressed in a dark blue uniform-like skirt suit, small and compact, looking more like an old-fashioned, efficient secretary than a housekeeper. Klara was to have breakfast with Ortega while they prepared the interview.

She was shown to a patio at the back of the villa. To her surprise, Carlos and the cameraman from Reuters stayed inside the house; she was to have breakfast alone with Ortega. He was shorter than she expected, with a moustache and thinning hair. Supple build. The big glasses he had used to hide behind in earlier photographs were gone, replaced by contact lenses. He looked nice, relaxed, almost attractive. He wore a short black suede jacket and jeans, dark blue shirt. They went through the interview questions, digressing here and there into all kinds of everyday subjects, as well as formal issues, the conversation flowing effortlessly.

"When can we tape?" Klara asked.

"Whenever you like," he answered.

"No time like the present."

With a certain malice, she decided that the interview should be recorded outdoors. She blamed the light, but the real reason was that she wanted to place this left-wing Sandinista revolutionary against the background of the villa, the garden and the lake with the black swans, that is, against a backdrop of luxury. There was a slight wind that might bring about problems with the sound, but she decided to take the risk.

She was high on the feeling of flow, making decisions that impacted men in power. She was in control. Ortega answered her questions seemingly sincerely and elaborately, and said some inspired and complimentary words about Sweden. When they were about two-thirds done, a car drew up outside the villa and they had to suspend the recording.

"It's the Colonel," said Ortega as a way of introduction.

Klara didn't recognize him but before she could ask, both men disappeared into the villa, and Carlos came back.

"That was Castro's right-hand man," he explained. "The boss has promised to mention that you are the Swedish journalist asking for an interview. Come and have a cup of coffee in the meantime."

The room to the left of the hallway was as coolly and austerely decorated as the rest of the villa – at least the part she had seen. A number of chairs along the walls, a long wooden bench at the table in front of the TV, which was on and broadcasting a Cuban morning program.

Almost immediately, another man appeared, someone Klara hadn't met before. He introduced himself as Alvaro, and initially his accent didn't reveal if he was Cuban or from Nicaragua. They had coffee at the big table, making small talk. The whole situation seemed unreal. There she was, while in a nearby room Nicaragua's president was talking to Castro's right-hand man *about her*. The only thing missing, for this really to be something to write memoirs about, was a romance. She told Alvaro that her suitcase had disappeared already before she reached Lima, half hoping that he, being so close to the powers that be, could do something about it.

After a while, Klara was sure Alvaro fancied her. She studied him from that point of view for a moment. Tall and fit, in his forties, "ugly-handsome", his face was unusual. He had high cheekbones, a pronounced chin, small eyes and a rather small boxer's nose.

He had joined the Sandinistas a long time ago, before Ortega regained the presidency. He came from a large family where brother fought brother on separate sides in various Latin-American conflicts. Later, when Ortega became president, Alvaro had been a public prosecutor for several years, but now he was in private practice. That was about as far as

101

they got before Carlos interrupted. The interview could be resumed.

While returning to the garden, Klara tried to analyze why she felt uncomfortable, as if Alvaro's interest was not entirely welcome. Gradually the thought faded as she concentrated on her work.

CHAPTER SIXTEEN

They changed the camera position to make the interruption seem planned and wrapped up their work. Klara checked the playback on the camera, found that it was all right and they finished at lunchtime.

Tomás Medina, the cameraman from Reuter, offered her a ride back to the hotel. Carlos called the guards and told them to let them out through the barriers. On the way back, Tomás suggested to tape some footage of the city.

"Great idea. What would be the most emblematic places?"

"The Malecón and Plaza de la Revolución," he answered.

She knew about the Malecón, a long, broad esplanade along the sea. "Is that the Plaza where the big picture of Che is on a facade?"

"Right, and why not add Hotel Nacional, while we're at it? That's where so many great musicians started their careers," Tomás volunteered.

"Sounds great," she answered, remembering Bebo Valdéz. The legendary Cuban had fallen in love with a Swedish woman and stayed in Stockholm when his orchestra left. He had supported his new family playing in hotel bars for years, until he was "rediscovered" as the great jazz pianist he was. A link to Sweden, if Richard decided to use it.

When Klara got back to her room, the telephone rang. It was Robert. He wanted to know how things were going and whether she would get the Castro interview. Klara told him that Ortega had promised to push for her. They talked about what to ask in case she got lucky, and she took notes to be sure not to miss anything. Suddenly the *telefonista* interrupted, informing that she had another incoming call. Both of them got excited hoping it might be someone from Castro's staff. She promised to call him back immetiately if that was the case.

It turned out to be Alvaro. He had talked to customs at the airport and her luggage should arrive in Havana around seven. He suggested he pick her up, go to fetch it, and then celebrate having a drink somewhere.

"Sure, and thank you for taking the trouble," Klara said, thinking she didn't want to have more than a drink.

She thought about him hitting on her, and the apprehension from the morning returned. *Does he expect to be compensated for the favor?*

When the limousine pulled up outside the hotel she couldn't help but feel special. It was a totally different car than the one that had picked her up in the morning. This one had diplomatic license plates and the Nicaraguan flag on each side of the hood.

So, Alvaro has diplomatic status.

The people in the lobby looked impressed when Alvaro held the door open for her. She secretly hoped the unfriendly hotel receptionist from last night was observing them.

At the airport, Lufthansa had messed up again and her bag was now in Caracas. Alvaro roared, screamed, and pushed people around like some kind of feudal lord from the Middle Ages. *This guy must really be somebody here,* Klara realized, and her dread grew. On their way back into town, he apologized.

"I can't stand all these idiots. Incapable, uninterested, un-motivated people. You have to be competent in the exercise of your duties, whatever your profession is," he claimed.

Klara nodded and tried to look like she agreed, but she was appalled by his way of treating people and may have not quite succeeded.

After a margarita at the bar where Hemingway used to drink, they returned to her hotel. Now, insisted Alvaro, she absolutely had to try a mojito. She liked the taste, and as he insisted, she had a second. They talked about her job, and he told her how well people still remembered Olof Palme in Nicaragua. Several important squares and streets were named after the Swedish PM.

"Shot with a Magnum," Alvaro said. "I have one of those myself, and with the ammunition the killer used, he made absolutely sure his victim would die."

A mental image of Alvaro appeared in Klara's head. Against the background of his somewhat nasal, monotonous voice and even though he was talking about something else entirely, she could see him in the jungle, shooting pinioned, kneeling prisoners in the back of their neck. She didn't know where that image came from, but it frightened her. From what he had told her, she understood that his activities as a public prosecutor had mainly consisted of removing opponents.

Can't he just leave, she begged silently. She had hoped Alvaro would get drunk and decide to leave, but it was clear that she had to think of some other strategy.

The threatening and unpleasant side of his personality had become more and more evident throughout the evening.

She glanced at her watch. "Oh, it's getting late. I need to call it a night."

"I'll see you to the door," Alvaro answered.

"That won't be necessary," she objected.

To Klara's great relief, he didn't insist. Alvaro had diplomatic status and she was a nobody; the hotel staff would probably not be of help to make him leave if he decided to not do so voluntarily.

"Well then, it's been a pleasure," he said with a wrinkle between his eyebrows as he crushed her hand in goodbye. He wasn't just disappointed, he was obviously angry about ending the evening this way.

Cerdo machista, Klara mumbled in the elevator up to her floor.

She washed off the makeup in the bathroom and considered taking a shower, but was too tired from the emotional strain. Cursing the airline once more for losing her luggage, she pulled off her panties and washed them, leaving the camisole to sleep in.

She had just drifted off to sleep when a sound woke her up. The door flew open with a bang before she had time to react.

Alvaro dangled the old-fashioned key fob in front of her face with a wicked smile. Then he locked the door behind him.

"You know you want this as much as I do," he wheezed between his teeth, as he grabbed her wrist and pulled her out of the bed. When the bedcover fell away, she felt utterly vulnerable; the fact that she was only wearing the camisole made it worse.

He shoved her up against the wall and pressed his body on hers. His hands were already all over.

Think, think fast! Do something! She was nauseous.

"I have to go to the toilet."

"I don't give a shit."

He could smell her fear, and it seemed to stimulate him.

"Scared of me, are you?" he asked scornfully and pushed her down on the bed.

"Please, don't," she said lamely.

He ignored her objection. With his forearm against her larynx he pressed her down against the pillow, simultaneously forcing his hand in between her thighs. There was no point in trying to resist. That would stimulate him more. Pressing harder against her throat, he studied her face as she fought for air. He licked away the drops of sweat that had formed on her upper lip and started laughing. It sounded hysterical, almost insane. She was running out of air. With his head inclined to one side, he was staring deeply into her eyes, savoring her pain and her fear, drinking it in.

She was hoping he would back off a little, to unzip his fly, and prepared to react. When he did, she brought up her knee between his legs with all the force she could muster. He froze, crouched and rolled to the side. She jumped out of the bed and ran for her handbag. She had to get her knife.

"Where the hell was it?" the panic was getting the better of her. *In the bathroom.* Pulling hysterically at the door she dove for her purse. From the corner of her eye she saw something shining in his hand, maybe a knife. He came after her and threw her to the floor. Her handbag flew out of her hands and ended up in the bathtub. Out of reach. Realizing that she had missed her only chance she tried to scream, but her larynx only produced a hoarse cackling.

Instinctively she crouched against the wall, praying to God to make her invisible. No one here would care if she disappeared. He was from a fellow socialist country and held diplomatic status. Witnesses would be bribed to say that she had left the island as planned.

Serena is going to be so disappointed, she thought, confused. *She's not going to understand why I don't turn up...*

There was a little snub-nosed gun, not a knife, in his hand. But Alvaro did not shoot. He was too aroused not to carry through with his sadistic desires. He walked slowly over to Klara and pulled her up from the floor. Twisting both her arms behind her back, he led her back to the bed.

Without putting his gun away, he hit her with both the back of his hand and his fist. Then he tore the camisole off. To faint would have been a blessing. Klara gave up, she stood no chance. Nobody would help her. There was no point in trying to defend herself. He was going to beat her, then rape her, and finally shoot her with that evil-looking gun. Unless he preferred fucking a corpse and shot her first...

The blood trickling from her nose into her throat made her want to throw up. The hope of survival floated through her foggy brain when she realized he was avoiding causing permanent damage. The thought slowly evaporated as she drifted into a merciful darkness...

CHAPTER SEVENTEEN

Stockholm

Pär called as soon as she got back from Cuba, and Klara invited him to her apartment. It would seem natural: by now they had officially spent a number of nights together at the hotel. He seemed surprised, but she insisted. She wanted Louis to know what had happened, but wasn't at liberty to contact him directly during this phase of the operation.

After closing the door behind them, she nodded for Pär to sit on the couch and sat down in Grandma's chair, just as when Louis had been there.

"I was abused and raped during the trip to Cuba. Ask Louis if that is part of my cover, too." She was angry, wanted to punish somebody, and Pär was the one at hand.

"You can't be serious," he said, looking angry too, but his expression changed as she loosened the silk scarf around her neck and he could see the bruises.

"What the hell?" he sounded genuinely upset, "What happened?"

Klara told him briefly. She had woken up in her hotel room and an unknown man, possibly a physician—he had a stethoscope around his neck—had been sitting by her bed. He had suggested she leave the country immediately. She was booked on the next flight to Acapulco, and from there on to Dallas, where she could connect to her original flight home. Her belongings were packed, including the hard drive with the recordings, and her bag stood beside the bed. Two nights had been booked at a hotel in Dallas, to allow her to recover before she continued home as planned via Chicago and Frankfurt.

"It is in nobody's interest for this incident to become known," the man had told her. She was allowed to leave on the condition that she remained silent. "There are enough Cubans who sympathize with our regime in Stockholm to make sure you have a nasty accident if you come within a block of a police station or make any attempt to report to the police or the press," he had threatened.

Naturally, they knew nothing about her plans to meet with Serena, and she didn't volunteer the information. Klara had to fight the tears when she told Pär about cancelling the meeting with Serena. It had hurt more than the physical bruises to hear her disappointment.

"I told you this was a bad idea. For heaven's sake, you're jeopardizing the whole operation," Pär interrupted her. After a brief silence he realized he was being unfair to her. "I'm sorry. I didn't mean it that way... Neither Alvaro nor this man asked any questions?"

"What do you mean?" Klara was regretting having mentioned Serena. She was emotionally vulnerable now and knew that Pär was thinking: *It's your own fault... You should have known better...*

"Are you absolutely sure they did not suspect that you cooperate with the CIA?" he waited for her to answer.

"He did call me a capitalist whore, but I didn't make that connection," said Klara thoughtfully.

"What an utter swine, that Alvaro," Pär conceded. "I am really sorry for you. Is there anything I can do? Surely you know that our case has absolutely nothing to do with this.

Believe me, Klara, our methods are much subtler... And what would be the point?" He was silent for a beat again, and then said: "In any case we can't have Cuban thugs hanging around watching you. It might jeopardize the whole operation."

"That is the only reason I'm not reporting this. But Louis needs to know."

"I will inform Louis. We'll think of something..."

Klara had never seriously thought that there was anything behind what had happened in Cuba other than Alvaro's perverted lust. On the plane home she had decided to take up martial arts. No one was ever going to hurt her that way again. Not without her retaliating in kind.

Pär got up and went into the bedroom. There he switched on the lights and waited for a while. Then he switched them off again and walked up to the window.

"There is someone on the other side of the tennis court. Now that the trees have cast their leaves, it is not a very good hiding place anymore... but because of all this we can't be sure if it is our client or some damned Cuban thug."

It was the first time Pär mentioned that someone had come for the blueprints. Klara's skin crawled. She had not been aware that he might already be in Stockholm. Things were getting serious...

CHAPTER EIGHTEEN

As the season's last current affairs documentary was ready for broadcast, Klara's contract-based employment with TV-Plus was headed to an end. The media environment was mostly populated by much younger and ambitious people, and quality of programing seemed to matter less than ratings. A feeling of being outdated was creeping up on her, and she had a hard time mustering the energy and enthusiasm the job demanded.

Sweden was short of simultaneous interpreters at the EU institutions in Brussels, and she had received an offer of an internship at the Parliament. She had mentioned to Pär that she regretted not being able to accept, due to the mission.

At their next meeting Pär told her that he would miss her terribly, but understood that she had to accept the offer to go to Brussels. She knew that included Louis' tacit approval. Pär didn't reveal to what extent the Cuban incident played a role in facilitating her move, but Klara was pretty convinced it had been decisive.

She arrived in Brussels on a Thursday and took a taxi to the bed-and-breakfast she had booked over the extended weekend, hoping to have found a rental by then. She was not particularly impressed by what she saw on the way from the airport. Only in the city center did the architecture get interesting. The taxi stopped in front of one of the typical tall narrow houses that resemble New York brownstones.

Or maybe it's the other way around, Klara thought.

Dragging the two heavy suitcases to the entrance, she rang the bell that said P. Van der Welden. It whirred and she said:

"This is Klara Andersson."

"I am Pascale. *Bienvenue!* Welcome!" said the voice, and the door clicked open. "Come on up!"

Inside, one narrow staircase led downwards to the basement and another one upwards to the first floor. It turned out to be virtually impossible to drag both suitcases up the staircase at the same time. A young woman appeared at the open door.

"Leave the suitcases there, your room is on the lower floor. My boyfriend will help out later. He's just out, picking up a pizza. Listen, I would appreciate if we can settle the bill now. We're going away to the beach for the weekend," Pascale explained.

Klara was disappointed to get a basement room. But she had booked one of the cheapest alternatives she could find, so she was hardly entitled to expect luxury.

Pascale beckoned her into the living room. Beautiful, broad sliding doors in white-painted wood and glass opened into the room with a big window facing the street. It was tastefully furnished in a classical way. The style did not agree with the young woman's look: she looked like a worn-out hippie with long blond hair, even though she could not have been more than 25 years old.

"Your booking includes breakfast, so buy fresh croissants around the corner and leave the receipt here. We'll refund you," said Pascale.

Pascale's boyfriend came in, carried her bags down, and showed her how the TV worked. In spite of being in the basement, the room was spacious and bright. The only thing indicating that it was actually located below ground level was that the big high-placed window only showed the legs of the passers-by. The glass was protected by a fine-meshed metal netting and artfully designed wrought-iron bars. That did not make her feel secure, though; to the contrary, it felt like a trap. If somebody came down the stairs, there would be no way out. She pushed the thought away. The bathroom was nice and spacious and on the same floor as her room. She had access to the kitchen on the upper level, and was allowed to prepare her own meals.

The bed was an incredible construction of cardboard, bought at the local IKEA. It looked inviting and she decided to take a nap before going out to dinner. For the moment she only unpacked the toiletries and the t-shirt she used as a nightie.

By the time she woke up, it was dark outside. Her watch showed twenty to nine, and she was hungry. She had eaten nothing since the food served on the flight. She looked up the way to Grand Place on the map on her phone. That's where she wanted to have her first meal in Brussels. She had travelled in Europe by car with her parents one summer when she was a child, and they had spent a whole day at the gorgeous square. She remembered the beautiful old buildings and knew that most of them housed restaurants on the ground floor.

According to the map it would take 50 minutes to walk to Grand Place. Perfect after a sedentary day. She just had to take Avenue Kortembergh to Rue de la Loi and follow that street to Saint Michel, then she would be almost there. But that route turned out to be deserted and depressing at night. Not a single shop window to brighten things up. She turned into a side street to find a more interesting route.

Somehow, she got completely lost, ending up on dark, narrow streets, with shady characters trading stuff in the gateways. She didn't dare to consult her phone, because that would reveal that she didn't know her way around. Somebody might get the idea that a tourist would carry cash. She was enormously relieved when she spotted the green light of an empty cab coming her way.

As it was rather late, she thought it best to ask the driver for a restaurant where she would still be served. He took her to a large, well-lit restaurant on two floors.

It was a typical tourist trap. As far as you could get from the charming, old-fashioned, candlelit restaurant she had been looking forward to. It was almost full of large groups of tourists. She listened around a little and chose a small table close to a group of Spanish-speaking diners. After a nice meal and some small talk with the neighboring table, the feeling of having got off to a bad start dissipated.

The next morning, Klara was up early. She went to the bread shop Pascale had indicated for the croissants and bought a local publication with ads for rental apartments. By 11:00 am, she had a full schedule of appointments for both Friday and Saturday.

The area around the Parliament seemed the best choice. If possible, she wanted to live centrally, with good public transport connections. By one o'clock she had found out that the apartments in the price range she could afford were awful: small, dark rooms, where the kitchen and shower room were, at best, separated by Masonite boards or just curtains, and at worst with a shared toilet on the landing, next to the stairway, often with hazardous gas-heaters installed in the middle of the room. All shabby and ugly.

She was still hoping for a stroke of luck, but on Sunday morning she was lying in bed dejected and wondering what to do, when she heard a noise of the door lock opening. Klara pulled on her black stretch-velvet trousers and a soft pigeon-blue sweater and went to meet Pascale and her boyfriend.

The basement room seemed considerably more attractive after having visited the array of affordable housing, and she wanted to find out if she could rent this very room for a few weeks, until she found a place to live.

"Sorry, no can do," said Pascale. "That's our bedroom."

Klara felt helpless.

"But my brother owns the house next door, and he has a vacant apartment."

Pascale gave her the keys and sent her to explore. Already from the outside it looked promising. The building was white and on the second floor there was a small semi-circular balcony with a beautiful wrought-iron railing. The entrance intercom had three buttons, which meant that the house was divided into three apartments. The door opened towards a staircase, just like the one in the house she came from.

You came right into the living room, and it was large, covering the entire width of the house. A big window and the French windows opening to the balcony let in generous amounts of sunlight. The flooring was hardwood. There was a classical fireplace on the far wall. A broad vaulted passage led to a modern kitchen with a glass stovetop and a large fridge. Another vaulted passage opened from the kitchen to the bedroom, with a large window facing the back yard. The bedroom was somewhat smaller than the other rooms, lending part of its space to a walk-in closet and a bathroom, all in white, both wall and floor tiles, and it too had a window. In the backyard there was a small garden, with a little fountain and a couple of swings for children.

Klara immediately fell in love with the place. The floor plan was eccentric but harmonious and the apartment full of light.

One problem remained. The apartment was unfurnished. The three-story villa where she and Manuel had lived in Madrid was large, and after separating, most of the furniture was stored, but she could only send for furniture if she was going to stay on after the internship.

Pascale turned out to be a resourceful woman. In no time she arranged for a desk with a chair and a lamp, a kitchen table with two chairs, and a mattress. She couldn't offer a bed, but did loan Klara a TV set, as well as the most basic things for the kitchen. The boyfriend helped move her that Sunday night, and Klara went to bed on a mattress on the floor in her new apartment feeling very happy, despite the sparse furnishings.

CHAPTER NINETEEN

The area around the European Parliament mainly consisted of big concrete office buildings with some lunch restaurants at street level. These mainly catered to civil servants, MEPs, lobbyists and conference participants, and thus were closed on Saturdays and Sundays. On weekends, the entire area was silent, deserted, almost spooky. Empty, black, curtainless window-holes in endless rows stared deadly at the street, giant buildings from the 60's and the 70's, devoid of any charm or beauty.

The old parliament building on Rue Belliard would have been difficult to spot but for the flag poles with all the member states' flags. Rue Belliard sloped downwards, and that gave the entrance a kind of basement feeling. Klara had been directed to that gate, rather than the impressive main lobby, to report for her internship. Large glass doors led to where security staff checked IDs and visitors put their bags through the metal detector. Identical glass doors then opened up to the central hall. The security control was not impressive. Those carrying a Parliament ID walked straight in, with bags and all.

Klara was delighted to see that there was a newsstand. It had daily newspapers from the member states, books and weekly magazines in many different languages, as well as candy and, still, some tobacco. Knowing what an invaluable support the press would be in her work, she was already reading daily news from the different countries whose languages she was covering. And she knew that the MEPs, Members of the European Parliament, struggled to get coverage in the newspapers. They were eager to voice their opinions because it seemed that anything not mentioned in the press in their home countries simply did not exist.

In the middle of the central hall, a straight brick staircase took you up to a balcony encircling the hall. It looked like an afterthought, not originally meant to be. The bank was right above the newsstand, and on the opposite side was an ATM and the hospitality desk. This was where Klara was heading. Trainees and new employees were assisted with practical issues like advice regarding discounts for cellphone contracts and cards for public transports.

By her Swedish colleagues she was, with few exceptions, met with ice-cold indifference, verging on pure hostility. She became conscious of plotting, turf wars and competition among the interpreters and made an effort to stay out of it. More women than men had hurt her and let her down over the years, and a so densely female-dominated working environment made her cautious.

Soon after her arrival the EU parliament convened in Strasbourg, as it did one week every month. The first time she was there, she was late booking a room and ended up at a centrally located but dirty old hotel facing the railway station. Not a great place, but at least it was easy to get to work with the special EU-buses that stopped right outside.

In Strasbourg, the plenary sessions engaged most of the interpreters. The sessions were shorter, but there were three of them in each booth. Just like in Brussels, party groups and commissions were also granted interpretation, which made it necessary to call in a number of contractors. Klara had not always been able to find an empty booth at relevant meetings in Brussels, but the Strasbourg week proved to be a great opportunity to practice.

She understood why the plenary hall often was almost empty. The MEPs had CCTV in their offices and could tune in to their native languages. That way they could use the time more efficiently without missing what was said during the debates.

More than ever, she tried to delve deeply into the world of interpreting. The work that until recently had just been a side job could now become her main source of income. She had on average worked only about 10 days a year, mostly in trade union contexts, because there had never been a huge demand for Swedish in Spain. English was a must, but virtually all Spanish interpreters had English as one of their working languages. Having had an interesting job in TV, Klara had not been terribly tempted to compete for jobs in the conference business. She had acted as a wild card, jumping in when work piled up and everybody else was already booked—and of course, on the few occasions Swedish was needed.

The basic idea of simultaneous interpreting is that a speaker expresses him or herself best in their native language. Members of Parliament should be elected on grounds of the values they represent, not for their language skills. Thus, the interpreter becomes an indispensable instrument for a smooth debate. At the EU institutions, you only interpret *into* your native language, from the source languages you work with. This was new to Klara, she was used to doing it both ways.

She wondered if everybody else deep inside felt as insecure about their own performance as she did. A good interpreter should ideally not be noticed. The idea of being invisible was unfamiliar to Klara.

That *must be why so few men choose the profession,* she thought.

CHAPTER TWENTY

At the breakfast table in a villa west of Malmö, Anders Källström suddenly looked up from his morning paper. His wife was sitting opposite him with her own newspaper. They had been married more than thirty years and had three grown sons. A happy marriage? He had always thought of it that way.

When their youngest son moved out a few years ago, they decided to take separate bedrooms. Many years before that, their sex life had gradually withered to a few times a year, usually after some special evening with a little too much to drink and with foreseeable results. They had known each other for so long that neither was inspired to try anything new or different during the act. He thought that he knew what to do to make her come as soon as possible. Then he'd think of a sexy image or film sequence and that was it.

Life is probably like that for everybody, he thought, *after such a long time together.*

Anders almost startled when he now, for the first time in ages, really looked at his wife. Karin was a physician, a GP, five feet four and slightly overweight. That kept the wrinkles in check. Her hair was grayish blond, cut short, with lightly bleached highlights that needed a re-fresh. No makeup, dressed in a classical dark blue skirt and jacket, with a suitably pale blouse and, he lifted up the tablecloth to make sure, comfortable walking shoes. Not bad for her age, just very plain.

Karin looked up over her newspaper and met Anders's eyes.

"What is it?" She'd instinctively felt that he had somehow assessed her. "Lipstick on my teeth?" she asked, knowing that she didn't wear any.

"I promise to fix the fence today," he said, just to say something.

There was nothing wrong with her. And she didn't look bad at all. The wives of friends and acquaintances the same age rarely looked any better. When he was first appointed, and then re-elected, to the EU Parliament he had been proud and she had been happy for him. He would make a great deal more money, and they could do some traveling and improvements to the house and garden. Instead, he realized, they had grown apart. There was too much that they did not know about each other's daily life to be able to catch up during the weekends Anders spent in Malmö. They slid further and further apart and no longer had anything in common.

"Lars won the regatta, don't forget to congratulate him," Karin said. Lars was the youngest son and the apple of her eye. Anders had had a vasectomy after they had Lars. Three were enough, they both agreed on that.

The doorbell chimed. It was the Polish cleaning lady. With both of them working full-time, however much he tried to help out it had never been enough while the kids were at home. As soon as they could afford to, Karin had insisted on having help with the cleaning. Deep in his social democratic soul it chafed. *Everybody ought to take care of their own shit*, he used to say. More than one party member had been publicly shamed for having illegal help at home. He was paying payroll tax for the service, but it still felt like a failure.

CHAPTER TWENTY-ONE

By now Klara had discovered the best opportunities to work on mastering her new profession. When no interpreting was scheduled and she was alone in the booth, she could record herself and listen to it at home. That had turned out to be particularly helpful. She could hear where she hesitated, when she had missed something and the sentence didn't make sense, and make sure she didn't catch any bad manners like humming, clicking with her ball pen or anything else that might distract the listeners.

The specific language of the Parliament had been a shock. She was painfully aware of how much she had to learn. The difference between a report and an opinion, a committee and a commission, between EEA, EEC and EU and some even more impenetrable acronyms. These were also pretty well-guarded trade secrets. Was *chairperson* always *presidente* in Spanish? More modestly 'ordförande'—*moderator*—in Swedish.

Spanish MEPs were often good speakers and loved to expand on their arguments, dazzling listeners with their eloquence and use of idiomatic expressions and proverbs. That kind of rhetoric was next to impossible to render into another language. It seemed an impossible task to read a speaker's mind, guess the intention behind the words, particularly as she knew nothing about the MEP's yet, nor about their ideas and the issues they were defending. She kept feeling that she could be both more specific and more general, more ironic or more factual depending on the speaker. Sometimes she wished she could work in the Spanish booth. It would be so much easier to interpret the concise Swedish speakers into Spanish than vice versa.

It was only after a while that Klara became aware of the moderator at the meeting. "Acting Chairperson" the sign in front of him said, but she couldn't read his name at this distance. She knew the chair of the committee, as she usually practiced at these meetings. The Acting Chairperson was Swedish. He was tall and wiry, slightly gray, not striking in any way, but still with a certain something. Passion for what he was doing, perhaps. The more she observed, the more fascinated she became.

She stopped practicing and just listened. He had a way of chairing the meeting that was much admired by Swedes, but disliked by other Scandinavians—manipulating to get his way instead of facilitating a discussion. He repeated what others replied with a variation in nuance, pretending to misunderstand until the sentence was worded the way he wanted it. The more Klara listened, the more impressed she became.

On the fifth floor in the Belliard building was one of the EU Parliament's most popular bars. It was simply a niche between rooms, with low, brown-speckled easy chairs and a small bar counter at the far side by the window, served by two waitresses. Maybe because it was one of the oldest bars, it was the most frequented hang-out place after work. A glass of wine, some bubbles or a whiskey blended well with the after-meeting conversations.

But at eleven in the morning, the bar was almost empty. Klara ordered a *lait russe*, the Belgian answer to the Spanish *café con leche*.

Before the coffee had arrived, she looked over and saw the Acting Chairman walk in, fast, with his head bent as if deep in thought. She scrutinized him so intensely that he must have felt it because, startled, he looked up and their eyes met for a second. The spell broke when a group of secretaries walked in, laughing loudly.

At home, Klara looked him up. That was easy, he was vice-chair and the only Swede in the sub-committee on Social Welfare Cooperation. The list of Members of Parliament, known as "the gray list" also showed all committees, with chairpersons, vice-chairs and board and committee members, with pictures. She found what she wanted to know: Anders Källström, Swedish, from Malmö, with a BA in Political Science, a Social Democrat, married. The information made it possible to track his meetings. She would be able to watch him work, as her only limitation as an intern was finding a vacant booth.

Having found someone who inspired her proved to be unexpectedly stimulating.

CHAPTER TWENTY-TWO

Anders was suddenly awake, aware of a powerful erection. That hadn't happened in years. Amused, he tried to recall what he had been dreaming, and remembered a pair of amazing green eyes. Then a slender neck and a shock of shiny, dark red hair came to him.

How the hell did this happen? I wake up with an erection in the middle of the night dreaming of some redhead? As he was about to discard the whole thing as just a dream, a blurry image of the woman turned sharp in his mind: rather tall and trim, but coming across as sensual, leaning a little lazily against the bar at the cafeteria in the Belliard building.

So, she is real...

He rolled to his side. Having concentrated on remembering, the erection had waned, and he decided to try to get back to sleep. A little light from the street lamps seeped in through the Venetian blinds, and he could just barely make out the objects in the room. His commuter flat in Brussels was rather drab. The thought of making it nice and cozy had never crossed his mind. Brussels meant nothing but work to him. He had got both cleaning and laundry thrown into the bargain when he signed up for the slightly worn, hotel room-like studio with a kitchen corner.

It was furnished with a brown couch in some soft material with short, frail metal legs and a low teak coffee table. A short bar with two high stools served as the dining area by the kitchen. Anders had never even made coffee there. The contents of the small fridge were mostly thrown away when the best-before dates ended up long past. An easy chair in the same style as the couch crowded against the wall completed the furnishings. And then there was the bed. The first time he laid down on it, he had been convinced that he would get a backache. It was soft and followed his body almost sensuously. The mattress gave way when he lay on his side, and didn't push his shoulder up under his ear. This bed was actually more comfortable than his own at home.

At the beginning of his mandate, he had put up a map of the EU, with information on the member states, population figures and finance statistics, as well as the number of MEPs, on the only wall available. A few thumbtacks held a newspaper clipping with a bad picture of himself from the last electoral campaign, and some holiday pictures of his family.

Later that morning, under the hot steaming shower, the erection came back. He closed his eyes and fantasized about undressing the redhead. She would have small, firm breasts he could cup in his hands, with perky pinkish-brown nipples, a flat stomach with just the suggestion of a curve... Pronounced hips and long thighs framing a perfect, dark triangle of curly pubic hair... Imagining her naked, he stroked himself. He wanted to feel her skin under his hands. Caress, kiss, lick her... Turn her around and take her from behind... When he thought of pulling her naked body towards him, with both hands on her hips and her warmth tightly closing around his swollen, pulsating member, he exploded in a powerful orgasm.

Afterwards he felt silly. It had been a long time since he had gotten excited without more tangible stimulus. He could count the women he had slept with on his two hands. Sure, a few times, inebriated and away at some convention he had screwed some nameless, faceless participant. Someone who had left no other trace but a fleeting feeling of discomfort when she was urged to leave in the small hours of the morning, with the excuse that he could only sleep if alone in the bed... Incidents that had been entirely without importance and never in the slightest way had impacted his marriage. Now he had consciously called up the image of another woman and desired her, enjoyed her. That had never happened before.

In the bathroom mirror he slowly shifted focus, from somewhere far away to the reflection of himself. He had lost weight since he started to commute, and that pleased him. It wasn't as if living in Brussels meant all those grand dinner parties people seemed to think, and the food in the cold, impersonal canteen was no more appetizing than food served in other lunch canteens anywhere else.

He examined himself in the mirror, turned around and studied his body profile and discovered that he actually liked it. He was tall, had thick gray-blond hair, grayish blue eyes and an angular face. No rolls of fat, so far nothing sagging.... No Greek God, but quite all right. When his eyes gradually reached his face, he had to smile. He knew that he was perceived as an unobtrusive person, but gray was the word. He was convinced that no woman—including his wife—in a long time had seen him as a sex partner; they just saw the stiff, boring Anders.

And she? The one with the dyed red hair? Could she see him any other way? Who was she? He was sure that he had not seen her before. Maybe a new interpreter. He had a vague idea he had seen her in the booth. They gradually became familiar faces, and voices, because of their language combinations, and the majority were women. Several of the Swedish interpreters were quite young and pretty, the very stereotype of the blonde, beautiful Nordic woman, but that redhead must be in her early forties. Well-kept, warm, sensual... His head started to spin again but leaning his forehead on the cold surface of the mirror, called him to his senses.

Anders was not in the habit of thinking a lot about what kind of impression he made on others. He had been appointed the social-democratic representative to various national offices based on his merits. He'd proved to be a good negotiator and had travelled all over Sweden mediating disputes. He had the ability to see what people had in common rather than what divided them. Precisely this had soon been discovered, and appreciated, at the EU Parliament, where he gradually had attained a rather solid position. Both in the committee where he was a regular member and vice chairperson, and in the party group, where he held the function of coordinator. The EU parliament had turned into something of a cemetery of elephants for Swedish politicians. The leadership in Sweden would get rid of those they worried might outshine them or compete for popularity, shipping them off to the EU, either as Commissioners or MEPs, and of course, those with a name would get to chair the more important committees. Anders had been appointed because the committee was not prestigious enough for one of the bigger names.

But he was more than happy. He felt that he was in the right element at the EU Parliament. The atmosphere here was different from that of any national parliament in the sense that you did not have to support a cabinet and its decisions. A member of the EU Parliament was free to act more independently and be more faithful to his or her own convictions than a member of a national parliament.

Next week was going to be quite heavy, with back to back meetings coming up. The parties of the same political colors from various countries were going to assess a report on cooperation in the defense industry. As usual among the socialists, not many were interested. Anything related to the arms industry was unpopular, in spite of being such an important source of income for Sweden. A strong public opinion back home resisted all attempts at discussing defense issues seriously and realistically. Protective of what they perceived as their neutrality, having stayed out of wars for 200 years, Swedes would need a long time, or a real threat, to turn the public opinion regarding NATO membership or even cross-border cooperation on defense issues.

At risk of later feeling ridiculous he dressed in a black shirt and a gray tie and sports coat. Those were the most audacious clothes he possessed. Uncertain as to how to interpret what had happened, the fact that he had desired this unknown woman so much that he had satisfied himself intrigued him, and he wanted *her* to see him.

When the morning had passed without a glimpse of her, not even at lunch in the canteen, he almost succeeded in forgetting all about her. He took the evening flight to Copenhagen, and his wife met him at Kastrup airport. At that, he considered the episode over, pushed it into a corner of his mind and tried to think of it as getting well after a flu and a fever, when things get back into focus.

CHAPTER TWENTY-THREE

Fahrid panicked when he realized that the woman had disappeared. He knew she had been traveling, and supposed she would be back in a week or so, like last time. After two weeks he waited at the bus stop several days in a row, but never saw her. Then he observed her apartment at different times of day and night, thinking she might be sick, but the lights were never on. Once more he cursed the secrecy around this mission. Nobody but Hamid knew he was there, and therefore he could not use existing sources to acquire modern surveillance equipment. Because he had to stay totally under the radar, his superiors had prohibited him from connecting with other operatives. He was in the blind. She could have gone underground again.

It was a cold, dark, windless night. His respiration turned into white puffs around his face, only to settle as shiny moisture on his skin. At least it wasn't raining, so he wouldn't leave wet footprints all the way to her front door.

He got into the building through the basement and walked up the four flights of stairs. His soft sneakers didn't make a sound. The door offered some resistance; it had two locks, but he mastered them in a few minutes.

Inside, he stood still, allowing his eyes to adjust to the darkness and deciding where to start searching. He kept the pair of thin rubber gloves on while stuffing the leather gloves into his pockets. In a flash of the penlight he saw himself in the hallway mirror. It had a beautiful frame with a pattern carved in pewter on a brass base. On the right side were three small paintings with Arabic motifs. Tunisian craftwork, painted directly on glass with very simple frames. Somewhat amused, he wondered whether he was going to find more souvenirs from the Arab world.

The door to the bathroom was on his right. Why not start there? With the flashlight between his teeth, he searched the cupboards. The shelves were almost empty. A few toothbrushes, mouth rinse, some half-full jars and bottles with cosmetic products. A tray on the bathtub edge was as uncluttered. Only a bottle of shampoo and a much-used scrub. He went into the kitchen.

The cup on the kitchen table made him jump. Had she not left after all? He picked it up. It was clean. His thumb automatically found a small inward curve that on the inside showed a corresponding bulge. Beautiful—deep blue with a coarse cracked white surface on the outside—but just an ornament. He continued to the fridge. It was empty apart from a jar of gherkins and a half-full bottle of Italian salad dressing. That confirmed his suspicion that she intended to stay away for some time.

In the middle of the room, he had to stop and look out the window. The view was amazing. It was a clear night and the city lights were competing with the stars. The trees had lost their leaves and through the branches you could see reflections in the water. You could also see anyone on the sidewalk beyond the tennis court now turned into an ice-rink. She could have seen him when he waited for the lights to go off on the nights he knew she was milking the guy from the shipyard for information. It annoyed him to have exposed himself.

He tore himself away from the window and went into the bedroom. There was a large chest of drawers in a light wood he didn't recognize. It was a beautiful piece of furniture with a big, matching mirror. He pulled out the top drawer. An incredible mess of papers and gadgets were rolling around. There were old receipts, wallets, discount cards to various shops, cheap jewelry and a lot of half-empty jars of cosmetic products. The next drawer contained t-shirts and sweaters. He picked up and unfolded one. It was a gray sweater, designed to be tight-fitting, with a square neckline. On a whim, he buried his face in it. He could smell traces of perfume. Putting it back he took a quick look at the bottom drawer. Tights and underwear. Imagining her in the skimpy thongs and lace garments he shut the drawer with a thump.

Clumsy!

He held his breath listening, but heard nothing from the apartment next door, so he continued to the desk in front of the window. There was a computer screen and a printer, a big cup with a lot of pens and pencils, and a notepad in the middle of the table. A handwritten note read Åsa, this is just for the first few days. I will mail you my permanent address as soon as I get an apartment. *Forward anything that needs to be signed or paid. Big kiss* and a heart. Underneath the notebook, there was a yellow plastic binder with receipts for the rent and bank papers. On the notepad was a telephone number with a country code and an address in Brussels. Fahrid carefully copied the information to his cell phone.

In a sense, he was grateful for her having left. In Belgium, he would be able to behave like he normally did and would no longer have to be so uncomfortably anonymous.

A thought struck him: *What if the documents he had come for were not yet complete? But she is a pro, no way she would give up so close to the goal.*

He left the building and walked down towards Tranebergsplan. There were some stairs well hidden among shrubs and trees leading to the subway station. On the way down, he called Hamid with the cheap prepaid cell phone he had found in the Volvo when he first arrived.

"Get the car and come," he said, short and peremptory in his tone of voice. "I am waiting by restaurant Sjöpaviljongen."

It was late and there wasn't a living soul about, but he still did not want to wait among the houses. There was a park behind the restaurant where he could hide in the bushes, in the unlikely event that a car or a person should pass by. The subway had clocked off for the night and the small square was empty. He ducked when he walked past McDonalds, but didn't have to. There was nobody inside. And Sjöpaviljongen was dark, closed for the night.

Half an hour passed until he saw the lights from a car. It turned at Vidängsvägen and came east, towards him. The car approached at low speed as if the driver was looking for something. Fahrid was just about to come out of the bushes when he saw that the driver was not alone. The vehicle pulled up outside the restaurant and stopped. Fahrid waited. The people in the car were so close he worried that they would see the condensation from his breath. He could make out their voices in spite of the idling engine. It was a man and a woman. She laughed loudly, sounding tipsy. Fahrid cursed them both.

Really? Grown-up people. Don't they have anywhere else to go?

He took a suppressor from one pocket and the Beretta from the other and screwed them together. If he had to, he would eliminate the couple. He had planned to use one single bullet in Sweden and get rid of the weapon. An unreasonable fury filled him, he hated being forced to improvise.

Bloody idiots. They deserve to die.

The man behind the wheel set the car in motion, rolling into the small parking area on the other side of the street and turning off the engine. The lights went out. Fahrid moved towards the vehicle, still hidden by the shadows. He glanced at the red and green neon clock on the Telia building. It was 02:27 am. Before leaving the cover of the trees, he stopped and listened. The sound of their voices was clear, the couple seemed to be arguing. Then the engine started and the lights went on, blinding him. The car left spraying gravel.

Breathing normally again, Fahrid tried not to feel how cold it was. After fifteen minutes Hamid turned up.

"Sorry it took so long, but I had to get the car from the garage. Where are we going?"

"Drive up to Drottningholmsvägen and turn left." Fahrid nodded, indicating the direction.

He had reconnoitered on several occasions when he had been in this area. Carefully and in a friendly tone of voice, he piloted them to Solviksbadet, by Lake Mälaren, a place where Stockholmers go swimming in the summer. When they turned on to the dirt road to the beach, Hamid got suspicious.

"Where are we going?" he repeated.

"Just drive," Fahrid answered.

Behind the yellow dressing rooms, he ordered Hamid to stop and turn off the engine. The old man was now frightened and dared not meet Fahrid's eyes, just kept staring stubbornly straight ahead.

"Look at me," ordered Fahrid while he took the gun from his pocket.

Hamid gaped like a fish, but did not make a sound. Fahrid wanted to hear the old man beg for his life, but by now he'd understood he would soon be in paradise and kept silent. He just leaned away from the muzzle pressed against his temple. A dull crack slung his head to the side, against the window. His body went limp. Careful to not let the blood seeping out of the small entry hole stain him, Fahrid kept his finger on the carotid artery until the heart stopped beating. He was disappointed. The old man had refused him the entertainment of resisting, maintaining his dignity until the very end.

He got out of the car, closed the door and walked at an easy pace along the water back to Alvik. There was plenty of time. The first train to the city wouldn't pass until four fifteen a.m. He would walk to the bridge and dispose of the gun and the cellphone. He chuckled, remembering that he got the idea reading about all the times they had been dragging for the gun that killed PM Palme there. It would be just as impossible to find his among the debris on the sea bed underneath that bridge.

After his errand at Centralbron bridge, he went to Mc-Donalds in front of the Central Station for breakfast and to kill time. When the clock struck nine, he collected the second-hand suit from the dry cleaners by Hötorget subway station. Then he picked up a bag from one of the coin lockers at Centralen, the railway station. It did not contain a lot. Only a new white shirt of excellent quality, a nice tie, a wallet, a passport and a silver key-ring. There were public restrooms with showers, and there he changed clothes.

Less than an hour later he was at Arlanda airport. He would be out of the country by the time the car with the old man's corpse was discovered.

CHAPTER TWENTY-FOUR

Klara's internship led to a loose cooperation contract with the Parliament, not the full-time employment she had hoped for. In spite of her disappointment, she decided to go ahead. She really liked the job, though most of her colleagues found it boring. Policies, rules, and regulations were proposed, discussed, and decided upon, and would affect the lives of all the people in the member states in a year or so. She got to see them in advance, hear the pros and cons, and that was exciting.

She was booked a certain number of days per month by the Parliament in exchange for a guaranteed monthly income, but not really a full-time salary, so in the long run she would need to secure jobs on the open market. There was no rush for now; she had hardly spent any of the money Louis had left for her in the safe deposit in Zurich yet.

Somehow, she was reluctant to use it until she had done her part.

As both Swedes and Spaniards were quite active in the Greens/European Free Alliance group, she was scheduled to cover their meetings quite often. She hadn't seen the interesting Swedish guy again, since she could no longer choose which meetings to attend.

"*Durante estos últimos años de inestabilidad, de crisis, casi de pánico ante los problemas económicos a nivel internacional, nosotros – y no estamos solos, por comentarios que hemos oído de compañeros de otros partidos...*"

Oh, come on now, give me the predicate! urged Klara silently. It was one of those very elaborate speakers who opens with a subordinate clause and now, after quite a number of those, had still not produced a usable verb.

"...*hemos observado*..."

Finally! thought Klara, and started:

"During the recent years of insecurity, crisis, almost panic, facing the economic problems on an international level, we have noticed, as have comrades from other parties ..."

This was the last Spanish delegate she was due to interpret today, and Klara turned to her computer to check out how to get some furniture from Madrid to Brussels. She was looking very much forward to having her own things in the apartment.

Anders walked with long strides along the underground passage that connects Espace Léopold with the Belliard building. It was colloquially called Jurassic Park, due to the modern-art, belligerent-looking and over-dimensioned sculptures that adorn the passage. They were said to symbolize the women of the European Union. To get to the Belliard building you had to—whether you were going to eat or not—pass through the canteen, unless you took an outdoor route.

Not practical, he thought.

Naturally, the buildings had originally not been connected; the indoor passages had been built retrospectively.

In the middle of the canteen he looked up and unexpectedly met her eyes. His knees went weak at the sudden impact. The sounds, the clink of knives and forks, the voices, everything seemed to fade. His vision softened at the edges. He couldn't see clearly; everything around him except her face was foggy and insignificant.

She was walking fast, straight towards him. A heavy briefcase on a shoulder strap, lead-gray jacket with a matching skirt and a glimpse of something electric blue under the jacket... He never had time to notice her legs; his gaze was fixed on her face. Her glasses flashed in the light and behind them, bright green eyes. They pierced through all his protective shields and read his thoughts. She looked him right in the eyes.

Anders felt helpless, as if caught red-handed. She knew. She could tell by looking at him that he had dreamt about her, that he had fantasized about her naked body while clumsily satisfying himself. There was no doubt that she was smiling at him. They had not yet exchanged a word, he didn't even know her name, and yet they shared a secret.

Their gazes locked so completely, so adamantly that they almost collided, in spite of there being plenty of space. The opening between the tables was probably ten or fifteen feet. Anders succeeded in looking away and made a half-turn to avoid the collision. She swept by so close that he could smell her scent, an expensive perfume with a flowery scent.

It made him feel strangely light-hearted.

He looked around a little embarrassed, worried that someone else had noticed the charge around them. The perfume and the visual impression remained etched into his memory.

Klara had spotted him from afar and wondered if he would recognize her. He looked so trapped, she almost giggled.

Obviously he had.

Anders had access to the list of interpreters and there they appeared with name, picture, and contact details. But where was she from? There were 24 official languages, and a number of interpreters for each of them. Knowing her name he could access her schedule, and then he would be able to approach her. He could not remember having wanted anything that much in a very long time.

He started with the Danish, but had no luck. Nor Finnish. Could she actually be Swedish?

Life seemed to have changed gears, be in slow motion, now that Klara was working. Assignments were scarce, some weeks only one working day, and now she couldn't very well hang out at the Parliament on the days she wasn't working. She was getting anxious and wanted to know what was going on with the CIA operation. Neither Louis nor Pär had contacted her in weeks. Maybe it had been cancelled and they had forgotten to tell her?

The phone rang. Work? Her private life in Brussels was next to nonexistent.

"Klara Andersson?" asked a man's voice.

Klara couldn't place the heavy accent. "Who is this ?"

"We have mutual interests," said the man. His French sounded better than his pronunciation of her Swedish name.

"I find that hard to believe," Klara said, as coldly as she could manage. *Friend* or *foe*? She tapped the table top with her fingernails.

"We shared a table at *Le Petit Paris* on Rue Lindthout about a week ago," the man continued in French.

Klara pictured the scene in her mind. There had been no vacant tables. She had ordered a small carafe of wine in the bar while waiting. Close to her, some elderly French-speaking Belgians in coveralls had loudly been discussing politics. They shared the table with a considerably younger man who looked uncomfortable and was not taking part in the conversation. It was obvious that he was not a member of the Belgian party. Klara had, for once, not given in to her bad habit of eavesdropping. When she was eating alone at a restaurant, which she often did, she always used to listen, curious about what people actually talked about and how many of the languages she could understand enough to follow the conversation. At a restaurant in Cannes, during one of the Media Markets, she had ascertained that the German at the table on her right, the Swedish at the table on her left, the French behind her and the English in front had been no problem to understand. She had been sitting at a Spanish-speaking table, herself, and obviously, no one had suspected her of eavesdropping.

The dark man from the crowded table with the loud Belgians had asked her permission to sit at her table, explaining that the subject the men were discussing embarrassed him. They had talked a little about the food, she had ordered steamed mussels with celery, and they were delicious. He had had "*le plat du jour*" consisting of a stew of some kind. The man was wearing an ill-fitting brown pinstripe suit jacket, a white shirt, open at the neck, and a pair of gray trousers in the same cheap quality as the jacket. He had watchful eyes and an almost handsome square-jawed face that contrasted with the cheap clothes and the bad shaving. His posture was bad but his large hands carried no trace of manual labor. The time had passed slowly and jerkily. They had spoken French. His name was Hassan.

There was a completely different timbre in his voice and his language now, though it had to be the same man.

"How did you get my phone number, Hassan?"

He laughed, but did not answer the question. Was he part of the mission or just someone who wanted to get acquainted? In the meeting between different cultures, friendliness does tend to be misconstrued.

"Let's meet somewhere to eat and talk," he said.

Friend or foe? Better find out.

"We could meet at Grand Place, at *La rose blanche* Thursday in two weeks, at seven," she said, testing him. It was an

141

expensive restaurant. His answer would determine who he was. Louis had instructed her to put off a possible meeting for at least two weeks, to make sure that the down payment had been made. Only then would she be preparing to hand over the documents. If he was the courier, he would understand the delay.

"Sounds good. I'll make a reservation."

Klara let out her breath. If he had been the unsophisticated immigrant he had seemed to be at Rue Lindthout, he would have backed out, suggested a cheaper place and protested about the delay.

"Shall I pick you up at Rue de Leys?" he asked.

Not only did he have her telephone number, he also knew where she lived. That made her uneasy.

"No, thank you, we can meet by the metro entrance on Schuman. I'll get there by myself," Klara said.

CHAPTER TWENTY-FIVE

Anders found her picture in the Parliament's internal database. Klara Andersson, the most recent addition to the Swedish freelance interpreters. After checking her schedule, he would know her whereabouts the next day.

The cafeteria on the second floor of the Leopold building was situated in a beautiful, open room with large windows facing the southeastern part of Brussels. He saw her standing alone at the counter, but before he gathered the courage to walk up to her, she took her cup and sat down at a table by the window with two male colleagues.

She was talking in a lively manner, but looked tense and strangely alone. A wave of warmth swept through him, so strong that he suspected he might be blushing. He wanted to make her feel safe.

When the waiter turned to him and asked what he was having, he realized that this was actually the first time he had ever ordered anything here. What do you drink at 10:45 am? Coffee? He was no addict, but could not think of anything else. The waiter fussed about by the espresso machine and returned with a cup. It had the EU symbol in blue. On the larger cups, *The European Parliament* was written in all the official languages underneath the circle of stars. He could not remember having seen that before. While he drank the rich, concentrated brew he turned to look at her again. Anyone he knew would discard what was happening as: *Impossible. Ridiculous.* Anders, a mature, solid, middle-aged politician who had come far, besotted by a total stranger with dyed red hair...

It was now or never. He knew he would never gather the courage to approach her again, and his next meeting was in fifteen minutes. He placed the cup on the counter and walked up to her.

"You are Klara Andersson, right?" he asked, less convincing than he had hoped.

She looked up, surprised, but when she recognized him there was a warm, amused twinkle in her eyes.

"Yes, that's right."

He liked her voice. It was clear and sounded young. He introduced himself.

"I was wondering if you could help me with the translation of a rather complicated report," he said. He had been told that the interpreters, especially the freelancers, often helped out with translations outside working hours.

"With pleasure," she said. "When do you want me to come by?"

"If possible, this afternoon," he said, encouraged. "Maybe we could have a bite to eat while we discuss the document?"

"That sounds nice. I'll come right after six," Klara answered smiling.

They both knew this was just a pretext to meet privately. After his meeting he remembered that he had never said where they were to meet and contemplated calling her cell phone. He was truly relieved when she knocked on the door to his office.

Klara and Anders' first dinner took place at an Italian restaurant on Rue Franklin quite close by, and they cautiously explored each other.

"I am married," he said, while they were having coffee after the meal.

She nodded and hoped he would continue. His marriage must be drawing to a close. *Why else would he be sitting here, with me,* reasoned Klara.

But no explanation followed; he remained silent.

After the dinner as they walked home to her place; he stopped and turned to kiss her.

"I don't know how long it is since I kissed somebody in the middle of the street," Anders laughed.

At the entrance to her building, he held her hard, and she felt how much he wanted her, but she decided not to let him come upstairs.

He looked nice, and somehow, he became more attractive the more she looked at him. The conversation had been entertaining and light, without being trifling.

The next evening, shortly after she came home, he called her landline.

"I've called your cell eighteen times. I thought you wouldn't pick up here either," he said, a little breathlessly. "I almost panicked: although I heard your voice on the voice mail I thought I might have the wrong number."

"I'm just back from work," she answered, surprised and pleased. "There were no messages on the voice-mail."

"I didn't leave any. I hate talking to electronic devices."

"Then how am I supposed to know you called? It comes up as a blocked number," she laughed.

"That's true," he said, as if it hadn't occurred to him, and then his tone changed: "Can we meet for a while?"

CHAPTER TWENTY-SIX

The dinner with Hassan, or whatever his name was, seemed so far off in the future that it became almost unreal. She cursed Louis for his imposed precautions, two weeks after first contact and then one month to the meeting. Klara was only working one day this week and none the following. Time simply would not pass fast enough. She was getting desperate. Anders was in Malmö for the week, and Klara had to do something or she would go mad. On a whim she decided to pick up her car in Madrid, stored on blocks in a garage ever since she moved to Stockholm.

First thing to do was to call Marcos, her stepson. As a linguist Klara much preferred the Swedish word for stepchildren—bonusbarn—bonus children. Manuel's children, Marcos and Serena, were definitely that, a bonus.

Marcos now shared an apartment in the old *Barrio de la Latina* with some friends, and after having checked that she could stay with him, she reserved a seat on the evening flight. She immediately felt better. The cell phone was all she needed if anyone, including Louis, needed to contact her. She loved driving and planned to drive non-stop back, even if it would be a long day on the road. That would give her two days with Marcos. She had not seen him since she left for Sweden, now more than a year ago.

But she had to notify Ferrín, the owner of the garage where her car was stored. After a long and thorough search, she found a file on the computer with his number.

"Auvisa," answered a male voice she immediately recognized.

"*Hola Ferrín,*" she said and added, "*soy Klara Andersson.*"

"Well, long time, no see! Where are you living now?"

Despite the many years they had known each other, Ferrín still addressed Klara with the formal "usted" instead of the informal "tú", in accordance with Spanish custom.

"In Brussels, but I was hoping to pick up the car tomorrow or the day after," said Klara. "Can you arrange a new battery and the insurance?"

"That is very short notice," he answered and Klara felt her spirits sink. "Wait a moment... "

She heard him speaking with somebody else in the room.

"You are lucky," he said. "There's a claims adjuster from La Mutua coming over this afternoon. Is La Mutua all right? I seem to remember you used another company before."

"La Mutua is fine! Anything, as long as I have comprehensive car insurance!"

The fiberglass vehicle body had caused problems before; not all companies were willing to insure cars like that.

"I think that will work."

Ferrín was a man her own age, rather attractive in a slightly rough-hewn way. A "what-you-see-is-what-you-get"-type of guy. They had always flirted lightly, bantered in a friendly way and joked with each other, ever since she had had a problem with her carburetor, which she didn't know the Spanish word for, on her first car, an old Renault 4L. He had then suggested that she say the Swedish word for the problem part and had immediately understood that it was el *carburador* she was talking about. Along the years, she had followed Ferrín to different car brands. At first, he had only worked with Renault, later he got into Ford. After the divorce Klara got to keep the little Renault Alpine, a beautiful little silver-gray sports car, a near cousin to the Porsche as far as the looks goes, and she had asked Ferrín take care of it. An antique from the late-seventies and thus not easy to find spare parts for, it had nonetheless become the apple of the mechanic's eye, and was in great shape. She had forked out for new black leather seats right before she garaged it.

What a lovely project! Klara's mood changed completely. She needed to feel that she was calling the shots, taking the initiative being in control of her life and not a victim of the circumstances. Marcos had been very pleased and told her he had a surprise for her. When she was now finally about to see him again, she realized how she had suppressed her longing for the children.

Out of consideration to Manuel and his new situation, she had not wanted to come between them and their father. Both Marcos and Serena had been in the U.S. then, but now Marcos was back in Madrid, trying to make a career as a film photographer.

The fact that she required so little to feel good again made Klara happy. When Manuel left her, she had felt her life had come to an end. She had been recovering after a bout of jaundice caught filming on location in Senegal, and Maria Jesus, a very sexy young woman, had substituted for her at work while she was ill. And of course, she'd seduced him. Klara's entire perception of life had collapsed. She had always believed their marriage would last, that it was final, the best win in the lottery of life. She had thought their marriage was immune to outside threats.

After they became a couple she had ceased to notice other men and had taken for granted that it would be the same for Manuel. They had been a solid, well-known couple in Spanish media for over ten years. In the early days they had avoided working on the same programs in order to not be away from home at the same time while the children were young, but gradually they had shared everything, both their family life and their enthusiasm for the work they were doing, she on the production side, he as a director. And they had enjoyed every second. That was why his betrayal had been such a shock.

Maybe she was even ready to meet her ex-husband and his new wife. Anders' total dedication, or fascination, maybe even love, meant a lot. She was enjoying life again. Manuel used to say: *no hay bien que por mal no venga*—there is nothing bad that doesn't bring about something good. Now every new day felt like something worth treasuring.

She put a small carry-on bag on her bed and filled it with clothes she liked and knew suited her. A dress just in case, trousers and turtleneck sweaters... Comfortable shoes for driving and one pair of heels. The purple woolen winter coat over her arm. Madrid could be cold in winter. She knew Marcos was busy during the day and in the evening. Before she got on the plane, she called Manuel on an impulse. They decided to have lunch together the next day. Manuel didn't mention if Maria Jesus would join them, and Klara did not want to ask.

Marcos came to Barajas airport to pick her up. He had become so grown up! Tall and elegant, with light brown hair and green eyes, broad-shouldered and with a better posture than ever before. He gave her a long, warm hug.

"You look taller. I used to have to remind you to straighten up all the time," she said, studying him at an arm's length.

"Yes, I'm doing manual labor now and it destroys your back if you don't carry heavy stuff the right way, so no need to go on about my posture anymore."

"What do you mean, manual labor? How about your camera work?"

"As assistant cameraman you're responsible for all the gear, tripod, cameras, lenses, and all. It ends up totaling a lot of kilos."

Klara had forgotten what it was like, Marco's job seemed like another world. Marcos only rarely worked with TV; he was into film. She herself had almost never worked with film. Still, at shoots, there was always someone who knew Manuel or Klara, and had worked with one of them. That created a certain confidence, working out rather like a letter of introduction, which Marcos needed until he had created a name for himself.

"Would you like to have dinner? Or shall we go somewhere for tapas?"

So like his father—considerate and charming...

"I could kill for some pata negra, cured manchego cheese and a good rioja. Throw in a tortilla española, and I might faint of pure pleasure."

"Tapas it is, then," he said and fished out his cell phone. "But if I may suggest, we make it Cabrales and a wine from Ribera del Duero."

Cabrales is a Spanish specialty, a blue cheese from the Asturias Region wrapped in fig leaves, that smells as bad as it tastes delicious. Marcos was only twenty-two, but paid attention to what wine suited the food and enjoyed both as if he were an old man, another thing he had learned from his father.

"I'm impressed with your expertise. It sounds great!"

While they walked to the exit, he made a call and arranged to meet someone at a bar at Plaza de la Paja, near where he lived, in the old part of Madrid.

"Are we having company?" Klara asked.

"That's the surprise," he said, with a big smile.

Klara worried that it was Manuel he had just talked to. She did not want to meet him yet, she wasn't ready. But she said nothing because didn't want to sabotage Marcos' surprise. She was so happy to see him again, her boy. Serena had been ten years old and Marcos eight when Klara had entered their lives. Their biological mother's death six years earlier had occurred at such a tender age that the tragedy had not impacted them too badly. Klara was the mother they remembered. She doubted that she could possibly have loved them more if she had given birth to them. Marcos didn't let go of her hand and gave her several hugs on the way to the car.

"You got a car? Can you afford that?" A black little Seat Ibiza in good shape, rather new.

"It's not my car, I borrowed it to pick you up," he said, not explaining further.

After driving around the block a few times looking for a parking space on the narrow streets of old Madrid, they descended three steps into a welcoming bar. The walls were original old brick, and the roof beams visible. On one side there was a bar running the whole length of the room, and the wall behind it was covered with well-filled wine racks in wrought iron.

The place was full of people standing around, but there were half a dozen rustic wooden tables and pallets. Marcos piloted Klara to one of them.

"I know that you don't enjoy eating standing up."

It was true. Klara had always had low blood pressure and used to get dizzy if she had nowhere to sit.

Just as they were about to order, a young woman walked into the bar. She was dressed in dark gray trousers with lacing at the waist and a short burgundy top under a black jacket.

"This is Eva," said Marcos proudly. "My surprise. We're in love, Mami." He had never called her "Madre", but "Mami" was informal enough not to offend their maternal relatives and still intimate and loving.

Eva greeted her and kissed Marcos on the mouth. He had complained that he was lonely and that he never met a girl that was right for him. He was good-looking, and Klara knew he had no trouble finding casual partners, but he had not had a regular girlfriend since he was seventeen.

Eva was a graphic designer. "She studied at St Martin's in London," Marcos explained with a hint of pride.

They were very much in love. Some part of their bodies was in constant contact, and they kissed from time to time. It warmed her heart, made her happy to see them together. The conversation flowed, and it felt like all three of them had known each other for a long time.

How very nice, she thought, *now he has company.*

It was almost two a.m. when they finally left the bar.

Marcos shared a large apartment with two girls. It was on the third floor, without an elevator, at Plaza Cascorro, where the flea market takes place every Sunday. The flat was old and worn, but the kitchen and bathroom were refurbished. All the rooms except for one faced the plaza and had French windows with classic French shutters. Almost all the furniture came from Klara's and Manuel's former home. A nice, brown Chesterfield sofa in leather, Marcos' and Serena's paternal grandmother's antique desk, the grandfather clock they had bought at an auction, easy chairs, mirrors, and paintings.

"Your father didn't keep anything?" wondered Klara.

"Well, you know, Maria Jesus wanted modern furniture, so they let me pick what I wanted from the storage. But if there is anything you want, just say the word."

"No, not at all, but Serena might want some of Grandma's things. Wasn't the chest of drawers and the mirror hers?"

"Sure, but she can't afford to have it sent to the U.S. yet, so I get to use it for now."

"How are you doing with Maria Jesus?" Klara asked.

"We're not that much in contact. She's all right."

"Please stay in touch with your father."

Klara got the only room facing the backyard, used as a darkroom. Much better than the couch in the living room. There was a bed with a bedside table and a lamp. Behind the door she found a couple of hooks to hang her clothes. After unpacking she placed the red picture frame with photos of Serena and Marcos on the bedside table. She never travelled without it.

When she was ready for bed, and had given Marcos yet another hug and told him how much she liked Eva, she withdrew to her room. She looked out the window and saw the jungle of obsolete TV antennas on the roofs, creating grotesque patterns against the night sky. Not needed anymore, nobody had bothered to take them away. She couldn't resist opening the window for a while, and took in Madrid's peculiar, very own smell. A mixture of dust, rubbish and burnt rubber, not gross, just so... *Madrileño*. The family, and Madrid, would always be important to her, but she was moving on in life. The children no longer needed her, they were managing well on their own.

A bitter-sweet sense of loss and relief spread through her.

CHAPTER TWENTY-SEVEN

At six the next morning Marcos knocked gently on the door and stuck his head in. He was going to work. In order to make a living, he also did commercials, and today they were shooting for a brand of chewing gum featuring a Spanish rally champion. He would be working late, but promised to call her during the day.

Klara decided to use the shower before the girls who shared the apartment got up. The water heater was a little on the small side and could only manage two showers, after that you had to wait a while until it heated up again. She washed her hair and blow-dried it. Made up discreetly and carefully. She chose a white lace bra and a thong under light gray trousers and a soft white sweater with a wide chimney collar. The jacket on her arm, for now.

Just before nine she went to the metro station at Tirso de Molina. She probably hadn't used the subway in Madrid more than a couple of dozen times during the twenty years she had lived here. The smell had always bothered her, made her feel unclean and anyway it was usually so cramped that women often were fondled: someone took the opportunity to rub themselves against some woman, only to deny it in an injured and aggressive manner when confronted. But Marcos had told her that the underground was the best way to get from downtown to Chamartín, the northern train station.

Now that rush hour was over it wasn't crowded. She even got a seat.

At Chamartín she took the commuter train to Villalba, forty kilometers northwest of the city. A little mountain village turned suburb with good communications. It had both detached housing and so-called *urbanizaciones*, condos in park-like estates with tennis courts and swimming pools. It was mainly inhabited by middle-class people commuting to the city. When Klara and Manuel had moved there, they could get to work at TVE by car in twenty minutes, but with time the traffic had turned impossible at rush hours, and nowadays it could take more than an hour by car.

The railway station in Villalba was remodeled and enlarged, but the core, the old building with white-washed walls and corners in natural stone, still remained. Klara studied the local community where she had lived so many years through the eyes of a stranger.

Calle del Rey, the main street, ran between the railway terminal and the mall at the other end, right by the highway. She glimpsed people she used to say hello to daily through the windows at the bread shop, the grocery store and the pharmacy, but although she saw them, they did not acknowledge her. Maybe they actually didn't recognize her. An eerie feeling of being invisible crept up on her, as if only she could see everybody and everything, but no one saw her.

At the mall, she took a left and there was the car repair shop. It had also been remodeled and modernized, the large windows displaying shiny new cars. She walked up to the reception not recognizing anyone there.

"I'm looking for Ferrín," she told the receptionist.

"*El señor Fernández no está, está probando un coche,*" the man said formally. Mister Fernández is not here, he is testing a car.

Klara had never realized that "Ferrín" was short for Fernández and thought it must have seemed disrespectful to inquire for him by his nickname. After all, he was the owner of the place.

"When is he expected back?" she asked.

"He should not be long," the receptionist said. "You are welcome to wait in the cafeteria if you like."

"Please tell him Klara Andersson is here."

Obviously, the name rang a bell. He looked at her again, smiling now: "You were in *Un, dos, tres.*" More a statement than a question.

"Yes. But that was a long time ago."

The move to Villalba with Manuel had coincided with the year she had worked as a TV hostess. *Un, dos, tres,* then in its first season, had become the most popular TV show ever: re-runs were still broadcast and new episodes still produced ten years later. At the time, Villalba had been thrilled to have a TV star, and she had signed autographs right and left. She was surprised that there were still people around who remembered her, and would definitely have preferred to be anonymous, as she was in Stockholm or Brussels.

She made herself comfortable on a high stool at the tiny cafeteria's bardesk and ordered a café con leche. Then she remembered that she hadn't had breakfast and added a *napolitana de chocolate*, *a pain au chocolá*, literally a chocolate bread, no English translation. It tasted heavenly, and the nostalgia trip was complete.

"*Y sigue tan guapa,*" said Ferrín behind her back. Beautiful as always.

He came over to her and suddenly Klara didn't know whether to shake hands or if they now, having known each other for so many years, should kiss on the cheeks. She held her hand out and immediately knew that was wrong. In Spain

156

a handshake seals a business deal, an agreement, but is hardly used as a greeting. She changed her body language and drew him closer.

"A kiss," she said and pecked him lightly on each cheek. "It's been such a long time."

"That's better," he said with a broad smile. "The kid is doing great and is ready for anything. I have just been out testing it. What a gem!"

At the office she got the insurance papers and the invoice. The sum was substantial. The American Express platinum saved her; she didn't have that much money. For a second, she wondered whether it was correct to spend the CIA's money on her car, but decided not to worry. All Louis had said were words to the effect of "keep receipts for cash withdrawals". She would simply take for granted that it was okay.

While she picked up the papers and got her card back, she became aware that Ferrín was studying her. She met his eyes.

"Are you never, ever coming back again now?" he asked, his expression serious and a little sad.

"Oh, you never know," she smiled. "I prefer not look too far into the future." To take the edge off she added: "I will have to come when the car needs an overhaul, won't I? I wouldn't trust anyone else to touch it."

The car stood in the arrivals parking. The license plate spoke volumes of its age, particularly now that the whole system for registration numbers had changed. It was clean and fresh inside, the seats smelled new and the body was newly waxed and shiny. She got in and moved the seat forward. Ferrín was tall and had been sitting comfortably when testing the car. The feeling of driving a sports car was emphasized by the fact that you sit low, with almost fully stretched legs, the seat only about ten or twelve inches high. The wooden dashboard had only four indicators: speed, tachometer, oil pressure and temperature.

After having tried the clutch to see at what point it caught, she turned the ignition. The engine was rather loud and had always verged on exceeding the allowed noise limit, but they had decided to keep the original muffler all the same. According to Ferrín, it had something to do with the performance. She waved farewell. He stood there waving back until she lost sight of him when she took a right out onto the highway.

There was little traffic and she could focus on getting the feel of the car again. The speed limit was 120 kilometers, about 75 miles an hour, but there weren't any cars around. A Renault Alpine's peak performance is at about 110 miles an hour, and she permitted herself to enjoy the feeling for a while, before slowing back down to 85 or 90. Annoying the *guardia civil* was not a good idea.

Once she had been waved over in her old Renault 4L, two young officers having followed her for a while, alleging that she was driving too fast.

"You are welcome to try, but I doubt that you can get this car to go faster than 80. That would be truly amazing," she had answered, smiling broadly, daring them. They had all laughed and instead they asked to see her license. There had been no consequences, despite not having a Spanish license, which she, after living in the country several years ought to have. The guards just wanted to confirm that she was the TV celebrity living in Villalba.

But now she was a mature woman and expected to obey the law. She would not get away that easily.

Halfway back to the city she discovered that the new ring road around Madrid, the M 50, was completed. Not in any kind of hurry, she tried it out to see where it would take her.

There were still hours to go before the lunch appointment with Manuel.

After a while there were indications to Aranjuez, and she headed there. One of her memories of the place was from shooting a TV program on glider planes in Ocaña, some miles south. They had flown over the city upside down in the sailplane and she had worried that the pilot might not succeed in finishing the loop before landing.

She parked by the Palace and went for a walk in the gardens. Time seemed to have stood still. The trees were pruned to keep the park looking the same over the years. The sun was bursting through the foliage as she arrived at a little bridge over a canal emptying out into the Tajo river. Many years ago, she had been on a photo shoot there. She still had the picture of her taken on the bridge, just as the stone dropped into the water splashed back up.

The river Tajo flowed in a slow dark green current, embellished by water lilies in lighter green. Where the rays of sun cut through the surface, it shimmered in gold. It was painfully beautiful, and Klara wished she had someone to share it with.

As if on cue her cell phone vibrated. It was Anders. After that first date, they talked every morning and evening, regardless of whether they had met during the day or were spending the night together. He was considerate and interested in her work and her daily life. He reminded her of things she had to do and kept her fully informed about his own ideas and projects. He showed all the signs of love: warmth and kindness, generosity and consideration, which filled a void in her, a void that she had denied ever since Manuel left her. In spite of mostly being flattered, not in love, the intimacy was something she had missed so intensely that this new relationship was becoming dangerously addictive. And they got along well in bed.

The fact that Anders was still married was no big deal. She was far from ready to renounce her newly acquired independence, but she wasn't willing to refrain from what he had to offer. She wanted to '*dejarse querer*', as they said in Spanish, enjoy feeling loved and cherished.

At a quarter to two she drove the car into the underground parking at Plaza Mayor. She walked through Arco de Cuchilleros to Casa Botín, Madrid's oldest restaurant. It was Manuel's choice. Again, Klara wondered if Maria Jesus was going to come. She hoped not, but checked her face in a shop window just in case, and then took a small mirror from her handbag for closer scrutiny.

"It doesn't get much better," she sighed. Maria Jesus was ten years younger than Klara and that was a fact, nothing she could do about it.

Manuel got up when she came in. He had chosen the ground floor, which lacked the charm of the brick walled caves in the basement. It was a table for two.

He hugged her. She perceived his familiar smell and embrace. They kissed formally on the cheeks even though it felt awkward. He had aged and looked a little tired. Well, no... he was looking his age. He was over sixty. The hint of a double chin was hidden behind a well-tended beard and he was suntanned.

"The short hair suits you, but you know that I prefer you blonde," he said.

"Well, you look fine," she smiled.

"Mariaje doesn't know we're meeting. I didn't want to risk her making a scene, but I really wanted to see you. She still sees you as the greatest threat."

"So, it's a secret meeting. That's exciting," Klara tried to joke. She sat down facing him and forced herself to relax, now that she knew Maria Jesus wasn't going to join them.

They talked a little about his work; he was in the middle of rehearsals for a drama and his present wife was assisting him. Like she herself had done so often... That hurt.

"But it's not the fun and excitement we used to share. Mariaje isn't you, and I'll have to live with that," he said.

Klara decided not to get into that. Instead she told him, without going into detail, that Louis had come to see her in Stockholm. Manuel had known Louis only in his capacity as a TV producer and friend. The true relation between Klara and Louis was the only thing she had ever lied to Manuel about.

They had shared the better part of her grown-up life and knew each other so well. She was the only mother his children remembered. They had been so close. An unbeatable tandem at work, a vivid, interesting, and fulfilling social life. People used to comment that they always saw them talking to each other.

And then he had destroyed it all for a fuck.

That was Klara's take on what had happened. Perhaps he was happy now? Maybe the animal unsophisticated sexuality of Maria Jesus stimulated him so much that nothing else mattered? When they first met, Klara had thought of the woman as utterly vulgar. Somebody, not Manuel, had commented "she smells of sex". She was too much, almost a joke, always bending over towards the men she talked to, her breasts almost falling out of her low-cut neckline, or dropping something on the floor to let her ultra-short dress reveal her sexy thong. Klara had never for a second suspected that Manuel, who loved *her*, would fall for those simple, cheap tricks. But he had.

Not so long ago, she couldn't stand the thought of him being happy with the woman he'd ditched her for; but now she wished him well. The pain had subsided, she no longer wanted to hurt him, or make him suffer. She no longer dreamed of revenge.

That was only in part due to Anders, it was to a greater extent due to Louis calling her back to action. Her new life was full and exciting. In her daily life she had a new, interesting job, and, she was involved in an important operation aimed at depriving a dangerous terrorist organization of some of its power.

"You're pale. You know you are free to use the studio in San Juan any time," he offered unexpectedly.

Manuel's writer's getaway… On the eleventh floor of a high rise, with a view of the Mediterranean and a miles-long beach. It was the summer paradise of the Spanish middle class. Klara suddenly longed for San Juan. A great place to disappear for a while… *incommunicado…* The climate was mild all year round, and the large balcony with comfortable sunbeds was protected against the wind, making it possible to enjoy every single ray of sun.

"I can't right now. Have to be back in Brussels in a couple of days. But I would love to take you up on your offer some other time."

She told him that she had picked up the car.

"I hope you have no objections?" she asked, not expecting any.

He looked unhappy. "You have no idea of all the shit I've had to put up with for letting you have that car!"

At that she got angry.

"For heaven's sake! It's mine! She took everything else from me. Thank God she couldn't take my relationship with Marcos and Serena, but apart from that, I was left with the car and a few items of furniture. I couldn't care less if she's mad!"

"All right, all right, just forget it," he said, soothingly.

The meal was over, and Klara had confirmed that her life with Manuel had definitely come to an end. She did not love him, and now it wasn't just something she told herself for comfort. He'd left a void, but it did not hurt any more.

The next day, she would be heading back to Brussels and her new life.

CHAPTER TWENTY-EIGHT

It was cold and windy on the Thursday evening Klara was meeting with Hassan. As she stepped out of the metro, the rain had stopped, leaving the sidewalks shining. Trying to think like Fatima, she had chosen a simple black crêpe dress with spaghetti straps and a waist length jacket in the same fabric. She was wearing thin, sheer black lace-top stay-up stockings, and she shivered each time the wind took hold of her clothes and the ice-cold dress lining met her bare skin. Her coat was a cobalt blue poplin with a thin lead-gray woolen lining. The string of pearls, a gift from the family for her graduation, was still beautiful and matched the pearls in her earlobes. Her handbag and stiletto-heels were black. She had made an effort to look her best.

The only car in view was a silver BMW Cabriolet parked on the other side of the street, in front of Europa and the bull, the statue by the entrance to one of the Council of Europe's large, gray buildings. She felt a little nervous looking up and down the street. Not a living soul around. The EU area was always deserted in the evenings. Only the wind rattling debris, swirling it along the street for a while, until it became too wet and heavy. Nervously, she touched the knife in her handbag. She kept it in a thin leather pocket that must originally have been intended for a comb. The weapon was supposedly Fatima's trademark. Ever since she had picked it up from the safe-deposit box in Zürich, she had practiced every day. Should she ever need to use it, it had to be second nature to her. Sometimes she just held it for a while, trying to figure out how Fatima, the woman she was pretending to be, would feel about it. She touched the knife with her fingertips and shivered. It had seemed so simple, when Louis explained the operation. The Sunni terrorist organization was convinced that she was Fatima Habib Sjögren, an Al Fatah sleeper, who, due to her "romance" with Pär, had gained access to the blueprints of the ship. They had advanced a large sum of money, Klara knew, and would double it once she handed over the documents.

Tonight was the point of no return.

The BMW started rolling. It turned at the roundabout and came toward her. She tried to think of the words in French to dismiss the John, in case he thought she was a hooker. As the car stopped in front of her, the driver leaned over and opened the passenger door. She hardly recognized him. He wore a dark well-tailored sports jacket, a nice white shirt and a tasteful tie. She couldn't see the pants. The bad posture she had spotted when they first met at the restaurant was gone. He looked like a fit, upper-class Arab, at ease with European ways, an impression reinforced by the car.

"Let's go, shall we?" he said, smiling.

Klara got in.

"How long have you been watching me?" she asked. She didn't know whether he was friend or foe, someone Louis had sent, or the envoy, but his answer would give her a clue.

"You mean now?"

Clear enough.

Before she could say anything, he continued: "Let us have a good meal and get to know each other before we talk business. And please call me Fahrid."

Not Hassan, then... "Klara," she introduced herself.

He looked at her and burst out laughing. It was a spontaneous and likeable laugh, contagious, shattering the tension between them. "I already know your name."

Momentarily disarmed by his charm, she still didn't relax. She placed her purse on her lap with instant access to the knife. They made small talk about Brussels and the weather. His American English was flawless, she could detect no trace of any other language. When he turned into an underground parking lot close to Grand Place, she stiffened. She knew from a prior visit that the restaurant had valet parking. Fahrid chose a slot close to the exit where the broad concrete columns created deep shadows. She studied the surroundings with her hand on the knife. The place looked deserted but there didn't seem to be any immediate danger. Not as long as he believed she was Fatima, and then not until he had got what he had come for. She lowered her shoulders trying to relax. He walked around and opened the car door for her.

At the restaurant he helped her take off her coat and held the chair for her at the table, the perfect gentleman. She couldn't help admiring how natural his very Western good manners were, and wondered where he was trained.

They had a Kir Royal and half a dozen oysters as a starter. She suggested lamb ribs with rosemary, roast potatoes and wok-fried greens for a main course, to show respect for his culture. Fatima would have adopted a western lifestyle if she lived like Klara Andersson. However, he insisted on red wine with the main course and helped himself to it.

The fact that he drank alcohol would seem to indicate that he was not a fundamentalist. That was a surprise. From the background material Louis had provided she had concluded that his organization had sprung from the most extreme hard-core Sunni Islamism... Maybe he was just really careful about his cover. He was intelligent, entertaining and well-informed about current issues. When he laughed, his otherwise cold eyes softened and the little wrinkles around his eyes made him look likeable.

Still, the tension was cramping her neck and shoulders. After the coffee, espresso, which he doused with copious amounts of sugar, he said: "I bring greetings from your grandfather."

The sounds in the room muffled and she swallowed saliva. This was a trap. Louis had told her that Fatima's paternal grandfather died in Israeli prison. She knew her life depended on her answer.

"Dead men don't speak." The lining of her dress stuck to her skin and she wiped away the perspiration on her upper lip with the napkin. The food felt like a stone in her stomach.

"Well, that's not my information. Aren't you happy to hear?"

Unable to meet his eyes just yet, she knew she had to take control of the situation and tried to remember how she had pictured Fatima's reaction. This was the most risky moment of the entire operation.

"I have mourned him long enough," Klara said.

If she failed now, her life would be entirely devoid of value to him, she would be reduced to an embarrassing mistake that he had to eliminate, leaving as little trace as possible.

"I want to leave," she said, getting up. She forced her movements to be slow and languid. The moment she got up, a plan formed in her head. Her courage came back when she broke eye contact. Her panic ebbed. She turned to him and smiled. He walked close to her on her left, with his arm loosely around her back gripping her right upper arm. Almost sensuously, she leaned towards him and whispered:

"What was the point in meeting before I was ready to give you the documents?"

He stiffened. The insult hit home. Her self-confidence increased. Discreetly and hidden by her own body, she reached for his crotch with her left hand. He did not pull away. Through the fabric she felt that he was hard and found his testicles. She squeezed them with all the force she could muster and felt him jerk away. Not much, less than any other man would have done. His self-control was admirable. Pretending to have tripped he gripped her arm so hard it became unbearable. Klara inhaled sharply and turned to him. He was gritting his teeth so hard she could see the muscles in his jaw play under the skin. There was a mixture of pain and desire in his eyes. She had got him off balance. Now she was in control. Under shelter of the subdued lighting in the wardrobe, with her back to the young woman who handed over her coat, she said:

"Wednesday in four weeks. Lunch. Café Le Nemrod at Toison d'Or. And if I sense that you, or someone you send, spies on me, the deal is off."

She walked away without waiting for an answer. His fingers had left five red marks on her arm that would turn into bruises and fade before they met again.

Klara hailed a taxi and chatted animatedly with the driver on the way home. High on adrenaline she could have burst out singing. She had succeeded! Someone would see the signal: her dress hung out to air on the balcony, and prepare for the last phase of the operation. Louis' instructions were precise once they knew it was going to happen in Brussels: at lunchtime on a Wednesday, four weeks after contact, at Le Nemrod.

While she prepared for bed, she thought of the next meeting. She would take the metro to Port Namur. The fact that it was a public place added to her protection. No one would want to make a scene. Both industrial espionage and security matters were handled with discretion and as little violence as possible, not like in the old days of the Cold War.

That thing she had said about spying on her had just slipped out of her. An improvisation in line with the character she was playing. She hoped it hadn't been a mistake.

Since she had come to Brussels, she had just gone on with her life. And waited. Waited for this to happen. There had been no personal contact with Louis since he visited her in Stockholm, but she could reach him the usual way, should anything unexpected happen. Sometimes she had seen signs, or just felt that someone was there, observing her. The dress on the balcony was the only sign needed to show that Fahrid had made contact.

As far as she understood, the blueprints had been manipulated, but it would take months of studies and computations before that was discovered. The agreement was that her part in the operation was completed once she handed over the documents. In return Louis had promised to re-establish her real identity and status. Every shred of suspicion regarding who she was, was going to be thoroughly and completely erased. Both Mossad and Al-Fatah would be informed about the truth.

Strangely, this thought did not produce the relief she expected. If anything, her feelings were contradictory. Now she had a second layer of meaning to her life. A secret and a purpose. How would she feel when that was gone? Would the interpreting work, and life as simply Klara Andersson satisfy her, now that she didn't have a family anymore?

She was not sure of it.

She went to bed, but could not sleep and got up to make a cup of tea. The adrenalin had subsided and now her hands were unsteady. She spilled tea on her dressing gown. Turning off all of the lights, she sat on the couch in darkness. The street lamps drew patterns of light and shadows on the broad floor planks. She wondered if Fahrid really had believed her. He'd said that the man who claimed to be Fatima's paternal grandfather was alive. If that was true, and not a trap as she had assumed, it was a problem. The old man was supposed to have died in an Israeli prison after confirming that she was Fatima, according to Louis.

She fetched a wire coat hanger from the wardrobe. Without turning the light on, she bent it up and went over to the cooking range. With the hooked part, she started picking at the slit between the stove and the kitchen cupboard. Soon she fished out a large brown envelope. She took it to the desk in front of the bedroom window and closed the Venetian blinds before turning on the desk lamp. She emptied the contents on to the desk. Together with a few other documents was her contract. Reading it again, she realized that she was only mentioned as Fatima, not Klara. She had not really thought about that before, just taken for granted that it was in order to keep her cover as tight as possible.

She gathered all the papers and stuffed them back, first in the envelope and then into the hiding place.

When she had emptied the safe deposit box in the bank in Zürich some months ago, she had only taken a quick look at the contents of the envelope. She had read the contract, made sure it was signed and that it said what Louis had promised. Now doubts spread like poison through her veins, turning into crippling fear.

Her sigh sounded ghostlike in the dark silence. Klara seemed to have disappeared into thick fog when she left Spain—and in her place Fatima had materialized.

The darkness got denser and it felt like the walls were closing in on her as she finally formulated the thought that scared her so much:

Is Louis the only one who knows that I am Klara Andersson?

170

CHAPTER TWENTY-NINE

Klara was determined to concentrate on the here-and-now. Four whole weeks would have to go by until she met with Fahrid again and thus concluded the task Louis had entrusted her with. In between the working days at the Parliament, she finally made the effort to contact the interpretation agencies operating on the free market to apply for freelance work. Brussels and the surrounding area hosted a surprising number of multilingual meetings: unions, business associations and lobbyists, really, anything you could imagine. The demand for qualified interpreters was great, and she seemed to be welcome everywhere. A few asked for references, but most were happy knowing that she had been approved to work for the EU Parliament. Meetings were planned a long time ahead, and interpreters booked months in advance, so she did not expect any actual job to come up within the month, unless someone got sick and had to be replaced. But she tried to keep busy with the applications and follow-ups.

Pär insisted on checking the blueprints in the cell phone at some point before she turned over the documents to Fahrid, and she decided to call him about it.

"If you can come to Stockholm, I can see you tomorrow," he said.

Now seemed as good a time as ever. She booked a flight the next morning and sent Anders a text message. He was in Malmö for a family get-together, but called back in seconds.

"That's great. I'll arrange to be in Stockholm tomorrow and Sunday too," he said. "When are you arriving? I could be at your place around five, maybe we can have dinner somewhere close?"

"I won't be landing until after seven," Klara lied. She had to make room for the meeting with Pär. "I'll call you when I get home."

The city met her with a glorious winter landscape. Clear skies and a few degrees below freezing kept the snow from thawing, white and sparkling.

When her front door closed behind her, a vague feeling of unease came over her. Something was "off". A faint, foreign smell floated in the air, like cigarette smoke. She instinctively reached into the handbag, and only when she touched the knife with her fingertips did she let go of the carry-on that she had been clutching. The knife was completely weightless in her hand and the dark gray, high-tech composite material had no shine. At a glance, it looked like a nail file. Only under closer scrutiny would you know that it wasn't. Simply holding it gave her a feeling of invulnerability, as if the knife automatically, all on its own, would carry out whatever was necessary to protect her.

The door to the bathroom was ajar. Had she really left it open? She entered, knife in hand, and pulled the shower curtain aside. Nothing... The bathroom cupboard was also not properly closed, but inside everything looked normal. In the kitchen everything looked as she remembered. She continued into the bedroom. On the desk was the steno pad with the address and the telephone number to Pascale's Bed & Breakfast, where she had first stayed in Brussels. Then she looked at the chest of drawers. One drawer was not properly closed. She opened it. On top was a gray jumper, a little rumpled.

Is this a message? No professional would have left so many clues, she thought.

She looked at the knife in her hand. Smiling at her overreaction she put it back into her handbag. Her cousin Åsa checked up on the place from time to time and forwarded important mail to Brussels.

But what was that faint smell? Not like Anders but remotely familiar: male, spicy, adrenalin-charged…

Just my imagination, she told herself, and pushed away the unease.

She had gathered the dust covers from the furniture and swiped the large surfaces when Pär rang the doorbell. Looking at her watch, she smiled.

One o'clock sharp, military punctuality. She wondered if he had been taking loops around the block to make sure he would ring the bell so precisely at one.

"Would you like a coffee, or maybe something stronger?" she asked. "But the choices are limited, the fridge is empty."

"No, thank you, I'm fine for now, I just had lunch." He paused. "Let me check the cell phone. I need to make sure everything that has to be there is."

She handed it over to him.

They sat in silence while he studied the blueprints. Then he plugged a strange looking device directly into the phone.

"What is that?" Klara was intrigued.

"A memory stick that fits the jack in the phone. I am transferring a few more pictures, and checking that the import dates are consistent with the time before you left for Brussels."

One of the pictures was getting stuck in the upload and he asked to borrow her laptop to fix it. When he was done, he leaned back in the chair and said: "Please rent a safe-deposit box in a bank and leave this phone there until the day of the delivery."

"Any bank?"

"Whichever one suits you, but go there a few times in the meantime. We don't want the bank staff to remember a specific date for your visit."

"Right, will do," Klara answered.

After a pause, he said: "You might want to check out the restaurant in advance."

"I already did," Klara answered. "Ever since I came to Brussels I have known that was where it was going to happen. I've been there for lunch a couple of times, and know all I need about the place."

"We will make sure that there's a table free outside on the sidewalk when you come," Pär assured her. "It is important that you take the metro, both there and back. Not a taxi."

"Yes, I know," she answered. She found his way of doubting her irritating. "It is the most sensible way of getting from the Parliament to Toison d'Or at lunchtime anyway." Her working days at the Parliament were booked months in advance.

He ignored her irritation and said that the lunch break was perfect. Then he went on repeating the details meticulously once more.

"Enough," she interrupted. "We've been over this so many times you'll just confuse me if you go on."

"It is important. It is the final stage of our operation and it has to be perfect."

"I know exactly what to do."

"OK, we'll leave it here then. Good luck." And he left.

For a second, she wondered if she would ever see him again.

Anders seemed not to worry at all about them roaming Stockholm together, just like in Brussels. They had dinner at Paul's, a very popular and much-frequented restaurant on Hötorget in Stockholm downtown. He did not stay the night.

The next morning she took the tram to Nacka for a nice lunch with her cousin Åsa. She had brought a box of Belgian chocolates.

Anders came back in the early afternoon. He loved her apartment and took numerous pictures, including a selfie on the balcony with the skyline of winter-Stockholm behind him. Klara wondered if he was that sure his wife would never check his phone, but didn't ask. They went for a long walk, had a wonderful dinner at Sjöpaviljongen, bought a pastry at Brioche on Alviks Torg and had coffee at home. Shortly before midnight he got up, dressed and left again.

She didn't ask, but the strange pattern puzzled her.

CHAPTER THIRTY

Klara's international background impressed Anders, and he liked to pick her brain regarding the cross-cultural issues he thought might be hurdles for his proposals. It happened often enough to make her feel she had something to contribute. Teamwork, a little like life had been with Manuel. After a big debate about compensations for cross-country social security spending, and having succeeded in getting his proposal accepted by a broad majority, Anders wanted to celebrate and asked her to pick a destination for a luxury weekend trip.

They passed Antwerp aiming for Rotterdam and stayed near to the coast, instead of taking the shortest route to The Hague. She was comfortable in the rental car. Anders didn't trust her old car and did not like to ride in the passenger seat. In spite of the season, they found a small restaurant with outdoor tables in the sun, well-guarded from the chilly winter winds. They had a simple but delicious lunch: a salad of fresh spinach and mushrooms with olive oil and blue cheese and a lightly fried fillet of sole with sweet peas.

It was almost four p.m. and the mist started rolling in from the sea. They were on their way to Hotel Atlantic, in Scheveningen. She had been there once before, in winter. That time the fog had been so dense that when the hotel, with its turrets and towers, slowly materialized, it looked like a fairy-tale castle, a vision detached from the rest of the world. She liked to imagine that it was possible to escape from reality. When life was tough, it helped to keep hardships at a distance until she had time to process them.

Sometimes she wondered about the fact that Anders never spoke of a divorce. When they started seeing each other, she had been convinced that Anders, this solid, honest, reliable guy, would never have initiated a relationship with her if divorce was not on the horizon. He rarely went home on weekends, and in Brussels, and now also in Stockholm, they hung out openly. If he took precautions, she never noticed. She never asked him about it, not quite sure yet what she really wanted.

In any case, now was not the time; now she just wanted to enjoy the moment. *Carpe diem.*

Anders drove slowly in the fog. Using Google maps on her phone she gave instructions about when and where to turn. From time to time, she checked the side-view mirror. They had had company since after lunch, a dark SUV. She wanted to believe that it just was a driver who found it convenient to let someone else take the lead through the fog. But when they approached a crossroads, the car behind them sped up, reducing the distance, and followed their turn. Looking alternatively at the map and the rear-view mirror, she gave Anders a couple of nonsensical directions, to see what the follower would do. The driver kept at their tail, and now there was no doubt. They were being followed.

Anders was looking forward to their romantic weekend, but sensed that after lunch Klara had fallen silent. She seemed distracted and edgy.

"Is my driving making you uncomfortable?" he asked. "Would you feel better driving yourself?"

She shook her head.

Dusk was setting in and the road was flanked by tall trees. Not a single house in sight, no source of light visible through the milky opaque fog, except for those from the car behind them. As it flashed the headlights, he slowed down to let the vehicle pass.

"What are you doing?" Klara's voice was high-pitched.

"Let the car behind us show the way for a while," he answered, pulling to the side of the road.

At that instant her hand landed on his knee, pressing down so hard that his foot on the pedal made the car gain speed. At the same time her other hand gripped the wheel steering out onto the road again. The car took a skid. He stared at her. *Had she gone mad?*

"Are you out of your mind?"

"Drive! Don't stop!"

"What's wrong?"

The maneuver had made them lose speed and the other car was closing in on them. Anders veered to the side of the road again, just in time to avoid a collision. The SUV, a BMW, quickly passed, braked and stopped, blocking the road. Understanding nothing, Anders saw Klara turn white.

The passenger window rolled down slowly, revealing a man with a balaclava and the muzzle of a firearm aiming at them. Instinctively, Anders shifted the gear to reverse and hit the gas, the gravel popping around them. Anders had never before seen a rifle with a sawed-off barrel in real life. Klara fumbled for something in her handbag. He pulled the handbrake while stepping on the gas to provoke a skid and turn the car 180 degrees, something he had not done since he was a teenager. A bang and a shot screeched passed, without hitting them.

From the corner of his eye, he saw her cock a handgun. *What the hell?* A new shot. The rear window exploded showering them with glass splinters. Anders ducked, shards of glass flying around. He lost control, skidding from one side of the road to the other. Then he regained control of the car and looked at Klara.

A heavy dark red droplet from a cut on her neck made its way down to her chalk-white shirt collar. The expression of panic was gone. She removed her seatbelt and got on her knees turning in the seat. Through the broken rear window, she fired several shots in a row. Anders was shocked, functioning only on instinct. He didn't count the shots. He turned to her for a second and saw her nod in satisfaction. In the rear-view mirror, he saw the BMW skid and lose speed. Both tires on the driver's side had deflated. The double-barreled rifle was now out of the driver's side window. On reflex Anders wrung the wheel to the right, then to the left, but not too much, knowing that they made a better target on the broad side. The fog was closing around them. He felt another two shots impact the car's body.

"Drive a bit further, then I'll take over," she said in a flat voice, while changing the cartridge clip in the weapon with surprising expertise.

"We need to call the police," he said.

"Just drive."

CHAPTER THIRTY-ONE

Klara's brain was working at high speed, processing the unexpected situation. First, they had to get to safety; Anders could take care of that. She needed to think. The material damage was the least of her worries. It was fortunate that Anders had insisted on renting a car. She didn't even want to think about the complications if her Alpine had ended up full of bullet holes. She felt her shirt cling and realized she was drenched in cold sweat. This was the first time ever that she had shot at anything other than a target at a range. She was surprised at how well it turned out, but then she concentrated on the damage control.

"We need to find a police station," Anders said.

"We can't involve the police," she answered, knowing it was going to be a battle.

"Of course we have to report it! Hell, somebody shot at us!"

"We got away without injuries."

"Fortunately. That madman could have killed us both."

"I don't have a license to carry a weapon."

"We don't have to tell the police that you shot back at them," he insisted after a brief pause.

"Think of the consequences, Anders. A police report would lead to complications, both for your career and for your marriage." Only an emergency situation justified such a cheap trick.

Anders looked confused, torn between his righteousness and the fact that he was on a trip that he would have a hard time justifying, both at home and at the Parliament.

"But look at this car. How are we going to explain that?"

"We'll have to report it stolen. There will be questions, but a lot less than if we file a report with the police. That's the only way you will be able to keep it secret."

"What about our clothes and things?" he was faltering.

She had to smile at his lack of imagination.

Anders turned silent. She seemed to know more about the event than she was letting on. He had thought that they were being subject to an attempted robbery, or maybe a case of mistaken identity. But Klara carried a gun. She hadn't thought twice about using it—and obviously knew how to handle it.

"Why are you armed?" he finally asked.

She didn't answer. His head was spinning, and he felt sick. He turned off down a narrow track ending by a barn. There he stopped and got out. With two fingers he pulled a handkerchief out of his trouser pocket and wiped the blood off his hands and neck. She came out and stood beside him. As she put her hand on his arm he noticed that she was trembling. He held her hard and stroked her hair and her back.

"What was that about?" he asked.

"I have no idea," she said.

He stiffened at her lack of candor.

"Why are you carrying a gun?" The question hung in the air, opening a gap between them. Anders had a hard time processing the situation. He had never been in the presence of an armed person, apart from police officers. Certainly not a woman—his woman.

"Not that strange, is it?" she answered. "I live alone in a big city. It's easy to get into my apartment from the garden. Sometimes I'm scared."

"That doesn't explain why you brought it along."

She moved away from him. "Lucky I did, or what?"

"So, you don't want to talk about it?"

He was painfully aware of her distance. She looked harassed, insecure, very different from her usual self. It touched him deeply, but he did not know what to do.

"Come sit in the car," he said and put his jacket over her shoulders.

He felt an infinite tenderness for her; at the same time he was a little frightened. The woman he loved, but in truth did not know much about, had become a stranger during those frightening moments. She had shown an instinct, a resolve and a cold-blooded determination he'd never seen before. He couldn't help being impressed, and suddenly he wanted her. Trying to bridge the distance between them and find a way back, he started caressing her.

The euphoria of having escaped death surged through him, a physical need to embrace life.

They made love in the car. She sat astride him in the passenger seat and her hair fell over his face. The smell of her stunned him, that mix of perfume and lemon shampoo. He wanted never to separate from her.

Klara had stopped thinking when Anders caressed her. The need to be close, to be alive and know that she was loved, overshadowed everything. They were quiet for a long time afterwards, in spite of the uncomfortable position. Slowly, reality returned. She was grateful for the time he had granted her. A small shard of glass had got stuck on one of her knees. He carefully picked it out and pressed a clean Kleenex against the wound.

Anders asked: "It was us they were after, wasn't it?"

She knew her answer would determine their path forward. She would have to tell him something. To try to deny any knowledge of the events would be to insult his intelligence. The question was where to draw the line. The whole truth would render him vulnerable and dangerous—that could hurt him, and her.

When he saw her hesitate, he said: "First things first," and started the car. "What do we do about the car?"

They abandoned the rental unlocked, in a dark corner of a big parking lot in the outskirts of Rotterdam, hoping it would take a while before someone discovered it. Klara wiped the fingerprints on the steering wheel, the shift stick and the handbrake. They left one of their bags with some clothes and toiletries belonging to both of them in the car, to lend credibility to their version of events. Anders called Avis and reported it stolen and declined the offer of a substitute car.

They first discussed returning to Brussels immediately, but the hotel in Scheveningen felt safer if the aggressor was still looking for her. No one knew where they were headed. They had not talked about the destination over the phone or by mail and were booked as Mr. and Mrs. Källström. On the way, Klara insisted on changing taxis, going to different places various times until she was sure nobody was following them. Only then did they board the train to The Hague.

The hotel room was as big as a suite. A short hall led to a spacious room with tall but narrow French windows looking out over the ocean. Heavy, beautifully draped silk curtains in gray and old rose framed the view exquisitely. The upholstery of a couch and a couple of old-fashioned armchairs matched the colors and the motif. In a beautiful walnut cupboard with a bar, a big TV was hidden. To the left was the bedroom with two enormous beds and past it a big bathroom with a Jacuzzi, a separate toilet and shower. Klara unpacked the most necessary items and put the red leather frame with pictures of

Marcos and Serena on the bedside table. Between them, she had wedged in the photo of Anders, taken on her balcony on his recent visit to Stockholm.

She opened the faucet to the bathtub while Anders ordered dinner from room service. Neither of them felt like being among people. The small cuts from the glass splinters stung when she got into the hot water. She lay deep down in the bathtub, feeling the heat soothe her tense muscles. Anders came in, tucked into the hotel's white terry-cloth bathrobe.

"May I get in with you?"

"Rather not, I am too sore," Klara hedged. "I'll be out in a moment."

She needed some time to herself, to decide how much she could tell Anders without involving him in the operation. She trusted him and wanted to tell him everything.

But that is impossible, she knew.

The bathrobe felt warm and soft. When she came out, the food was already served on a big dinner wagon with a single rose in the middle matching the color palette of the room. Domes in a silver-like metal covered the plates, keeping the food warm. They sat down face to face, still in silence. Anders served wine.

"We've been avoiding the topic for hours now," Anders started. "You owe me an explanation."

"I don't know who or why..."

Anders interrupted holding his hand up.

"Whatever you do, Klara, do not lie to me," he said. "I deserve better than that."

"Okay," she said. "But you have to understand that there are things that you are better off not knowing."

"Then this is very serious?"

She told him the essentials and stuck to the truth: that she, through an interpreting assignment had got involved in something that she was not at liberty to discuss, that it had to do with the Swedish Security Service. He wanted to know when they had approached her, and she told him it had happened before she came to Brussels. He did not press for more information, but asked about her weapon skills. She told him about her father and his interest in weapons and hunting. It had been natural in a small town like Boden, dominated by the military, to shoot as a hobby. She gave him the name of the club in Stockholm that would confirm that she was a member, her ranking in terms of skill, and the telephone number to the shooting range at Fridhemsplan in Stockholm, encouraging him to check her up.

The next day they got an early train from The Hague and split up at the central station, the Centraal, in Brussels. Klara needed to be alone.

CHAPTER THIRTY-TWO

Klara moved restlessly between the rooms in her apartment trying to decide whom to alert. She left her cup of coffee on the kitchen counter and went to the landline at the desk in the bedroom. Sitting down she stared at the old-fashioned black telephone. When she bought it at the flea market on her second Sunday in Brussels, she had found it picturesque and charming. Now she hated it. She made the decision: someone had tried to kill her, and even if the danger was over for the moment, she was going to use the emergency number Louis had given her.

"The number you have dialed is incorrect; please try again," said a recorded, metallic voice.

She tried again, with the same result. *Have I memorized the wrong number?* She dialed again, slowly and carefully. Panic drawing closer with each intent.

"The numb…"

She planted both feet squarely on the floor and forced herself to think.

The code for outgoing international calls, maybe it wasn't 00 as in Sweden? She was too impatient to check and instead grabbed the cell phone. Pressing the plus-sign she dialed the number again.

"American International," a woman's voice answered, almost immediately.

She hadn't expected it to be a direct line to Louis, but still felt disempowered.

"Mr. Hornett, please."

"May I ask who is calling?"

"Klara Andersson... I'm calling from Europe," she added, in a lame attempt to make the woman hurry up.

"One moment," the operator said and put her through to an extension.

Nothing happened in what felt like an eternity. Klara checked the screen on the phone to make sure the call was still active.

"Miss. Andersson? I'm very sorry, Mr. Hornett is on another call right now. He will be in touch with you as soon as possible."

"This is an emergency. He told me I could reach him any time for emergencies at this number," she said. He had promised to be there: in an emergency, you don't have the luxury to wait for a call back. *This was an emergency.* "I'm afraid I can't assist you," said the voice coldly.

"Tell him to get back to me as soon as possible," Klara insisted, knowing the woman had just told her that.

"I will forward your message. Goodbye, Miss Andersson."

And she was gone.

Louis' behavior was becoming a pattern, he wasn't available when she needed him.

She tried to reach Pär, but he didn't answer either. Feeling utterly abandoned, she walked up to the eight-paned French windows leading out to the tiny semi-circular balcony and looked down at the street below. It was every bit as empty and deserted as the streets back in Boden had been around dusk when she was a child. Not a single car, not a single human. No movements behind the curtains in the windows across the street. Suddenly she felt dizzy and she had to steady herself, grabbing on to the handle to the balcony door.

Sweat broke on her forehead. A threat, a terrible intangible sense of danger loomed over her, like a bottomless vacuum sucking her down into an endless black hole. Everyone else in the whole world had left, had been evacuated, leaving her alone to face the terror...

The sound of the phone ended the compact silence and brought her back to reality. She swept the receiver off the hook.

"Hey, you sure answered quickly. I saw you called..."

Klara let out a long sigh. It was Pär. Maybe Louis had asked him to call?

"This is an emergency. Somebody shot at us yesterday in the Netherlands."

"What happened?" Pär said. "In detail."

"Anders Källström and I were on our way to Scheveningen for the weekend." She wasn't sure how much Pär knew about her private life, but the relief that someone she could trust was listening made her go on talking. Like therapy.

"A number of bullets hit the car before I got a chance to retaliate."

"Please don't tell me you killed someone," he sounded faint.

"Of course not, I aimed for the tires, and we were able to drive away." Klara hadn't really thought of the risk of killing someone, the implications, complications, of something like that. Now she realized how lucky they were to escape with nothing more than material damage. Pär asked what they had done after driving off and seemed for once somewhat impressed by her resolve.

"Look, Klara, I saw your call and thought you were going to tell me about the bank safe, to know where you chose to open it," he paused and she could almost hear him thinking. "But this is very serious. I'm calling Louis right now. I'll ask him to contact you immediately."

"Well, good luck. I called the emergency number a while ago, but he didn't bother to get on the line."

"You know that you are under close surveillance in Brussels. He knows, as well as we do, that you are under no immediate threat, right there and now."

She just remembered something she thought Pär should know, and his comment about the surveillance didn't sink in.

"I had to give Anders an explanation for the fact that I am armed. He's smart. He didn't believe that it was just for personal protection, so in the end I had to tell him that I'm cooperating with relevant Swedish authorities about something that I'm not at liberty to discuss. I hinted at Säpo, I don't know if that was OK?"

"We may have to do some damage control. I'll take care of that," he said. Then he asked: "Was there only the driver in the car?"

"I never saw more than one person. If there had been two, the passenger would have done the shooting, don't you think?"

"OK. I'll have Louis call you on a secure line. I sincerely do not think what happened has anything to do with our operation. They have paid 50% and you haven't delivered yet. The Sunnis wouldn't want to hurt you."

He didn't actually say it, but she sensed the words "at least not yet" like an echo, at the end. It felt like a death sentence momentarily suspended.

She had been to the bread shop at the corner for fresh croissants that morning on her way home from the Centraal, but never managed to eat them. At lunchtime she went down to Au bon coin frais, just across the street, but once there, she knew that a yoghurt was all she could stomach.

When Louis finally called, the cell phone hummed with electronics, making sure no one else could hear them.

"Klara, I'm so sorry about what happened," he said. "From what Pär told me, I suspected that Mossad might have something to do with the events, and have been in contact with their Chief of Operations. That's what took so long."

"Did you tell them that Fatima is just a fictitious character?"

"Not exactly. That wouldn't work at this stage of our operation. We can't risk a leak to the Sunnis. But I fixed it. In any case, they just wanted to talk to you."

"What? Using a masked shooter and live munition to approach me for a chat? You'll have to do better than that. They could have caused multiple casualties, I wasn't alone. How did they intend to explain what was going on to Anders?"

"It was an operator wanting to make merits with his superiors. He knew they wanted to confirm their suspicions regarding Fatima. There's no proof whatsoever, but they think she may have helped this guy, Atef Bseiso, to escape in Madrid, when he was on his way to Paris in the summer of 1992."

She felt the hair rise on her arms. It was what Reuven Levi had talked about in the TV interview. Mossad must have deduced that she, Klara, and Fatima were the same person.

"Louis, I'm in their crosshairs now," she said, controlling her voice. "You know that I interpreted at the Madrid Peace Conference in October 1991. I know that Bseiso was one of the guests."

"Relax. Now Mossad's chief is informed that there is no connection."

"Connection between what? Because they still think that I am Fatima."

Her knuckles had turned white from the grip on the edge of the desk.

"I have fixed it. That is all you need to worry about. Just go on doing what you're doing. You have no reason to worry."

Easy for you to say.

"I quit," she said, her voice breaking. "I can't do this Fatima business. I'm not cut out for this. Mossad is much too aggressive and powerful. They'll end up killing me and maybe even people I care about."

"That's not going to happen, Klara. Let me explain how we are playing this: As of about an hour ago, the chief of the Israeli Secret Intelligence Service knows that you are an extremely valuable double agent, working for us in a sensitive operation. He has given orders to all his agents to stand down. To leave you alone."

They continued talking for a long time, allowing her to vent her fears. He sent her the encrypted file of the conversation with the Mossad Chief of Operations and waited patiently while she listened to it. For all she knew, it could have been performed by an actor, but the voice, the jargon and the accent rang true, and in the end, Louis managed to convince her that she was safe.

CHAPTER THIRTY-THREE

Klara had rented the safety deposit box at a Spanish bank, Banco Santander-Central-Hispano, due to some kind of loyalty ties to Spain. It was one of three possible options, at Rue de la Loi close to Schuman, only a few blocks from the Parliament. She had been there a couple of times since, just as Pär had suggested.

The day she was meeting Fahrid the only item in her briefcase was the cell phone with the photos of the documents. She had stuffed the glossaries and notebooks interpreters carry around but rarely use in her locker at the Parliament.

She walked back one block and took the metro line 2 to Clemenceau. From Port de Namur she would walk the Toison d'Or on the right-hand side, towards Place Louise and Café Le Nemrod. It was 12:27 p.m. Perfect timing... By one o'clock she would be having lunch at an outdoor table. The sun was shining, and the temperature was pleasant. Her shoulders and neck were stiff, but she was in a good mood. In an hour it would all be over.

She couldn't help looking up at the Hilton Hotel as she passed, hoping to see a movement behind a curtain or the flash of a pair of binoculars. That would have felt reassuring, but the entire facade seemed lifeless, as if set in stone. There were a few foreign cars in line at the Q8 station. She sauntered past, thinking that maybe she would get a glimpse of Louis in one of them, but no such luck.

When she reached the restaurant, there were no free tables. She stood on the sidewalk looking around. At that moment, a young couple called on the waiter to pay. She walked up to them and asked if they were leaving. They invited her to sit, just as planned.

Klara ordered *salade niçoise*, a Perrier and a lait russe. She needed to have something to do to mask her nerves. The café offered their guests newspapers and in the pile she found yesterday's El Mundo. It wasn't important which, she would have grabbed any newspaper.

There was a light article on the last page that didn't seem to demand too much concentration. She put the paper on the table, in case her hands might shake. The seconds seemed to resist turning into minutes. The electronic clock on the shopping center facing her, showed the same time so many times she had to check her own watch, to make sure it was working.

On one side of her sat an elderly French-speaking couple, on the other a group of beautiful young women from the elegant boutiques around the Place Louise. Nicely made up and elegantly dressed. There was still not a single table free. She studied the people sitting there, one by one, but saw no one who could be Fahrid or someone sent by him.

The food came. The salad was supposed to be lukewarm but had turned cold by the time it was served. She forced herself to chew carefully, as much to make time pass as to avoid a stomach ache. How stupid to order the coffee together with the meal. When she had finished eating, it was undrinkable. She beckoned to the waiter and ordered another.

None of the surrounding tables had changed occupants. It was almost two thirty, and she felt the panic creeping up on her. What should she do? Her shift would start in an hour and nobody had turned up yet. Just leave the briefcase? She longed for a brandy, but did not dare to drink a single drop of alcohol, first because she was going back to work, but also because she needed to stay fully alert. Something was wrong. Once more she scrutinized the people around her. Could Fahrid have sent the young man in the gray suit with that hideous wine-red tie? A woman the same age joined him. They kissed and seemed at ease making small talk.

For heaven's sake, Louis, do something, she prayed, aware that that was impossible.

Shortly before two she got up and paid her bill. She left for the metro, walking slowly. The briefcase felt heavy in spite of containing next to nothing.

She had no idea what to do.

What had happened? Had the whole operation failed? Was it her fault?

She wasn't thinking clearly and was on her way to the wrong platform in the metro. To get to the other side she had to go back, up and over, through a narrow and sparsely lit passage. Almost half way through, somebody gripped her arm hard. Every finger fit with the memory of the five bruises Fahrid had left there last time they met. She spun around on her heel so fast she would have lost balance had he not held her. It was him, in baggy, ill-fitting clothes. The relief exploded in her breast.

Without a word he pressed her against the wall with his body. He kissed her and bit her lip while patting her down, searching for the phone.

"In the briefcase," she said to get his hands off her. He grabbed it and pinched her nipple so hard she gasped and twisted in pain.

The revenge for what she had done at the restaurant.

"Never forget that I give the orders," he hissed and disappeared as suddenly as he had appeared.

Catching her breath, she slid down against the wall. This was not how it was supposed to happen. Small flicks of light danced before her eyes and she was afraid she would faint—from the anticlimax or simply from the relief. A man came running, glanced at her, then turned and ran back the way he had come. She was too woozy to wonder why. Some school girls hurried to help her to her feet. All three of them were talking at the same time and she didn't understand a word. She didn't have the energy to think in French and just said: "I'm okay, I'm okay."

The girls looked disappointed, but the train was entering the station and Klara ran to catch it while brushing off her clothes.

The afternoon at work passed in a fog. She left the Parliament, and as soon as she was outside she switched on her cell phone. She longed to hear from Louis, to tell him that the operation had been accomplished, even if somewhat differently from the plan.

It had started raining. Stubborn microscopic droplets gathered on her glasses and prevented her from seeing clearly. At the corner of Rue Froissart, a warm diffuse light was shining out of the stationery shop window.

The telephone rang. She pressed the green button, eager to hear his voice.

"You blew it," he said.

The cell phone turned heavy in her hand. "What..." she started, but there was only silence at the other end.

CHAPTER THIRTY-FOUR

Klara threw her coat on the couch and went to sit down at her desk by the window. Why did Louis accuse her of failing? She had handed over the blueprints, and that was how the operation was supposed to go. The end of impersonating Fatima. She dried her tears with the back of her hand. The tension and disappointment ran off her with the tears. She turned silent, staring straight ahead.

Outside it had stopped raining. In the rear garden, the house sparrows were bathing and drinking in the granite dolphin-shaped fountain. A tired jet of water spurted out of its mouth with irregular pressure. Right now, she envied the birds and wished that she also could hide from the world that way, to blend in with the background and become invisible.

Night fell while she was sitting there. The sparrows were long gone, and the fountain swallowed by the darkness. She realized that the red leather frame with the pictures of Serena and Marcos, and that recent one of Anders was missing from her desk. She must have left it at the hotel in Scheveningen. The windows of the apartments in neighboring buildings facing the back yard were lit, mercilessly revealing their inner life, normal people's everyday lives. Fussing about with food in the kitchens, school kids coming home, filling washing machines with laundry...

She sat there, exhausted, waiting for an explanation to *"You blew it"*. She wanted to leave the nagging unease behind, be finished with the operation once and for all.

Far, far away, she heard steps on the staircase. Her upstairs neighbor coming home from work, she registered, indifferently.

The sound of a lock being tampered with, unwilling to yield...

Her lock.

She shot up from the chair, snatched the knife from her handbag and the gun from its hiding place in the kitchen drawer on her way to the living room, and was on her knees behind the couch just in time to see the door slowly swing open.

A short man was standing in the doorway raising his arms in the air.

"Don't shoot! For heaven's sake!" he said in the south Swedish *Skåne* accent, looking harmless and mildly ridiculous. A herringbone-patterned wool coat was flapping out around him.

"Who are you?" Klara was still aiming at him.

"May I get my badge out? It's in my pocket." He made no attempt to fetch it.

She nodded. There was no way the coat pockets could hold a weapon; the garment was hanging loosely around him.

"Put it down on the floor and kick it over. If you take one single step or do anything unexpected, I will shoot."

He fished out an ID card with his left hand, the right one still raised. Then he bent down and shoved it along the floor. Without taking her eyes off him, she picked up the card.

"May I come in now?" he asked.

"Go out and close the door. If I am satisfied with your ID, I will let you in."

He obediently did as she told him. She heard the lock click. Even though he obviously had the means to open it, it would take several seconds to get back in. She studied the ID card. Mats Larsson FRA, it said, and then in a smaller font: Försvarets Radioanstalt, the Swedish Armed Forces Radio Center. That was where they did all the signals intelligence collection. It looked legit, but what was he doing here?

Feeling less vulnerable she opened the door leaving the knife on the floor behind the couch, though still with the gun in her hand.

"Come in, Mats. Is that your real name or just an alias?"

"No, no, we're not that sophisticated," he said, smiling for the first time.

She picked up her coat from the couch and the wide-open pizza-carton with leftovers from the coffee table. The whole apartment was untidy, the bed still unmade.

"What do you want? Why didn't you just ring the bell?" she asked and nodded to him to sit down. Angry with herself for caring about the mess, she folded the pizzabox in half and dumped it in the rubbish.

"You've been silent so long we thought you might be sleeping. I have been working eight-hour shifts surveilling this apartment for a while now, so you'll have to forgive me, but to me we are practically old friends," he said.

"What? We never discussed bugging..." She stopped when she realized the enormity of the intrusion. It felt even worse that it was Swedes who were listening. Americans might do things like that, but not Swedes. That was not right.

"Becoming a sex therapist was never part of the bargain!" she said, spitting out the words. "Do you wankers jerk off when I have company in bed?"

"Mind your language, please." Mats said, his tone of voice strict and avuncular. "You know the purpose of the bugging."

"I don't. And I certainly wasn't consulted. Do you have camera feed too?"

"No, that was not considered necessary." His voice was matter-of-fact.

"Well then, what do you want?" She felt nude and exposed—soiled, and wanted him to leave. Immediately.

"We want to know what went wrong."

She only had a vague idea of what might be his role, and none at all about how much information he possessed. But he obviously had a connection to Louis and the mission, she thought, so she nodded to him to continue.

"The plan was to take your friend in and have him sing a little, you know, applying modern methods and devices if necessary, but you conveniently let him slip away."

"Fahrid? He is not my friend."

Mats ignored the comment and Klara continued: "That's not correct. It was never about taking the guy in, as you put it. That was not the objective."

"It was *the* objective. We had people everywhere, in the street, at the cafeteria, at each entrance of the metro and on both platforms, but we lost you in that corridor, and he got away because you're the only one who knows what he looks like... Was that your idea?"

"I can't believe this," she sighed.

"He ditched the briefcase, and it was only when we found it that we understood you two had actually met."

She wasn't listening anymore.

She had accepted to play the part as Fatima to hand Fahrid the documents. That was the deal. But the CIA and their Swedish counterpart had had other plans that had failed because she changed platforms in the metro. So now they blamed her. It would have been laughable, had it not been tragic.

The consequences of what Mats was implying scared her. She had to put an end to this.

"So now you are blaming me? Because you have behaved like incompetent idiots? Louis owes me an apology!"

"Who is Louis?" Mats voice was suddenly hard.

Klara turned ice cold. She jumped to her feet and raised her gun, aiming at him.

"Who are you really?" she asked, emphasizing every word. "Why are you here?"

Mats automatically lifted his hands again, like a puppet pulled by strings. Once more he looked frightened.

"My name is Mats Larsson and I work for the Swedish Armed Forces Radio Center. We have orders to cooperate with you."

"And who, then, am I?" she asked, her voice calm.

Gesturing with one hand to her to drop the gun, he said: "If I understand correctly, you are an undercover Palestinian agent who promised to help us catch an extremely professional and dangerous Saudi operative."

"Go away! I have nothing to say to you. Get out!"

Mats got up from the couch and walked backwards towards the door, not taking his eyes off the gun in her hand.

"Take it easy," he said. "I'm leaving."

At that moment something made Klara change focus. Before Mats reached the door, it slowly and silently swung open again. The doorway framed three tall men in some kind of uniform she couldn't identify, each with a well-oiled Ingram aimed directly at her.

"You'd better come with us now," said Mats a little pompously. "Thank you, guys. I think the lady is getting nervous," he added, and both his posture and his tone of voice had changed entirely.

She wouldn't have time to move a finger, she knew, before they shot; they were trained to act instantaneously. Faced with the inevitable, the tension, the anger, and the disappointment literally drained off of her. Her gun clattered to the floor, miraculously without going off. Giving up, she felt somehow relieved. Mats took a sealed plastic bag out of his trouser pocket. There was a piece of white fabric in it. The smell of ether spread through the room, leaving nothing to the imagination.

Swedes? she thought, when the cloth covered her mouth and nose.

CHAPTER THIRTY-FIVE

Anders had moved in to his new office only a few months ago and it was still a bit unfamiliar. On the eighth floor of the Espace Léopold, commonly known as Léo, the EU Parliament's impressive building in steel and glass, he had a lovely view southward, over the Parc du Cinquantenaire and the enormous triumphal arch at the other end. The building on Avenue Renaissance in front of Klara's apartment on the street behind, glimpsed through the trees. The dimensions of his office were unfamiliar. In the old place, he could reach up to his binders from his seat at the desk; here, he had to get up each time he needed one.

After his great success last week, this week had been a quiet one, and it was drawing to an end. He was often staying in Brussels over the weekends lately because of Klara. Words like passion, infatuation, or even love, weren't part of his vocabulary, though those words would describe his feelings rather well. The shocking events of the weekend had brought their relationship to a new level. She had told him that she was in the final stage of a cooperative endeavor with Swedish Authorities—it was unclear if it was police or military—in a matter he himself would have approved of, had he been in the same circumstances. Her conclusion was that the shooter must be someone who wished to see that mission fail.

He believed her, and found her even more fascinating now. It added to the mystery around her that had captivated him from the first moment.

He sat drumming his fingers against each other, wondering if Klara would be at home or if he should call her cell. Just as he had started keying in her telephone number, there was a knock on the door.

"Entrez," he said loudly, but without getting up.

The door opened and two men came in. Anders looked at the business cards they handed him. The older man's card read Reuven Levi, Red Sea Investment, and the other one Abraham Nathanson, University of Tel Aviv. Nathanson appeared to be in his forties, about six-foot-tall, pale, with poor, flaky skin and a permanent five o'clock shadow. Levi, on the other hand, was a short man, about sixty years of age, compact and powerful, with a neck like a bull and short, light grayish brown hair. The eyes were steel-gray and watchful, the face angular, with character, and was only slightly mellowed by age.

"What can I do for you, gentlemen? It's rather late and I was just about to leave." He was not a big fan of all these lobbyists who pestered the MEP's at all kinds of inconvenient times.

"It's about what we can do for you," Levi said, as he sat down uninvited and waved to Nathanson to do the same.

"I don't know what you are hinting at, but we will have to get back to that some other time," Anders said. He was getting really annoyed. "As I said, I'm leaving now."

"It's about Klara Andersson," Nathanson said, with a deep and beautiful voice that did not seem to fit his looks.

Anders froze.

"Who is that?" He tried to keep a straight face.

The men definitely did not look like vulgar thugs. Their clothes were elegant and their appearances distinguished, at least the older man. *Does this have to do with the shoot-out?* he wondered.

"If you let us cut straight to the point, instead of interrupting all the time, you will be able to leave before she starts missing you," Levi said, studying his fingernails.

"I have nothing to discuss with you."

The fact that these two foreigners knew about his relationship with Klara was threatening in itself and the willpower both men exuded was tangible, overpowering. Anders felt his resistance wane.

As if he had not heard Anders, Nathanson started talking: "I am responsible for Mossad's database on hostile agents and terrorists. The woman you know as Klara Andersson is registered in that database, and has been so for quite some time. She has been a sleeper for years, but we believe she is now active again. Her present work here at the Parliament offers interesting opportunities."

Anders had somehow suspected that the men represented some organization, something official. But Mossad? Somebody there must be suffering from acute brain hemorrhage.

"That's the most ridiculous..."

Levi interrupted him: "We know she's sleeping with you."

Not we know you *are sleeping* with her, Anders thought. *Does that mean something?*

"That's why we want you to help us," Abraham said, before Anders had the chance to object. "But first you should know that it is with the approval of the Swedish government that we are approaching you," he continued. "And you have the right to refuse to cooperate. We have to inform you about that, they insisted."

"You Swedes are so finicky about individual rights," Levi practically sneered, making it sound like something bad.

Anders was speechless, both startled and angry. He was as stung by Levi's disrespectful comment as he was confused about Nathanson's completely absurd allegation. He had never been into conspiracy theories, and this was a bad one.

"What kind of stupid nonsense is this?" he bellowed. "I refuse to listen to another word! OUT! Immediately!"

It was obviously some attempt at extortion, but he had no idea what they thought that they could make him do.

Nathanson made a move and pulled something out from his inner breast pocket. For a second, Anders thought it might be a gun; that would really have crowned the insane situation. However, it turned out to be just a bunch of papers. Abraham took the top one, and handed it over to Anders.

"Read it!" bawled Levi.

Anders looked suspiciously at the paper. It was a stiff card, the size of a postcard, with the royal blue logo of the Chancellery of the Swedish Government, the national coat of arms with the three crowns at the upper left, and The Prime Minister's Office printed in the middle of the card. He turned it around. There was a handwritten message on the other side.

"Recognize the handwriting, do you?" It was more of a statement than a question from Levi. Nathanson continued:

"I'm sure you understand that a message of this nature cannot be signed. The risk that it falls into wrong hands is too great."

Anders, please listen to the bearer of this card, it said, simply, with today's date at the right-hand side and a badly drawn flower. Anders was in no doubt about whose handwriting it was; what shocked him was the flower. It was an internal partisan joke they had come up with when the nominations committee had had real trouble finding the right candidates at a party rally some ten or twelve years ago. They had sent secret messages to each other, and the flower had been a kind of password.

Since then, it had become the symbol for the special friendship between an inner circle of party members. He didn't understand the context, but now he could no longer dismiss these men's errand as an absurd fabrication, invented by some overheated Mossad brain. Somehow, they had been in contact with Sven Åmansson, an old friend who had become Undersecretary with the Ministry of Interior. Anders respected and had great confidence in him.

He rubbed the palms of his hands on the trousers. So, people knew about his affair. That was disturbing. A certain part of the pleasure in his relationship with Klara had been precisely the fact that their relationship was his fantastic secret. It gave him a sense of power to know that he—gray, reliable, down-to-earth, straightforward, honest and rather boring Anders—had a woman that other men would envy him, had they known. When they looked at her, which they often did, he thought: *she's mine.*

The Israelis nodded in unison, when they saw he had finally understood. They seemed to sense that Anders' guard was down, and to make the most of it, Nathanson started speaking again.

"This woman was present at the Middle East Peace Conference hosted in Madrid in 1991."

"Nothing odd about that, she is an interpreter, for heaven's sake," Anders reacted.

"Don't interrupt, if you want to be able to leave here within in a reasonable time." Levi's voice was sharp.

"A top man from the PLO, Atef Bseiso, was at that conference too. A cold-blooded murderer and hit man, and one of Chairman Arafat's confidants. A year later, when he returned to Madrid, CESID, the Spanish intelligence organization at the time, advised us he was coming," Abraham explained. "We planned to bring him in for questioning, suspecting he was actually part of Black September."

"You are familiar with Black September and what they did, aren't you?" Levi asked.

"Of course I am, but what has any of this to do with Klara?" Anders didn't like where things were going.

"Will you let me finish?" Abraham asked harshly. "Someone helped Bseiso to escape from Madrid to Paris. That forced us to improvise and he ended up getting killed in the middle of the street. The incident was unfortunate, and brought about a serious breach of trust between us and the French, not to mention the CIA, who were cultivating him as a key contact within the PLO.

"But why on earth do you think Klara was involved?" Anders was sure it was all a stupid misunderstanding.

"Recently, among the belongings of a man in Israeli prison we discovered a clue. It was a dictionary, big as a brick, Swedish-Spanish. At some time, it belonged to her; her name was penciled in it," said Levi drily.

"It had a hiding place, the pages had been cut out in the middle, to fit something, God knows what—a small gun, drugs— inside. In any case, the book brought Klara Andersson's name to our attention. The lead took us to Spain, and eventually to a plastic surgery clinic in Madrid. There, after digging deeply, we found out that a change of identity had taken place, in the early 90s."

"Change of identity?" Anders shook his head, uncomprehending.

"The real Klara Andersson was a Swedish girl from a small town up north, who made a living doing bit-parts and modelling in Madrid. When she decided to have a nose job done, to be more photogenic and improve her chances, a well-trained Palestinian agent, Fatima Habib Sjögren, took her place," explained Abraham.

"The poor girl didn't have a chance, she never woke up from the anesthesia," Levi said. "And believe me, the woman you're fucking has no qualms of conscience regarding the murder of the true Klara."

"It was a perfect occasion; the agent was not much older and thanks to her Swedish mother, she had the right complexion. A good cosmetic surgeon did the rest," continued Abraham. "The replacement was successful, went practically unobserved, and Fatima has lived as Klara Andersson ever since."

"Oh, come on. Nobody noticed? Nobody ever missed the Swedish girl?"

"No. Klara Andersson was a single child and not close to her family at the time. She spent the best part of twenty years in Spain, only going back for her parents' funerals. They died in the mid-nineties, within months of each other. People change over the years, and the relatives knew she had had a nose job. Fatima is clever and skilled, and when she recently returned to Sweden, she obviously integrated successfully with a few of Klara Andersson's relatives."

There was silence. Anders was confused, sick; it was like a bad movie. He tried to think of something to prove them wrong, that their story didn't hold water.

"The Palestinians," he said, "aren't they just into suicide attacks? I mean, they don't have resources for something like this." Anders could not remember having heard of anything more sophisticated.

"That's what most people believe. It's not in our best interest to spread knowledge to the contrary. But in the 80's, helped in part by Swedish foreign-aid money, a group of Pal-estinian elite agents were trained in Libya and the Soviet Union. The woman you know as Klara Andersson was one of them."

Abraham looked Anders in the eyes while talking, and at the same time he was picking out some grainy black and white photographs from among his stack of papers. One picture showed a smiling, young blonde woman in a khaki uniform in front of a tent, proudly holding a Kalashnikov. The landscape behind the tent was desert-like. The other one showed a woman in a strict dark blue pant suit and white blouse standing by an interpreting booth. Much as he wanted to, Anders could not deny that both photographs looked a lot like Klara, years ago. But pictures could be modified, photoshopped.

He looked again at the photo from the desert-like landscape and his resolve returned. He made a firm decision not to allow himself to be impressed by the two men and their story. He needed to talk to Klara herself.

The one little thing that chafed at the back of his head was the way she had acted when they had been attacked, the other day. Her familiarity with the gun, not doubting for a second to use it.

All three were silent for a beat, allowing Anders to catch his breath.

"Did she ever show you how she handles a knife? No? Well, believe me, you would be impressed," Levi said.

"Fatima collaborated with the Basque terrorist organization ETA for a while, then she married a Spaniard," Nathanson continued his story. "No children, but since then, she has been laying low. Turned into what we call a sleeper. We thought that maybe they questioned her loyalty. It happens with undercover agents."

Right there Anders stopped listening. Hope budded in his troubled brain. If she had ever been who they said she was, she had obviously defected long ago.

"Some of this she has told you herself, isn't that so?" Levi asked. "Apart from the change of identity, and her true background, of course."

He nodded stiffly. Now he started to suspect that the two men might be after something else altogether.

"I don't believe a word of all this. The story is too construed and complicated; there are too many things that could fail for it to be true. You must have been working hard to construct this incredible fantasy." He paused to give his words the proper emphasis. "I thought that, by now, you would have concluded that we didn't come here to kill time with unfounded allegations and false accusations. Both Mr. Levi and myself are busy people, and we would not waste the time had we not considered this important. If you are still in any doubt at all, I remind you of the message from a person in your own government. I insist that you refrain from interrupting me and let us explain what we expect from you. After that, you will have the opportunity to ask questions," said Nathanson.

Anders shivered in spite of himself. He shut up.

"*We* are not the bad guys in this story," Levi said, his smile sarcastic and arrogant.

CHAPTER THIRTY-SIX

Fahrid needed a powerful laptop and a high-quality printer, plus a comfortable work space to scrutinize the documents handed over by Klara. He had to print the photos to know that they indeed were what they had paid for, only then would he be passing them on. If the pictures were good and contained the technical specifications to the YS 2000, she was valuable. He wondered how much of the money she would eventually get.

He still found it difficult to think of that woman as Fatima, there was really nothing about her that indicated Arab origins. Those green eyes. She seemed far too westernized to him. But her mother had been Swedish, that must be it. In any case, her cover was impressive.

Dressed in his cheap, baggy clothes, he left his simple rental in the immigrant quarters for good. He bought a prepaid cell phone, wrote a few words on a piece of paper that he stuffed into a stamped, addressed envelope and shoved it into a postbox. Then he went to the garage, changed in the toilet, picked up the BMW and drove to Hotel Sofitel by the airport. It was suitably discreet and not too large. The rooms were spacious and comfortable, with a desk broad enough to fit both computer and printer. He saw to getting a room on the ground floor, to be able to exit by the window and get to his car in seconds, in case of emergency.

Then he returned to the city, to an electronics shop close to La Bourse, and bought a laptop with all kinds of accessories. Not because he needed them all, but because he wanted to come across as a spoiled big spender, in the improbable case anyone would remember him. After returning to the hotel, he worked purposefully, printing and studying the documents, for hours. He forgot to eat. The next day he only left the room while it was being cleaned, but took the computer and print-outs with him, and then continued working until late. Only when he heard voices in the corridor did he look at his watch. It was already eleven. He went to the lobby and asked for the address to a porn club, in order to fit the part he was now playing.

The premises were painted black and had a mirror ball in the ceiling above a minute dance floor, which was right in front of a small stage where the strippers worked shifts. There was a bar along one entire wall, and on the other side there were booths for smaller groups. He looked at the girls, saw nothing he found exciting and made a gin and tonic last all night. That first time he was left alone at the bar.

The next evening, he didn't have the energy to find a new place, as he was totally uninterested in what was being offered. This time, a young hooker approached him. She was not tall, not particularly pretty, but had stunning legs, which she showed all of. She was blond with long hair, heavily made up and dressed in very tiny jeans shorts and a white top under which you could make out a black bra.

"You look lonely, handsome. Buy me a drink?" she asked, smiling.

"Not interested," he said.

"Don't you like my type? I have several clients like you, and they loved my company," she said and stuck her arm under his while pressing her pelvis against his thigh and leaning close.

The bartender's watchful eyes caught on to them and he came up and asked her what she wanted to drink. Fahrid realized that he had no choice and offered her champagne. He knew that she would be served cider at best, more probably a fizzy soda, not what he paid for, and played with the idea of tasting the contents of her glass and making a scene. But he kept his temper.

It was unavoidable.

Half an hour later they were in her room, which conveniently was one floor up in the same building. It was small, with a sink and a bidet behind a curtain and a large bed with a wrought-iron headboard taking up the better part of the room. The sparse lighting was wrapped in pink gauze. He had no wish to have sex with her. He was annoyed, felt forced into the situation. The last time he remembered really wanting a woman was that night he had had dinner with Klara, but that was more due to the excitement of the operation, and because she was enigmatic—not a professional who fucked for money. The very idea that he was expected to comply was enough to turn him off. Forced to pay and forced to fuck.

The girl turned on some music and started stripping. Soon she was completely naked in front of him, seated on the bed looking up at her. She began unbuttoning his shirt and stroking his chest while she continued moving to the music. Her pubic hair was very curly, and she had full round breasts, probably filled with silicon, as they did not change shape whatever moves she made. He was as uninterested as it is possible for a man to be, and anger was building up inside him.

"Darling," the hooker said in her obsequious manner, "would you like me to suck your great big cock?"

When that had no effect, she turned around and wriggled her hips at his eye level, then she bent over and spread her buttocks apart.

"Is this where you would like to be, gorgeous?" she asked, while she stretched her hand out, between her legs, stroking his penis.

"I don't want you, damned whore!" Fahrid shouted, getting up and pushing her away.

She fell forward, on all four. He pulled her up. While holding a firm grip around one of her arms, he struck her with full force across the face.

"You're not allowed to hit!" she screamed, trying to break away from him. "I'll call for help if you hurt me!"

It was only when he saw a drop of blood slide down from her nose and her cheek slowly turning a deep red from the blow that he felt something akin to excitement.

The alarm, verging on fear, that shone out of her eyes succeeded in producing a rather lame half hard-on. He shoved her down on the bed. She landed with her legs spread and her feet on the floor. He never undressed, just pulled his trousers down and pushed it in. He then closed his eyes and imagined something entirely different to be able to ejaculate as soon as possible.

The whole thing took only minutes. As soon as he finished, he got up and pulled up his trousers. She remained lying on the bed. He fished out a few hundred Euro from his wallet, threw them at her and left the room without a word. On the way out, he buttoned up his shirt and put his jacket on. It was only when he was sitting in his car that he permitted himself to react. He hammered hopelessly with his fists at the wheel. The frustration was suffocating. It had been so close to turning really ugly. He had wanted to strangle the slut to prolong his pleasure, but had managed to control himself. He could not risk an unnecessary murder.

A few days later, Fahrid was driving to Saint Petersburg. In line with his role as a playboy, a Louis Vuitton bag was in the back filled with new shirts and suits, and the high-end laptop rested on the seat next to him. Everything fit the passport he was carrying, stating that he was from Saudi Arabia and had a name reminiscent of the royal family.

As far as he had been able to determine from the scrutiny of the documents Klara had given him, they were first class. He couldn't help admiring her. She had done a great job, was professional, and could hardly be suspected of treason. She might prove useful, he thought. During the long drive, he kept busy preparing a new plan.

Approaching Hamburg, the phone rang. Somebody reported that his superiors had arrived, and were waiting for him in Saint Petersburg.

Fahrid was excited. Turning over the documents was a major accomplishment and would smooth the way for his new plan. He expected them to approve it.

CHAPTER THIRTY-SEVEN

When Levi and Nathanson left an hour or so later, Anders was pacing back and forth in the small office. Klara was no terrorist that was impossible. He had to talk to her, face to face, see her reactions when he confronted her. Grabbing his coat off the hanger behind the door, he took the lift downstairs and left the building.

The cold night air cleansed his head and had a soothing effect. Once at Rue Belliard he decided to walk to her place; it wasn't far. On the way, he went over and over again what he had learned in the last couple of hours. The men clearly had information about Klara that he knew was true. In addition, they had provided some unconfirmed data, and maybe a handful of blatant lies.

It was hard to believe that she would knowingly have exposed him to danger, but he had to confess that what the two men from Mossad had told him explained her reaction and behavior in Holland better than her own version.

He looked up at the apartment window. It was dark. *She must be taking a bath,* he thought, and pressed the entry code. In spite of being upset, he felt his body react to the prospect of her in the bathtub, and he ran up the narrow, steep staircase two steps at a time.

Just as he was introducing the key in the lock, he noticed that the door wasn't properly closed. He panicked. He wanted to turn around and run away but stood frozen to the spot. He remained completely still for more than a minute and only then started to listen intensely. Not a sound from inside. He pushed the door open a little, not knowing what to expect. When nothing happened, he stretched out his hand and turned the light on.

Apart from the fact that she wasn't there, everything looked normal. The unlocked door was the only indication that something was wrong. His unease increased. He could hear his own breathing, as well as muffled noises from the flat above. In contrast, the absolute silence inside the apartment seemed even more eerie. A little out of breath from the quick walk and running up the stairs, he moved towards the kitchen. In the doorway he turned and looked back at the living room. Behind the couch, in the middle of the room, there was something on the floor. He went over, staring at the object for a long while before picking it up. At first, he thought it was a nail file, but when he tried the edge it cut deep into the flesh of his thumb.

He cursed. It bled profusely, and he pulled a handkerchief out of his pant pocket and wrapped it around the wound. Levi's comment about Fatima's expertise handling a knife rang in his ears. The cold, hard, dark gray artifact burned in his hand. It was well balanced and surprisingly heavy for its modest size. He had never seen anything like it. It did not have a nice handle as if it would be a letter opener or a decorative object. It was deadly. Must have been specially made.

Anders felt his world waver again. Did it belong to Klara, or had someone planted it here? With the knife still in his hand, he went to the bathroom to look for a band-aid. He wasn't holding on to the knife out of fear; he was sure he was alone in the apartment; but it was a kind of link to her. On the way he observed that she had left the bed unmade. She often did. A quick look in the rubbish bin revealed only a crumpled-up pizza carton.

Once his thumb had stopped bleeding, he stretched the band-aid hard around the cut and went to the old walnut escritoire in the bedroom window. She had insisted on bringing it from Madrid because it was just the right height to see out through the window over its top. He turned the key opening it. The old-fashioned writing surface had an inlay of dark green leather with a narrow golden border. He picked carefully at it, to see whether she could have hidden something underneath. It didn't budge. In the upper part there was a row of four small drawers, and two more at each side of an open space. She kept a vase with a bouquet of dried roses in that middle compartment, the first flowers he had sent her.

He methodically searched all the drawers including the three big ones underneath. She used to say she thought it had a secret compartment somewhere, but they had never seriously looked for it. Finding nothing unfamiliar, he pulled the drawers out and scrutinized the sides and the back of each. He moved on to study every inch of the desk's inside, in vain. No letter or envelope, not a single clue anywhere. He sat there on the floor, among neatly stacked small and large drawers, trying to think.

The passport. She usually kept it in the top left drawer inside the desk but it wasn't there. He went back into the bathroom; the toothbrush and toothpaste were also missing.

She had gone away.

Why hadn't she told him? Why hadn't she called?

When he tried to put the drawers back, they would only fit into the desk the way they had been placed originally, and he spent some time figuring out the right order.

Exhausted and hungry, he locked the door and went out again into the cold evening. Without any real hope, he dialed her cell phone. Her friendly voice made him shiver. Where was she? He turned onto the busier Avenue Renaissance and hailed a taxi.

"*Centre ville,*" he said in French, having no idea of where he wanted to go.

He had never before experienced anything like this. Never felt so bewildered, verging on physically sick, and at the same time afraid he would never see her again. Was it true that she was some kind of terrorist or spy? Had she disappeared from his life forever? He couldn't bear to think of the possible consequences—for his work and his marriage—of being involved in something so alien, so strange and unbelievable. It was unreal.

He stopped the taxi and got out close to Grande Place, walking listlessly around the magnificent square. On his third round he went into *La Chaloupe d'Or.* It was more a snack bar than a restaurant nowadays, with walls of dark wood and small benches. It wasn't crowded, and he quickly found a free table. He ordered a sandwich and a glass of white wine. Since he had been seeing Klara he had become used to having wine with the evening meal. While eating he decided to return to her apartment. He couldn't understand why she had left so suddenly without telling him, but he wasn't yet ready to believe what the men from Mossad had told him.

Maybe he could find something, anything, that would give him a clue as to what was going on.

He took the metro to Schumann and walked the familiar street for the second time that evening. Already on the stairs he heard her phone ring, but when he unlocked the door and picked it up, the caller had hung up. He sat down on her broad, comfortable unmade bed, picked up the pillow and pressed it to his face.

The smell of her lingered.

After a sleepless night, Anders arrived red-eyed to the Parliament. He had stayed in Klara's apartment, hoping that she would come home or that someone would call. In the morning he had cut himself several times while shaving and felt grimy in spite of the shower.

He was going to turn to the interpreters' office for information. The administrative departments would be working on a Friday; only the MEPs were free to travel home. It was a long shot, but Eva-Karin, chief interpreter of *les cabines suédoises* might know something about Klara's absence.

Her office was on the third floor in one of the old buildings. Both of the elevators were busy, and Anders was about to take the stairs, but changed his mind when he saw the left one arriving. It was empty. He got in and pressed the button for the third floor. The elevator started, jerked and stopped between the ground floor and the first. He pressed the 3 for the third floor again. Then once more.

Nothing happened.

He went completely mad hammering at all the buttons and beating at the door at the same time.

"Help," he bellowed.

After what seemed like ages he heard a male voice yell: "Hello. Did the elevator get stuck again?"

"Yes, damn it. Get me the hell out of here, will you?" Anders shouted.

"Just a moment. Calm down. I'll call the janitor."

It did not take many minutes, but Anders was cursing and sweating profusely.

"We never use this one," said the young man, when the door finally opened. "It always gets stuck between the ground floor and the first."

Anders recognized him, he had an office in this building, housing the administrative staff related to the interpretation services. He was in charge of the documentation service for the interpreters, an Englishman in his thirties who had already quit working as an interpreter.

A too female-dominated environment? Anders wondered. "Why don't they block it or put up a bloody sign, for heaven's sake?" he hissed, fully aware that it wasn't the guy's fault.

"Got claustrophobia, have you?" he asked, obviously pitying Anders.

"Yes, that, and I'm in a hell of a hurry," he answered, not wanting to explain further.

Feeling even more grimy now after the episode in the elevator, he found the door to Eva-Karin's office open. He knocked on the doorframe.

"Come in."

Passing the doorstep, he got tongue-tied.

"Can you help me out?" he managed to ask.

"Excuse me. What did you say your name was?" the woman asked, very reserved, inspecting him.

Anders introduced himself.

"How can I help you?" Eva-Karin's tone was slightly more accommodating now that she knew he was a Member of Parliament.

"Klara Andersson had promised to help me with a text yesterday, but she never showed up. I've called her a couple of times, but nobody answers. I'm wondering if she suddenly had to go to work in Luxembourg or something?" Anders knew he sounded stupid.

"Klara is on sick leave. Acute appendicitis. Anything else?"

Anders didn't quite succeed in hiding his reaction. He had kissed the tiny scar on Klara's tummy so many times. He wanted to ask more questions, but the words wouldn't come to him.

"Thank you," he said stupidly, and left.

He felt Eva-Karin's questioning eyes burn at his back. Acute appendicitis, she had said. A sloppy lie or an excuse?

After a few hours in his office, he had come up with something like a plan. He took a taxi to the airport. On the way, he realized that he couldn't turn up unannounced at the Cabinet Office at Rosenbad. They would work on a Friday, though, and he reached for his cell phone.

The battery was almost depleted.

He hadn't remembered to charge it at Klara's. Sven Åmansson's personal assistant picked up his call and promised to check if she could squeeze him in sometime along the afternoon. She asked him to check later for confirmation. Sven was the person who had endorsed the two Mossad agents, and at present that was his only lead.

Bloody charger. He would have to buy a new one and find somewhere to plug it in. It felt like a matter of life and death to be reachable. What if Klara called?

First, he got a return ticket to Stockholm and paid with his private Mastercard; it was a private trip after all. Then he found an outlet. The cell phone rang almost immediately.

"Yes, Sven says he was expecting you. We'll squeeze you in at five-thirty, you can have dinner while you talk," said the assistant. "But you'll have to make do with three quarters of an hour. He has an important finance-related meeting after that."

That would be plenty, Anders thought, encouraged.

On board the plane, he tried to put his thoughts in order. Why had the information been conveyed through Levi and Nathanson? Why not personally by Sven? Was there any actual evidence that she was not Klara? Here his thoughts took another turn: he realized it didn't matter so much to him who she was. After all, it was the woman he knew that he cared about. But then again, he faltered: Could he possibly have fallen in love with a cold-blooded murderer and a terrorist?

CHAPTER THIRTY-EIGHT

The first thing Klara saw was a transparent tube. She followed it with her eyes. It led to a butterfly needle on the back of her left hand. Her wrist was fastened to the side of the bed with a broad strap. The right one was also immobilized. The tube was fastened to a bottle of fluid hanging close to the headboard. She was too droopy and indifferent to try to read the text on the dispenser. Apart from a slight stomachache she felt comfortably indolent and lethargic and was about to drift away in a light haze, when someone said:

"Hi, Klara! Time to wake up."

She couldn't identify the voice, but knew it was faintly familiar. Then it moved into her line of vision. She tried to focus. A fair man with short hair, about her own age... An angular face with a jutting, decisive chin and a flat, small nose—a boxer's nose.

"Do you recognize me? No? What a blow to my vanity," he said. "I'll turn you loose." He continued approaching the bed.

He removed the adhesive tape and then carefully the cannula, before ripping open the Velcro bands around her wrists. She rubbed them, they were red where the straps had been. Then he handed her a glass of water, a white capsule shining in his other palm.

"Take this, and you'll recover in no time. There are some people who want to talk to you as soon as you are ready."

223

Klara took the pill and drank greedily of the water. She fell back upon the pillow when he left the room. A low-key mumbling arose on the other side of the door, but she couldn't make out what was being said and didn't care enough to try. Instead, she tried to clear her head. The memories were like cobwebs, going all kinds of places. The last thing she remembered, she was standing in the middle of her living room and three big guys in dark clothing had been aiming at her with automatic weapons....

"Hasse Broberg," she croaked. Was she hallucinating? Hans Broberg, Hasse for short, her very first boyfriend, back in Boden. They had been at the ball for cadets, having just finished their training, last time they met. It was the year she was studying in Stockholm. Next only to the Nobel Prize dinner in prestige, the press covered the event with an abundance of pictures and comments, and her classmates had been flabbergasted when they saw that *she* got to go to the famous Cadet Ball.

Hasse had hit her that night, when she refused to sleep with him, and that had been the end of their relationship.

He had got heavier, stouter, with age. He had always loved extreme sports, ski-jumping, parachuting, checking out survival equipment in cold weather, in short, constantly challenging fate. Through the grapevine she had heard that soon after becoming an officer he had left the military.

Mats Larsson worked for the Armed Forces Radio Center and Hasse was an officer once upon a time... So, maybe the Swedish Armed Forces links them somehow? she thought foggily. *Better than being captured by Mossad.*

She pulled her fingers through her hair. It was sticky with sweat. The thought of how she looked drifted through her head without settling there. Next to the door Hasse had left through was another door. That had to be the toilet. The sparse, sterile interior and the alarm button on the side of

224

the headboard indicated that this was not a home or a hotel room.

When she tried to stand up, she got dizzy and had to hold on to the bed for a while. The door did lead to a toilet. Her clothes were hanging on hooks on the wall. On a stool by the shower were her watch and the few items of jewelry she always wore. After a pee, she went over to the mirror above the sink. The sight of her reflection was a shock. Her skin was tight over the cheekbones and she had dark shadows under the eyes. The chalk-white garment she was wearing emphasized her pallor and made her look emaciated and hollow-eyed. Her hair was impossible, matted and tousled. She turned the shower on. Her legs started trembling, and she had to sit down on the floor with the warm water flowing over her.

After having washed her body and hair, she brusquely changed from warm water to cold and let it sting her for as long as she could stand it. That cleared her head somewhat and she felt stronger. There was a comb on the shelf under the mirror, and after using it she thought she almost looked human again. Only then did she think of checking the date on her watch.

It wasn't working.

She cursed the Rolex for winding up with movement. It would have worked for about a day after they had taken it off her. So, she deduced, she had been out for more than 24 hours.

Before dressing in her own clothes, she checked her body for bruises or needle marks. There was nothing apart from the one in the hand. But were these really the clothes that she had been wearing when those guys invaded her apartment? Black velvet stretch trousers, a tight-fitting black top and a large, gray, low-cut cashmere jersey? She blamed her difficulty to recall details on the drugs they had given her. For what purpose remained a mystery.

By the window, she got another shock. Snow covered the ground. It was pitch dark outside, no sign of human life, not even another house in sight. She put her forehead against the ice-cold windowpane and blocked off the light from behind with her hands.

There was a big birch tree a few feet away. It glowed with ice and frost, the branches heavy with snow. It was so beautiful that she caught her breath. She hadn't experienced proper winter weather for a long time.

The lights from two windows to the right and another one to the left were reflected in the snow. Hardly a big hospital, then. She couldn't see anything above, but below her there was a diffuse illumination on the ground. She calculated that she was some fifteen feet up, presumably on the first floor. The window had a white three-glass-frame, without any kind of opening mechanism.

So, she was a captive.

There was a knock on the door and three men came into the room. Hasse was not with them. The oldest one, around fifty, spoke.

"I'm sorry we're not meeting under more pleasant circumstances," he said.

Klara sat down on the bed and pulled her legs up. The men stood surrounding the bed. She wasn't frightened. This was Sweden, for sure, a state under the rule of law where inexplicable abductions simply did not occur.

Now she would finally find out what the whole matter was about. In a hazy way she was mostly curious.

"I should perhaps start by introducing us. My name is Lennart Svensson, you may consider me the project manager. This is Doctor Olle Lindström, who has been watching over your health like a bloodhound. And this is my colleague, Lieutenant Colonel Åke Svedenius."

She nodded to the men as they were introduced, but remained silent.

"The reason for bringing you here is that the operation failed," Svensson continued. "And that triggered doubts regarding your identity."

She frowned, but still said nothing.

"You have a Swedish passport in the name of Klara Andersson, but we suspect that you are Fatima Habib-Sjöström." Now it was Lieutenant Colonel Svedenius talking. "What's your comment to that?"

She took time to think before answering. They had gone to a lot of trouble to get her here, and that had to mean something. Something positive, she wanted to believe. She decided to be cautiously accommodating.

"My name is Klara, and I was born in Boden. I am the only daughter of the late Britt and Carl Andersson."

"We are not convinced that that is true," said the Lieutenant Colonel and then continued talking in a different language.

It could be Arabic. Was he testing her?

"Please talk to me in a language that I understand." she asked him.

"You don't seem to understand how serious this is. We could accuse you of murder," he continued, in the same unpleasant tone of voice, but now in Swedish. "To do that, we only need to confirm if Fatima killed Klara or if it was the other way around."

CHAPTER THIRTY-NINE

Klara grabbed the bed frame to steady herself. The room was spinning around her.

"I haven't killed anyone," she slurred. *I don't want to be the enemy,* she thought. *Not to these people. Not in my own country.*

"Do you recall the 1992 Peace Conference in Madrid?" Åke's question sounded like a gunshot, his voice hard and demanding.

"Yes, I interpreted there," she said, trying to keep her voice steady. She felt under attack. *Why is that such a big deal?* she wondered. And then she remembered: *Atef Bseiso...*

"You did more than just interpret, perhaps? Contacted a dangerous terrorist, maybe? Mossad insists that you played an important role in helping a member of Black September escape them a year later."

No, Klara thought, the panic spreading. *They cannot seriously believe that I had anything to do with that shit! If I only could think clearly, I would know what to answer...*

"Well?"

She remained silent while she tried to remember what Louis had taught her, in case she would ever be interrogated. Tell the truth, he had said. Cooperate. We can find solutions and make things right afterwards; the important thing is to gain time. If she told lies she later could not remember, she would make things worse. Three pairs of eyes never left her face. When she started talking, she had made up her mind to put the cards on the table.

"I am a CIA asset. They recruited me to inform about the public opinion regarding political decisions and other major and minor events in Spain before it became a member of NATO," she explained. "And I assisted them in Czechoslovakia, because of my work with TV there. I have never been an agent or spy. I have received no training to that end. Recently, when I worked at TV-Plus in Stockholm, I found out about Mossad's attempted assassination of Atef Bseiso in Madrid and that they killed him in Paris shortly after. They claim some Swede helped Bseiso to escape in Madrid, but they have no hard evidence. It could be pure fantasy on Mossad's side. I don't even understand why you are concerned. It's nothing to do with me—with us, or with Sweden."

"You informed…? Please be more specific. What do you mean by 'inform'?" Lennart Svensson asked.

"I wrote reports. What's there to specify? Informing means imparting information, surely?"

"Who is Louis?" Åke asked.

"The guy who started this awful mess!" she snapped, scowling.

Seeing their expressionless faces she decided to try to keep her anger in check.

"He is my handler," she added.

"Elaborate, please."

"Oh, come on, you know who he is. He's the reason I'm here, isn't he?"

"All right, all right. We know who he is," Lennart Svensson admitted. "But the relationship between you and him, and your true background, are things we can't take his word for."

"Where is Fatima now?" Åke interrupted.

Klara felt that every word she said was being carefully assessed.

"She never existed. It's just a cover. I saw the name for the first time early this autumn, beside a photograph of myself, in Mossad's database on terrorists."

The men nodded as if on cue. It looked stupid and she almost giggled. A little startled she realized that she was still high on something.

"Soon after that, Louis Hornett, my CIA handler, turned up at my place in Stockholm. He asked me to pretend to be Fatima, just this once, to turn over some false, or modified, documents about the stealth ship YS 2000 to a courier from a Saudi terrorist organization. That was it, then both Mossad and the Palestinians would be told the truth about Fatima… or me, I guess," she continued. Everything was so convoluted and confusing.

Nobody said a word. When she couldn't stand the silence any more she added: "So Fatima can't be dead… I mean, she never existed."

Trying to see the bright side of things, Klara clung to the idea that it was better being questioned by Swedes than by Mossad. Somewhere, right past the limits of her capacity to think for the moment, there was a solution. She knew that she had a trump card, only could not now, for the life of her, remember what it was.

"We've got the hospital records." Åke said, gloating. "They tell a different story."

"Hospital records?" she had only been in hospital twice, once when she had had her appendix removed and then when Louis had paid for the abortion.

They gave her a thick envelope, with the logo of the German Hospital in Madrid. Were they hinting at abortion being illegal in Spain at the time? Confused, she opened the binder. There were a lot of photographs. She couldn't read the text, it was faded and she was unable to focus. She stared at the pictures.

The first few were the ones Doctor Hasselberger had taken, she remembered, before fixing her nose: front, right profile, left profile... but there were many more photos of another woman. She had long blonde hair and green eyes, rather coarse features with a large, slightly bent nose. The chin was strong and square, but her cheekbones not well-defined. The other woman must have been there for cosmetic surgery too. All the pictures of her had red and blue lines drawn with an indelible felt-tip pen.

This was Fatima. And now they said she was dead... Klara's breath caught in her throat. Her hands were shaking and she had to put the pictures down on the bed. She was nauseous and closed her eyes to keep the photographs from spinning around like a kaleidoscope image. The bigger picture emerged in front of her inner eye. This obviously described the surgical interventions necessary to make Fatima look like herself: the blue lines where something should be removed, and red where something should be added.

She looked up from the file. Three pairs of eyes looked at her as if they thought they could penetrate her brain and read her thoughts. They didn't look away from her face for even a fraction of a second. With a mixture of fear and admiration, she looked down again.

The last picture in the binder was one of herself with a plaster cast on her nose and bruising under her eyes. That had surprised her when she woke up from the anesthesia. Doctor Hasselberger had told her they did not need to touch the nasal bone, and therefore the convalescence would be short and her eyes wouldn't get bruised. She had never questioned him about it though, just taken for granted he knew what he was doing. She remembered that first stinging pain on her left buttock. The removed birth mark. The only trace of the abortion, the most important matter on Klara's mind, had been her shaved pubis and that she bled for several days.

Inside the envelope there was one more picture, dated a month after the operation. It was also of her. She looked happy. Klara tried to retrieve that feeling. Her nose had turned out just like she wanted it. The same as before, but without the little bulge. A great surgeon, Doctor Hasselberger.

Fascinated against her will, she opened the binder again. Covering the marked parts of Fatima's face with her hands and squinting at the result the pictures actually resembled herself a lot. This was better than an invented cover. These photographs and the medical records were convincing, tailored to show that she was the one who had disappeared and that Fatima had taken her place. She was overcome with a crippling fear that it might become difficult to prove that *she* was Klara.

The family had not made much of a fuss about the cosmetic surgery. Her father had died a short time after, and her mother was too exhausted and bereaved to bother about her nose when she came home for the funeral. They were both gone now.

She had been framed and didn't know where to start, or if there was any point in trying to contradict the story these documents told. There was only one person who could ratify that she was Klara—and that was Louis. The horrible doubt that had come over her the other night, was now confirmed. The very person who had put her in this Kafkaesque situation, was also the only one who could save her from it.

Lennart must have noticed her despair.

"Let's take a break and have dinner," he said, his tone of voice a little friendlier. "You must be hungry."

She didn't think she could swallow a bite.

A winding wooden staircase led to the ground floor. They walked down the stairs one after the other, with Klara between them. The building was not a hospital, she now saw, but a spacious two-floor building with a large living room and an adjacent dining room on the ground floor. There were rag rugs in nice colors on the blonde wooden floors and rustic birch furniture. A large open fireplace in natural stone dominated the living room, and there was a tiled stove in the dining room, both of them with fires going. A door stood open to the right and showed a library, the walls covered with well-filled bookshelves and inviting easy chairs in bottle-green leather with individual floor lamps in brass. Hasse was in the living room watching the news on TV.

"Fancy a drink before dinner?" he asked. His tone of voice was a little wait-and-see, as if he still wasn't sure she remembered him.

"Not porter. I haven't had one of those since we last met," Klara said, smiling. The mere thought of liquor made her feel sick.

"Is that so?" Hasse asked, willing her to say more.

She decided not to accommodate him, but only answer direct questions and said:

"Some bubbly water and a slice of lemon is as strong as I'll have on an empty stomach."

The others helped themselves to whiskey from a liquor cabinet by the wall. Hasse went out of the room, to the kitchen, Klara presumed.

"So, you recognize him now?" Lennart Svensson asked, scrutinizing her.

"I do, but I haven't seen him for over twenty years," she said. Then she got really angry. "I recognized him right away but didn't place him. Is that so strange?" she said. "After being kidnapped, held captive and drugged, and waking up in a strange place?"

"It's our job to be suspicious," said Åke Svedenius, the Lieutenant Colonel.

233

Klara scrutinized him. He was stiff and stubborn, and precisely what he'd said—suspicious. He kept his distance and was impersonal, while the others seemed to be curious about her. The contempt for women she perceived from him frightened her. It reminded her of Alvaro and Cuba.

The doctor spoke for the first time, his manner friendly: "I have used nothing that could lead to permanent damage or impairment, but of course, you must have been confused when you woke up."

"Is it addictive?" asked Klara, with a sting of unease.

"How do you feel now?" he asked, avoiding answering her question.

"Not that great," she said. She had to let it go, save her strength. No point in wasting energy on something she couldn't change. Her grandmother had taught her that. She'd also taught Klara that it was useless to worry in advance, because sometimes those things we fear never happen. The location, snowy and isolated from the rest of the world, just as the farmhouse up in Randijaur, brought Grandma close. She had been important in Klara's life. Her right breast had been removed, and Klara fantasized that she was an Amazon. She had shown Klara the beauty of thunderstorms and how the aurora borealis would move when you whistle. Remembering her grandmother made Klara regain a certain peace and strength.

Nobody introduced the stout stern-looking woman in her late 50's who served dinner. Klara thought she looked like a strict nurse or a housemaid from some old TV program.

"Hjördis Petterson," Klara said when the woman left the room.

"What did you say?" Åke looked confused.

"She looks like Hjördis Petterson," Klara said, nodding towards the door where the woman had left. She was referring to a Swedish actress, famous in old movies from the fifties and sixties. Everybody around the table fell silent for a spell. Klara was just starting to worry that she had said something offensive when a general merriness broke out.

The smell of smoked whitefish and mashed potatoes with dill reached her nostrils and she realized that she was indeed hungry. After eating in silence for a while, she made another attempt at conversation:

"It's beautiful out there. Where are we?"

"Let's say north Sweden, you don't need to know the specific location," Lennart answered.

"How did I get here? It's a long way from Brussels."

"With plane and helicopter. Your insurance is first class," the doctor said, smiling.

"Is my absence justified to the Parliament?"

"Acute appendicitis with complications. Yes, I know that happened long ago, but they don't. Medical records are private, so you don't have to worry about explanations when you get back," he grinned.

His last comment cheered her up. She was going back. The food did wonders and Klara felt a lot better. The men continued their small talk until after dessert. They all got up to drink coffee in front of the fire in the living room. The men helped themselves to brandy, but Klara declined. She needed to think. She needed to recall that something that she knew would solve all her problems...

"Tomorrow we'll start the debriefing," Lennart said when she left to go to bed.

She wanted to plan for that in depth when she closed the door and was alone in her room, but as soon as her head hit the pillow she was sound asleep.

CHAPTER FORTY

Anders asked the taxi driver to take him to the City. Downtown was often referred to with the English term, but the name of the neighborhood was Norrmalm, north of the Old Town. He got out at Fredsgatan, across the street from Rosenbad, the Cabinet Office. He had seen the buildings along this street turn into government dependencies one by one during the last couple of decades and knew most of them were connected by complicated inner corridors and tunnels. The area was convenient, just across the bridge from the Swedish Parliament.

When he went to pay, he realized he didn't have Swedish krona, and had to use his credit card. Anders had campaigned for joining the monetary cooperation, the Euro, and had been very disappointed when his countrymen opted out.

He pushed open the heavy metal and glass door, applying weight. On a mezzanine up from the ground floor was the booth with the security guard, a pretty young woman in a brown uniform.

He told her his name and who he was seeing. She nodded, picking up the phone.

"Your visitor is here," she said, then, turning to Anders: "Please take the elevator on the right, second floor. His assistant will be waiting for you there."

That turned out to be Birgitta Axelsson, a robust woman in her 50s who never had qualified for very prominent positions, but had always been around. He knew her from party meetings and rallies along the years.

"So, how's Brussels? Are they spoiling you as much as they say?" she asked, a tone of envy in her voice.

"It's mostly work. Just like here," Anders said. He didn't want to fight the MEPs' corner right now, but he knew his party comrades believed his job was a ticket to a life in luxury.

"The small dining room was vacant. Very fortunate, because the only time Sven could see you on such short notice is over dinner. I've arranged for you two to be alone. But I don't understand this hush-hush business, rushing here from Brussels. You ought to be more sociable, Anders, I mean, see more old party friends, now that you are visiting. For once."

He ignored her sarcasm, mumbling something about an urgent matter.

Birgitta saw him to a beautiful dining room in royal blue and gold and told him that Sven would be there in ten minutes. It was one of the smaller rooms, with two large windows facing Strömmen where Lake Mälaren meets the Baltic Sea. The view was breathtaking. It was dark outside and the city lights sparkled in the water. Anders turned around to take it all in. The porcelain was white with small blue crowns, on a white tablecloth covering a blue one, that reached all they way to the floor. The national coat of arms adorned the cutlery, and the glasses were crystal with a broad gilt-edge. Did his party comrades enjoy this standard daily, here at the Government Offices, he wondered?

He sat down to wait. A young waiter appeared from nowhere and asked if he wanted something to drink.

"A Ramlösa, please." Bubbly water would be just right.

His old friend came rushing in before he had finished the bubbly water and gave him a bear hug. Sven was wearing a dark suit, but had loosened the knot of his tie and opened the top button of his shirt, which was soiled at the cuffs.

"You can't meet the finance crowd like that," said Anders, nodding at his tie.

"I have a spare shirt in the office. But, how are you? How is Karin?"

Karin, his wife… The question was like a bad omen.

CHAPTER FORTY-ONE

When Klara woke up, it was so dark she couldn't make out the shapes in the room and didn't know where she was. She was floating in a soft, snug nirvana. The fluorescent hands of her watch showed twenty to seven. There was complete silence. In big white cotton socks and a way too large t-shirt she padded to the window and peered out. No sign of dawn on the horizon. No stars, no artificial lights from anywhere... The birch looked compact and heavy against the sky.

She walked to the other side of the room and opened the door. A warm yellow light escaped from under the door across the hall. At least she wasn't the only person on earth. She wondered whose room it was. Then she discovered the guard who sat sleeping on a chair. She wanted to wake him up, so he wouldn't be rebuked for falling asleep on his post, but decided against it. She might have scared him and woken everyone else up.

After a long warm shower, she took some time to do her make-up. Mascara and discrete brown eyeshadow; anything more would look out of place here. Her handbag, a small pigskin bag with a narrow shoulder strap, was under the stool in the bathroom. As expected, it did not contain her knife. It did, however, hold her passport. Somebody must have taken it from her apartment. She shuddered at the thought of strangers searching her drawers and pawing through her belongings.

Her fingertips touched the key ring. It was a present from Anders. A miniature copy of a bronze statue by Eduardo Chillida, his first gift. She caressed its rounded surfaces. It linked her to another reality—to memories of love. She felt a warmth surge through her at the mere thought of Anders and had to smile at her fetishism. To touch certain objects produced strong feelings in her, an echo from parallel realities. She missed his big, warm hands on her back, his way of burying his nose in her neck when he lay behind her, satisfied and exhausted after making love.

She wanted all of him. But he never spoke of divorce and that was wearing on her. He had never actually said that he would break up his marriage, and she was far too proud to ask. Slowly but surely, she had grown afraid of not getting the right answer. She was clinging to the idea that things could change in a moment, as they often did in her own life. Sometimes, for the better... His wife might fall in love with somebody else.

She wanted to believe that the reason for his cowardice was that he did not trust her to stay with him. That he thought she might meet someone else and dump him. He did not know how rare it was to meet someone worth loving.

Poor Anders.

A knock on her door made her thoughts return to the present. "Come in."

"Good morning, Klara," Hasse said. "I thought you'd be up and about."

His hair, so fair you couldn't make out the gray at first glance, was still wet from the shower.

"Good morning," Klara answered. "To what do I owe the honor?"

"I wanted a word with you alone, before the debrief. They are going to check how much of what they already know tallies with what you yourself tell them. To be on the safe side. But I'm curious, what is your background, actually? Were you trained by the CIA?"

There was a hint of envy in his voice. They had summoned Hasse to confirm her identity, that much was clear to her. Now she wanted to understand the purpose of this visit.

He must have come to establish his position as my ally, 'the good guy', she thought. Lull me into feeling safe.

Her silence provoked him into continuing.

"This is the first time you work with us, and you came in kind of slipping on a banana peel. But I don't know your background," he said, and added, laughing. "You can't be Fatima, for sure, but you might be Mata Hari incarnate, for all I know."

'Us' spoke volumes, and it was all she needed to know.

"Don't be silly. How about yourself?" she countered. "What is your role in this?"

He pretended not to hear her question.

"I must admit that my first thought, when I was summoned, was that this could not be you. Timid, strict, middle-class Klara," he said. "You didn't have balls back then. I knew that you went to Spain. There was an article about you in the local paper, Norrländskan, with pictures and all, saying you were an actress or a model, or something like that."

A non sequitur, she thought. This wasn't leading anywhere.

"Must have been a long time ago."

"Yes, my mother was still living in Boden. She sent it to me. I imagined you married to some prosperous Spanish hacienda-owner with a bunch of kids. I would never have expected you to be into something this risky. You used to be so meek and controlled—holding back—like Daddy's little girl. I don't even remember having seen you drunk. This doesn't become you."

"What does that mean?"

241

"I mean that it doesn't fit my image of you. But maybe I'd better revise my impression?"

He looked at her.

"Your impression of me is incorrect," Klara said. "We were both very young and inexperienced back then. Time doesn't pass in vain."

To divert the conversation, she asked: "How about you? Do you have children?"

"No, no way! No woman has been able to bear being around me for long enough. Just as well, I guess. Having kids makes you vulnerable. They can be exposed to risks. You don't have any kids of your own either. Why not?"

"Not that it's any of your business, but it was a deliberate choice. I did not want Manuel's children to have to compete with a newcomer for our time and attention. I got to be a mother all the same. And I had my work."

How conscious had that choice really been, she wondered? The reminder that she would never experience pregnancy and breastfeeding made her sad. It was too late.

Hasse ignored her snub.

"Well, the way things look, that's probably for the best. I won't bother you anymore now. You're going to have a long, hard day. Fight them a little, don't make it too easy for them."

He left the room. *What was that last bit about? Are they seriously still doubting my identity?*

Her stomach rumbled. She was hungry. Breakfast had always been her most important meal. It had also been the most precious time of the day, when the whole family gathered, with time to discuss whatever they were up to at the moment. She hoped that the kids were still eating a proper breakfast.

CHAPTER FORTY-TWO

A nders cleared his throat. "It's not about Karin."
"I can't believe this. Are you getting a divorce?" Sven asked "Surely you've had affairs before? Though I must admit that Klara sounds hot. I've never seen her, not even a recent picture, but after what I've heard––we have audio surveillance of her apartment, you know––I wouldn't mind jumping in bed with her myself some time."

Anders felt himself go cold at the same time as he was exuding sweat. *What the hell is he saying?* Talking about *his* woman with such blatant disrespect? Had he completely lost his self-control? The comment about listening never quite registered.

"It's not what you think," was all he managed to say.

Sven went silent. It dawned on him that he had put his foot in it.

"All right, all right, rewind please. And sorry, I had no idea it was serious. But wait, let them bring the food."

Anders picked at his fillet of pork with mushroom sauce and Hasselback potatoes while he told Sven the story. Every morsel seemed to grow in his mouth and despite chewing dutifully, it was hard to swallow.

"Then Mossad came, with that note from you, and now she has disappeared..." he finished.

"No, no. No reason to worry." Sven actually patted Anders on the shoulder. "She is here, in Sweden, safe and sound, I promise you. In the safest of safe-keepings... I called them right before I came up to see you. They are still investigating whether she really is Klara Andersson."

"*Safe-keeping*? Are you out of your mind? In this country we don't just take people into some kind of *safe-keeping* like that!" Anders' confusion was turning to anger. "And what's your role in this? You've got nothing to do with the police, the Armed Forces or intelligence agencies."

"No, that is entirely due to you. I have been appointed as a kind of acting liaison, because you and I are old friends. The guys from Mossad contacted SÄPO, and they arranged the meeting. Somebody here met with them, I'm not at liberty to tell you who, but when he heard that she was sleeping with you, he called me in. The guys from Mossad were pretty upset about us protecting a Palestinian agent and they pretended to do us a favor snitching on you. They asked for permission to contact you." Sven paused. "Trust is vital in this kind of case. Wasn't it ingenious—signing with the flower?"

Anders had a feeling he was gaping like a fish, then said peevishly: "You should have contacted me yourself."

"This was the way those Mossad people wanted it; they wanted to see your reactions first hand. To make sure you actually are clean and not acting as her accomplice." Sven paused again to let the words sink in. Then he continued: "Have you ever thought about the kind of gossip, I mean the scope of it, if this got out? That Anders Källström, the Swedish MEP, the old wet blanket, is sleeping with a foreign spy? You'd bloody outshine Profumo! Come on, admit that it is incredible!" He stopped only when he saw how hurt Anders looked.

"I do apologize, but I had a hard time believing it myself. If I hadn't heard your voice on those tapes, I wouldn't have."

He continued in a more factual tone of voice.

"The CIA had cleared her, but our military secret service became suspicious when the plan didn't work out. And right at that moment Mossad turns up. We didn't quite know what to believe. She embezzled information about a Swedish military secret, turned it over to the enemy, and we got nothing in return. We've kept her under surveillance ever since she met with the Saudi guy the first time, and when she failed us, we brought her in for questioning."

Anders stared at his friend while he explained what the plan had been, and how it had not worked out. He felt compelled to tell Sven about the attack in Holland.

"It wasn't Swedish agents, was it?" Anders asked anxiously, no longer knowing what to believe.

"Hell, Anders, you're really playing with fire!" Sven said, with an undertone of envy. "While I'm stuck here pushing papers. No, I would have known. I don't think we good old Swedes would get into violent stuff like that. Particularly not abroad. Who do you think it was?"

"I have no idea, and Klara says that she doesn't know."

"The thing is," said Sven, a little stiffly, "that whether you want to or not, you have to follow up on this."

"What do you mean?"

"We need to know why Mossad has become involved. Why are they interested in her? Why right now? Or is it about our stealth ship? You'll have to cooperate with them. They say Klara's job at the Parliament offers interesting opportunities, but that would only make sense if she is this Fatima. We suspect that it is actually about something else, but, as I said, we don't actually know what. You will be reporting to me, and you'll report *before* you do anything. What you can share with them has to be cleared by me personally. It's probably only about keeping an eye on Klara, and you won't mind doing that, will you? At least that's what they said they wanted."

Anders nodded absentmindedly.

"They told me differently," he said.

"Really?"

"It's about this Palestine agent they executed in the middle of the street in Paris in 1992. They claim he was a Black September operative, involved in the massacre at the Olympics. They had planned to get him in Madrid and believe this Fatima helped him to escape. The Paris assasination was an improvisation and ended up all over the press. It caused trouble for them with both the French and the CIA."

"Fatima was a trained agent by then, she is supposed to be about ten years older than Klara," Sven said. "I agree, it is pretty far-fetched, but not impossible that that is Mossad's motive... They have forever after been determined to exterminate all of those involved in the Olympics massacre. She is being questioned employing very sophisticated methods." Anders couldn't bear imagining what that might mean.

"If she *is* Klara, there is nothing to worry about.

We expect her to lead us to Fahrid, the Sunni organization's super-agent. It is us that he's spying on, and it's our property they came after. She is our only lead, and the only person who can identify him with certainty."

"How is she supposed to do that? If he already got what he wanted, he will be far away by now."

"At any rate, it's our only chance. I myself don't know anything about the details, and the less you know, the better. We have an agreement with the CIA regarding this woman. They promised to release her for good in return for us agreeing to cooperate with them on this mission around the Karlskrona shipyard. It might not have mattered much whether she is Klara or Fatima; the problem is that Fatima is guilty of several criminal offences, apart from the eventual murder of a Swedish citizen, namely the real Klara. And obviously we cannot *cooperate* with such a person.... You understand that,

246

surely? We have even had to find an old boyfriend from her teenage years, in order to make sure of who she really is."

Anders startled. An old boyfriend? Something that could only be jealousy stung him, and he did not quite succeed in hiding his irritation.

"Was that necessary?"

Sven continued as if he hadn't heard.

"As luck would have it, this guy works for Celsius nowadays, so there won't be any leaks."

"Can't you just leave her alone? If she is Klara, she is no real agent. The way I understand it, she has had no professional training or anything like that."

"Think about it, Anders, we are determined to exploit the situation, and if possible score some political points if we can capture this Arab agent. In the best-case scenario that could also boost the marketing of the stealth ship."

Anders didn't really listen. He was sickened by his own words. To openly question Klara's identity, not just secretly in his head, felt like betraying her. Regardless of who she was. The other woman didn't exist, was just a figment of somebody's imagination.

Sven looked at him with an expression akin to pity and spoke in that tone of voice grown-ups use when explaining something to a recalcitrant child.

"You have to realize that this is an exceptional opportunity. We would never have been able to create a character like Klara, or Fatima, ourselves. It takes a long time and requires far too many resources. The CIA has obviously been grooming her for a long time, without even knowing if she would be of use. All they've had in return so far is some chicken-feed information. This is gold, my boy! Surely you understand that? In the name of the sacred Swedish neutrality, in the unlikely event that she would get caught, we can claim that she is a Palestine agent, or a double agent from the CIA, without actually lying. We can attain our objectives at no risk to us, as regards the press and public opinion… But don't worry, she doesn't actually have to be a trained sniper to manage. This is child's play compared to stuff she has done before!" Sven paused. "At least if she really is Fatima."

"This has gone to your head! It's madness! You sound like you're talking about a drone on remote control or something!"

"The condition is that she accepts, of course, and then there's no problem, is there? I have to go now, bit of a rush actually, but you'd better bank on staying for a couple of days. First of all we have to go through your talk with Mossad in detail. Take a room at the Sheraton, it's on us. I'll come by some time after ten tonight and we'll schedule a meeting."

Anders felt sick. His friend had changed, he had lost track of reality. A puppy in company of the CIA and Mossad wolves. Anders' brain felt hot, too swollen to fit his skull. It was like standing up to his neck in a quagmire. He folded his napkin and put it on the table. On his way out he silently prayed to be spared meeting anybody he knew.

CHAPTER FORTY-THREE

Klara was tired. They had spent the entire day in the library. During the morning she had answered thousands of completely nonsensical questions. Most, it seemed to her, were about things that she would have learned had she been Fatima. That was why they were so senseless. What did they expect to reveal by asking about the name of Kerstin's cat, the color of the Klassons' country cottage or even at what age she got her first dog? The general air of boredom and stagnation changed only when Åke Svedenius finally spoke.

"Describe your secret hiding place."

The atmosphere became electrified, and the temperature rose by several degrees. Tension settled like a veil over the room. Fatima would not have been able to answer that, she realized.

In her mind she was back to the white summer nights in Boden. After midnight, when she was sure her parents and most other people were asleep, she would sneak out, take her bicycle and pedal past the house her great-grandmother lived in, by the railway station, towards Svartbjörnsbyn along the road that rounded Lake Bodträsket. Across from the church on the other side, there was a narrow gravel lane with a small concrete bridge.

The bridge was supported by a pillar, and on it were three steps formed by reinforcement rods, serving as a ladder. It led down to a platform, about one and a half feet wide and invisible from above. There she used to sit and think, dangling her feet. There was a current, and her feet made two grooves in the water; like two ships on the ocean, they created a v-shaped pattern of soft waves.

A few years later, as a teenager, she had crossed that bridge with Hasse. They stopped and she had shown him the platform. Something you do when you are in love and want to share everything with your beloved.

Impressive. Hasse was doing a good job. It was a very personal memory, something not even her parents had known about. He was not present in the room, but he somehow confirmed when her answers were correct.

After that they spent the afternoon looking at photographs. They were asking about the names of the people in the pictures and where they were taken. Sometimes she remembered, others not. Probably some of the photos had nothing to do with her. She felt they already had made up their mind about her and relaxed a little. With the other half of her brain, Klara started to plan.

When they broke off for dinner, she was sure she had convinced them that she was indeed the true Klara, despite the number of questions she had not been able to answer. Some because they were nonsense and others because she just didn't remember. Although she wasn't nervous, the strain had left her shoulders and neck sore.

After the meal they sat down in front of the living room fire, and when they had watched the news, the men helped themselves to a second whiskey.

Klara was prepared.

"Hasse, I hope you destroyed the negatives of those pictures I agreed to pose for when we were engaged," she said, laughing a little.

First, he just looked surprised.

"I took so many..." he started. Then he realized what she meant, and a blush crept up from his throat and soon covered his entire face. "Oh, those..."

Laughing and in a slightly provocative manner, she told the men how Hasse had insisted on photographing her in sexy underwear when he was leaving town for his military training.

"I wouldn't want them to be posted on Facebook or something..." *Got them now,* she thought. This was her chance of getting the upper hand.

She had calculated that the drinks would work in her favor. They were relaxed and a little dulled, and she had pointed their thoughts to the sexy underwear Hasse might remember, but the others could only imagine. And she felt the atmosphere change. It was the same phenomenon as when she had grabbed Fahrid by his testicles in the restaurant and squeezed. She sensed that Åke Svedenius was fantasizing the most.

True to his misogynic personality, she thought. She had counted on that.

Now she was going to snub them.

"I have corroboration in writing as to how the operation was planned. Step by step. The plan, my role in it, the lot," she said, and couldn't help sounding a little triumphant.

"Of course we know that," Åke answered, unwilling to confess that she was right. "The question is why you changed the original plan without informing us."

He was like a bloodhound who refuses to stop once he's on the scent.

"There never was a change of plan. When neither Fahrid nor anyone else turned up at Le Nemrod, I thought he had got cold feet. Or that he had spotted something suspicious and aborted. There never was a Plan B, I simply didn't know what to do."

Hasse sat on the other side of the couch drumming his fingers against each other. His sudden reaction made several joints crack.

"Dammit! It's always like this with you people! So bloody clumsy! Not even the chain of command is clear," he grumbled.

He and Åke had a bone to pick, the hostility between them was palpable. She must keep focused. Lennart raised an eyebrow, but said nothing.

"My instructions were to hand over the briefcase or just the cell phone, and that's exactly what I did," she said, trying to sound indifferent.

"Our priorities are not necessarily the same as those of the CIA," Åke stated.

"How on earth was I supposed to know your priorities?"

"There was no reason to inform you. As soon as we knew who he was, we would step in and start surveillance. That was none of your business. Maybe we didn't trust you to cooperate under such conditions." The moment he said it, Åke seemed to realize he had said too much. His facial expression became even more somber. He had painted himself into a corner.

Pleased with her strategy, Klara went on.

"Fahrid is no ordinary terrorist. He may be a religious fanatic, I don't know, but he is not stupid. He is fearless, has a high level of education, is very intelligent and a true chameleon. I seriously doubt you could tail him or keep him under surveillance without him noticing."

"And you are the judge of that having met him for a couple of hours," interrupted Åke.

"It's dangerous to underestimate your enemy, you ought to know that. If he had discovered that he was being tailed, the consequences could have been disastrous. He doesn't mind dying as a martyr, if he gets to take as many infidels as possible with him to the grave," she continued, her tone of voice as indifferent as she could make it. "You people risked a lot of human lives, mine included."

She didn't want them to shut down, she wanted to continue and finish this discussion once and for all. Therefore, she kept her emotions and her voice in check. She had made her point. She was innocent, whether or not Åke was ready to recognize the fact.

"You took too much for granted. It was a mistake not to inform me about your intentions, and you can't blame me for that."

She looked at Lennart. Although no one was willing to admit it, she felt that all of them knew that she was right. Only Åke obstinately continued sulking. He must have been the one in charge of the Swedish operation, she concluded. *That explains why he is taking this so personally.*

"When nobody turned up at the restaurant we checked that you took the briefcase into the metro station," Åke said. "We had guys outside and, on both platforms,, and radio communication with all of them. They saw that you carried it down to the wrong platform, then turned around and went back up. You were out of our line of vision for twenty-two seconds. That was all. He had disappeared before anybody realized what had happened. Keep in mind that you are the only one who has seen him in real life. He must have dumped the briefcase before he reached street level, or we would have nailed him."

It confirmed Klara's impression of Fahrid. He had obviously stuffed the cell phone in a pocket and got rid of the briefcase before reaching the street. *Not taking any chances,* she thought.

"It was a good plan," Lennart finally entered the conversation. "We had people everywhere. If Fahrid had sent somebody else, that person would, in time, have taken us to him.

And when he met with his superiors, we could have made a grand slam. The idea was not to kill him, but to take him in and pump him. He is spying on us, stealing information about Swedish military equipment, and that's our turf. The CIA chose to stay out of it at this stage; the matter is sensitive due to their relations with the Saudis. We know that Fahrid is part of a very well-funded and secret terrorist organization, but so far there's little hard evidence. The real question is whether you just made a mistake going to the wrong platform, or if you lost us on purpose, to protect him."

That hurt. *So, it's not only about the identity,* Klara thought. *There are doubts about my loyalties too.*

"He took the opportunity when I changed platforms. I don't think he would have approached me anywhere where there might be surveillance cameras, like in the metro. He would have rescheduled the meeting. In any case, I did my bit. I delivered the cell phone with the documents and fulfilled my commitment," she said. "Your plan to take advantage of the situation without my knowing and consent, has nothing to do with me or my performance."

"Not so fast, sweetie-pie," said Åke with a sneer.

Klara had to turn away to hide her anger.

"My name is Klara," she said, her tone of voice sharp.

"I suggest we sleep on it. There is still a lot to talk about before you can return to Brussels," Lennart said. He seemed to realize that the conversation was derailing.

Hasse got up first and walked towards the stairs. Klara followed him. Halfway up, he turned.

"They are not all incompetent," he said, half-smiling. "But when they offer you the job I advise you to be cautious about how your assignments are planned. Never agree to anything you can't accomplish alone. Back-up always sucks, and abroad it's practically non-existent."

So that's the way the wind is blowing, Klara thought.

CHAPTER FORTY-FOUR

The snow squeaked underneath their feet. It was cold. The small lake they were walking on had a layer of ice of about four inches, and then a layer of snow packed tight of about the same thickness. The only sign that there were other people somewhere were the jig holes drilled for fishing. They had frozen over again. On the other side of the lake was a conifer forest of skimpy spruces with sparse branches, the way forests mostly are in the far north. The soil remains frozen a few inches down even in summer, and the white nights were not enough to give a proper push to the growth. The vast untouched nature reminded Klara of her Grandmother's place.

There was no wind at all. Klara walked fast. Her breath stayed in the cold air, like a thin cloud around her face. Seen from afar she must be leaving a track of breath clouds.

"What a pity the sun isn't shining," said Lennart, not needing to take long strides to keep up with her. "But it is still lovely, isn't it?"

"I had forgotten about this. It makes me nostalgic," answered Klara quietly.

"Do you like it in Sweden?" Lennart asked. Finally convinced that she was Klara, he had just asked her to cooperate with them, without yet entering into details.

"I really like it here. I must admit that when I decided to leave Spain, I could have moved to some other country with a language I speak, but now I'm glad I came back. There's more gender equality here than anywhere else that I know of. Nowhere does a woman have as much freedom as here. Hardly even in the rest of Europe."

"An interesting thought," Lennart said. "Here the discussions tend to focus on what doesn't work so well."

"I know, and we're still not there. Salaries aren't equal here either, but I can't help getting a little angry sometimes because I feel Swedish women are pretty spoiled. On the other hand, nothing would ever change if we didn't speak up," Klara paused. "I came into Manuel's daughter's life quite early and I always told her that there is nothing in the whole wide world that she couldn't do if she really wanted to. That kind of thinking wasn't very common in Spain at the time. I'm very proud of her. She is only twenty-two now and already flies tourists between the Caribbean islands."

"A big airline?"

"No, a small charter company. Apparently, they only have three or four planes. She's accumulating flight hours in order to apply for a job with a bigger company."

"Have you thought about our suggestion?" Lennart asked, after a moment's silence.

"I'm not thinking about much else," Klara answered, "but it seems like walking into a trap blind-folded. What's the catch? What are you trying to hide? So far, what I've seen of you people has hardly inspired confidence, and I'm definitely no selfless heroine. I have no intention of risking my life. Letting Mossad believe that I'm a terrorist was dangerous. What happened in Holland was a shock. I don't want to spend the rest of my life in constant fear, looking over my shoulder."

"I already told you that it would only be about intelligence for KSI."

"KSI?" She had never heard the acronym before. "I thought you were SÄPO.

"No, we're military. It's short for *Kontoret för Särskild Inhämtning*, something like The Office for Special Intelligence Collection in English. It is a department within MUST, which translates Military Intelligence and Security Service."

"Military. So, that's where you guys are from." It made sense. Mats Larsson, who had drugged her in Brussels, was from FRA, the Swedish Armed Forces Radio Center, and Åke Svedenius had been introduced to her as a Lieutenant Colonel.

"We operate all over the world on specific missions," Lennart explained. "We badly need someone inconspicuous to closely follow the discussions about military cooperation in Brussels, at the EU Commission and Parliament. Your present job provides a perfect lookout post. Louis Hornett tells me your reports are outstanding, that you have a talent for weeding out what's unimportant. We want to know who the real players are, what their motives are, who the lobbyists are and what they are after... well, I think you understand. That's it for the moment, but our needs may shift from time to time," answered Lennart. "And you should know that we can make sure Mossad leaves you alone."

"I want to know exactly how you plan to do that, and I'll make a decision only once I know. If you can eliminate that threat, it's tempting. I tend to be passionate about what I do. Interesting projects can turn me into a workaholic. So, maybe. But there are a few people I would like to talk to before I make up my mind."

"You're thinking of Anders Källström? I have to ask you not to reveal anything specific, at least for the time being... Who is the other one?"

Klara stopped in mid-stride. It surprised her that the relationship with Anders was common knowledge, but then she remembered that they had both bugged her apartment and interviewed her under the influence of sophisticated drugs. Her woolly-headedness was receding and fragments of scenes that must have taken place during that time had started coming back to her.

She started walking again.

"The other one is Louis. He knows enough about it all to not compromise you, and you will need his consent, anyway. He is an old friend whose views I respect. I haven't talked to him after completing the assignment."

"I'm afraid that's our fault."

"What do you mean?"

"That he hasn't got in touch. He contacted us to ask if it was okay to call you, but at the time, that didn't suit us." He added the last sentence a little doubtfully. "Louis is actually in Stockholm right now, for a mutual assessment of the operation. From their side, it is mission accomplished. And that's really what's in your contract, you know. Our part of the deal wasn't spelled out there, so you were right all the time. But we didn't think it necessary to inform you of our part. We were just going to take over where you left it."

Louis's words over the phone had come as a complete shock. He'd said that she had failed. She had thought about what they had agreed, over and over, not getting any the wiser. Now a weight fell off her shoulders. Lennart's confirmation meant so many things, not least that she was entitled to a greater sum of money than she had ever owned. But she was disappointed in Louis for not having been sincere. He could have spared her all that anguish if he had only explained. It also undermined her confidence in him.

"So, what is your agreement with the CIA, then?" she asked.

"Just that Fahrid was going to be ours, when you had identified him and after he had handed over the documents to his superiors. We had hoped to identify the leaders... And to take you over from the CIA."

258

"I beg your pardon?" Klara stopped walking again. "Isn't my consent a requirement here?"

Lennart stopped in front of her.

"Don't get me wrong. Of course it is your decision and yours alone. What I mean is that we are authorized to try to interest you in cooperating with us."

She didn't want to walk about in the snow any more. She needed to be alone.

"Please arrange for me to talk to both Anders and Louis, as soon as possible. I am not going to make any decision before that."

"I might do better than that," Lennart said, very cooperative now. "Louis can be here in about three hours. In the meantime, you can talk to Anders on the phone." And then he repeated: "I guess I don't need to remind you to be discreet?"

The conversation with Anders was a disappointment. He sounded confused, distant, and cold.

"What's wrong?" Klara asked.

"It's all this commotion. Please Klara, try to understand. First we get shot at, and then you disappear. I had to turn to the Government Offices to find out what was going on. Hardly very discrete, surely you realize that much?"

"The Government Offices? Why on earth did you turn to them?"

"I asked Eva-Karin about you and when she said that you had acute appendicitis, I got really scared. I didn't know what to do. Finally, I contacted an old friend at the Government Offices."

Something was very off, but it wasn't the right time and place to delve deeper.

"Do you know where I am?" she asked instead.

"Only that you are here in Sweden and that you're safe."

"Well, that would depend on the point of view, but we can discuss that some other time. When can I see you?"

It had taken months to get Anders used to talking on the phone, to say important things, things that she needed to hear when they were not together, and not just empty phrases. Now he seemed to have completely lost the hang of it. *Or care less?* She felt cold and lonely at the very thought.

"As soon as you're back," he said. "I'm flying to Brussels tomorrow evening, and from what I've been told, you will be back in a day or two."

"Well, you're better informed than I am." In a different tone of voice, attempting to find a way back to the intimacy that used to characterize their conversations she asked: "Do you miss me?" She missed him. Right now, what she wanted most of all was to feel his arms around her and lean her head against his chest.

His voice had also changed when he answered.

"More than ever. Come as soon as you can!"

At least the call ended on a good note.

CHAPTER FORTY-FIVE

Anders looked at his phone, uncertain what to do. He had made no mention of Mossad's visit. That felt like a betrayal. His longing for her had materialized as soon as he heard her voice, but now he reacted:

What the hell am I doing?

He had a long, lonely evening ahead and almost panicked at the prospect of spending it brooding in his hotel room. In an attempt to bond with his family, he called Krister, his oldest son, who lived in Stockholm, to see if they could meet.

He dialed the number. After four rings, when he was about to hang up, his son answered.

"Krister, it's Dad."

"Is something wrong?" Krister asked.

He takes for granted that I'm calling because something is wrong, Anders thought with a sting of guilt. "No, not at all. I've been working here in Stockholm for a couple of days, but we've finished now. I'm going back to Brussels tomorrow and wanted to take the opportunity to see you on my only night off." The lie made his ears burn. "So, I was wondering if I could see you for a while? Unless you have other plans."

"No, I'm just hanging around watching TV. Elin is at her parents' place."

"Well then, why don't you come over to the Sheraton. Let's have a gin-tonic or something in the bar."

"Your treat? I can't afford such luxuries."

"Deal! When can you be here?"

Anders had become more generous towards his sons since he was seeing Klara, perhaps due to a guilty conscience. Swedish kids, once they emancipated, were not used to parents paying when they met somewhere away from home.

"In a hurry?" wondered Krister, sounding uneasy. His father was not in the habit of inviting him for a drink or calling unexpectedly.

"No, not at all, it would just be nice to have time to talk for a while."

"Half an hour?"

"Good! See you then."

He heard that Krister sounded surprised and a little bewildered, but he thought his explanation was believable. At home he never talked much about his work, and saw no reason to discuss why he was in Stockholm.

He was already sitting in the bar when his son came in. Krister was tall and fair. Fit, almost sinewy. He was studying law with little diligence, but he was diligent about mountaineering in all kinds of impossible places around the world. He had been living with his girlfriend Elin for three years. Neither of them seemed to be in a hurry to finish their studies. They tested different academic fields, but nothing attracted them more than going off somewhere and climbing rocks.

Anders shuddered at the thought of the student loans Krister was accumulating, but Karin had forbidden him to raise the issue. They only ended up arguing about it when they met, which wasn't that often.

Now his heart warmed as he saw his son approaching. There was so much of Karin in him. He was completely uncompetitive. That was probably why he climbed mountains instead of some other sport where he would be compared to others.

They gave each other a dutiful and slightly clumsy hug. Anders had never been good at physical contact and had hardly touched his sons since they entered their teens.

"You sounded so strange on the telephone, you almost scared me," said Krister, relieved, studying his father at arm's length for a moment.

"No, well, you know... Not very well planned. We finished too late to fly back to Brussels and too early to go to bed. I just thought it would be nice to see you if you could spare the time. Find out how you're doing..."

They ordered a whiskey each and some nuts.

"Mother says you work too much. You're away almost every weekend."

Again, Anders felt a sting of guilt. So, Karin had commented on this to the boys.

"Mostly it's really stressful."

"Good thing she's so busy herself, the choir is performing in Heidelberg soon."

"Sure, that's right," Anders lied, he hadn't heard a word about that.

Karin and he were used to limiting their calls to check that all was well. He didn't share her interests. She was active in the church choir, went to concerts once a week and was a member of the Inner Wheel, a Rotary spin-off for the wives and daughters of Rotarians. She also frequently met her sisters and her friends. It was almost as if she was trying to make up for lost time since their sons had moved out. He had done odd jobs about the house and played bridge and golf when he had been coming home more often.

An hour later Anders knew a good deal about Krister's and Elin's plans for their studies, and about a three-month-long trip in Spain that they were planning, on bicycles, not mountaineering this time. And that they were doing well together.

Half of Anders' brain was elsewhere. His thoughts swung brusquely between his family, his sons and Karin, and Klara. He was sure that neither Krister nor Lars nor Magnus could imagine for a moment that their parents might divorce. Or that he could have an affair. Thinking of all the times they had ridiculed friends' and acquaintances' divorces, convinced that would never happen to them, made Anders break a sweat.

The very thought of facing Karin and saying the words was impossible. That would shatter thirty years of their lives. It would destroy their lifelong self-deception: that healthy, lasting relationships are based on sense, not passion. He had believed that to be true, until he met Klara.

CHAPTER FORTY-SIX

Klara waited for Louis' arrival in the library. The days were short up here; it was already dark outside. The indirect light from under the bookshelves created an inviting atmosphere. She chose an easy chair and switched on the floor lamp next to it, then looked for something to read. The books were organized according to title, not author, which was unusual and at first confused her. She found a Swedish translation of a book by P. G. Wodehouse that she had read in English. That suited her perfectly, entertaining and not demanding. There were CD's on the bottom shelf, and she found the player, a somewhat old-fashioned stereo hidden in a corner. Gershwin's Rhapsody in Blue suited her, for the same reason as the book.

When the CD ended, she searched for another. The Planets by Holst caught her attention because she could not recall having heard it, but before the music started the sound of a helicopter drilled a hole in the compact silence around the house. Only minutes later, Louis was standing in the doorway. He was wearing a light camel-hair coat with a beautiful paisley-patterned silk scarf in moss green loosely tied. She recognized his ostrich skin briefcase; he had had it for years. They hugged for a long time before he took off his coat. As always, he was well-dressed in a discrete grayish blue wool blazer that combined nicely with the mustard-colored shirt and dark trousers. His once so fit body had somehow shrunk. He was sinewy and almost scrawny underneath the clothes. A painful reminder that he was aging.

"How are you?" she asked, a little uneasy.

"The Big C," he answered.

She froze. "Where?"

"Old man's disease," he said. "The prostate. It's not the most aggressive type of cancer, there are good medicines and they say the progress is slower the older you are. Something about the cells not dividing as quickly as when you're young. A blessing in disguise, one might call it. It can take years."

Klara needed a moment to take in the news. Louis was a CIA operative and probably often at risk, but plainly aware of being ridiculous, she had always stubbornly blocked out the idea that he could die before she left this world. Their bonds were strong. He had been present all her adult life, sometimes far out in the periphery and other times close and present. An almost incestuous relationship: first the lover, then the mentor who pulled strings that impacted her life, time and time again.

But also made it interesting and exciting.

They hugged again. Klara couldn't think of what to say. His obvious vulnerability frightened her.

He moved an easy chair to sit facing her. She liked that; it was important to be able to read his reactions as they spoke: disapproval, affirmation, possibly appreciation—but his dark skin made that difficult in the scarce light of the library. She suggested that they move to the living room. There seemed to be no one else about anywhere on the ground floor.

Only when they sat on the couch in front of the fire did Louis speak again:

"Enough about me. I've come to talk about you."

"Why did you never get back to me? The last thing I heard you say was 'you blew it' and I never got an explanation."

"That's because of our agreement with your present hosts."

"I should have known the whole story." Thinking about it made her angry. "That was really stupid, Louis."

She was angry about her own reaction, too, immediately assuming the blame, believing she had failed, when in fact it was due to someone else's mistake. "It affects my confidence in you," she added. "I never thought you might deceive me or expose me to greater risks than we had agreed to. That was the foundation for our cooperation. I carried out the assignment the way we had agreed." She paused a moment, doubting whether to say it, but finally did: "I feel betrayed, Louis."

"I owe you an apology. The message got in the way."

"The message?" *Was she being obtuse?*

"About my health. It happened so fast, they did some tests a few days before you were going to deliver the documents. It was cancer, and they told me it was vital I have surgery immediately."

Same old Louis. He knew exactly which button to press. It was an acceptable excuse. Again she thought: *what if he had died?*

"How about Mossad, have you informed them about who I really am?"

"No, not yet. That's on hold, for as long as you are here and safe, anyway. The Swedes have ideas regarding that. They would like to exploit your cover further." He raised both hands to prevent her from interrupting. "It's up to you, so calm down. And it can be arranged to your total satisfaction."

"Oh, yeah? Lennart said so, too. How?" she snapped.

"You only need to know if you accept to work with them. If not, we'll follow the original plan."

"I cannot live in fear. The shooting in Holland, was that Mossad?"

267

"Yes, but they only wanted to talk to you. Something like the Swedes, now."

"Says who? The Mossad? I don't believe that, Louis, not for a moment. I was there, they were using live ammunition."

"Klara, I promise you that I'll take care of it."

"And what happens when Fahrid's superiors discover that the blueprints are fake? Do you really expect them to just grin and bear it? Or is that when you expect him to come after me, so you get a second chance to trap him?"

"Not at all. Nobody will accuse Fatima of having provided false documents. What they've got is next to perfect and only the slightest bit incomplete."

"I don't understand."

"Certain necessary materials are only available from a reduced number of sources in the entire world. Our aim is to track the deliveries to where they plan to build the vessel. Then we can destroy it, along with everything else hidden there."

"Sounds like an idea."

Louis nodded thoughtfully.

"I'd like a drink," he said, unexpectedly.

"Is that ok? With your medication?" she asked.

She worried about his health, but realized it was ridiculous to try to influence his lifestyle.

"It's fine," he smiled. "But thanks for your concern."

She went to the cabinet by the wall to see what it contained. There was a well-filled ice bucket, a small bowl with slices of lemon and a number of bottles.

"I don't think they have your brand."

"No, I didn't expect them to. Here." He pulled a bottle of 18-year-old Glenmorangie out of his briefcase. "I was flying private, so I took advantage of not having to pass security," he smiled. "Only one ice cube."

"Think I'd forgotten?" She couldn't help smiling.

268

Klara helped herself to a tonic with ice and lemon, but without gin. The drugs were almost out of her body now, but she was still a little queasy and had a tingling sensation in her fingers. She thought it important not to add any other poison until her system had cleaned out completely.

"So, what's your advice?"

"Accept the offer, of course. You've got a knack for this. The Swedes have not explained their plans for you in detail, but they know your reports are excellent. Operation Absinthe Angel in Prague was a success, and the results were exceptional. I don't think you ought to take on anything of an operational nature. That kind of work is risky and you don't have the training." He paused. "And the Swedes don't have reliable back-up abroad."

Hans Broberg had said that, too, Klara recalled.

"Remember: there is no way to un-recruit an agent," he said, once more.

"What does that actually imply, Louis?"

"It means that even if you quit, there will always be somebody somewhere who believes you are still active. Your best protection is to be linked to an intelligence service."

"I'm marked for life, then?"

The question went unanswered. Surrounded by all that snow, the vast emptiness, it was as if the house was embedded in cotton, isolated from everything. For a long while the only sound was a clock somewhere, ticking away the time, and the crackling of the logs in the fireplace.

"The first and most important condition for me to accept, is to have Mossad stand down," she said. "I cannot live with that kind of menace."

"Are there other conditions?"

"Don't try to distract me. I feel completely compromised. There's no point in discussing this. I want to know exactly how you are planning to deal with Mossad."

"I said: we'll handle it," he got impatient. "What are the other conditions?"

"Not important for the time being."

"So you'll take it on?"

Monitoring political decisions and their impact on people's lives; having the power to secretly influence the course of events… It was like observing life from a balcony. She had done it in Spain—and again in Prague. It was addictive—intoxicating, but not with her life at stake.

"No way. Not unless I get proof that Mossad no longer considers me a terrorist."

"Okay," said Louis. "This is how we will do it: we, the CIA, will tell them that you are a valuable double agent and promise to share some of the intelligence you provide. That will make them leave you alone." He was a master at removing obstacles and getting things done, making quick decisions in difficult situations. That was why she had trusted him with her life. To try to discard Fatima/Klara as a mistake would leave many more doubts. This was for sure the best way to keep her safe. The CIA and Mossad were close in many matters, so if they believed she could be useful, they would leave her alone.

"What is this nonsense about Fatima's assassination?" she asked. There were a number of questions only Louis could answer. "I thought it was just the legend to create my cover?"

Now Louis looked troubled. He took a sip of the whiskey. She waited, but was not about to let him off the hook.

"You remember when you were at the German Hospital in Madrid? That's where it all started."

CHAPTER FORTY-SEVEN

Klara tensed up. She had believed the photographs of Fatima were something fabricated for this operation, a recent reconstruction.

Her head felt empty. *Had he orchestrated events in her life that long ago without her consent?* She felt her skin contract and got goosebumps all over.

"Have you seen the medical records from the hospital?"

He reached down for the briefcase and half-way into the movement he stiffened. Small beads of sweat became visible in his hairline. She saw the pain in his face.

"What is it?"

"Nothing that doesn't pass as quickly as it turns up," he said and took a brown envelope from the briefcase.

"Lennart showed me the records, but I didn't have the energy to read. I got completely hypnotized by the photographs."

"I told you it was watertight."

He put the file on her knee, opened it and pointed to a place in the text.

"You were never pregnant. We were together every day that week. It was simple to find the opportunity to slip the right doses of hormones into your food or drink to produce the symptoms of a pregnancy. It was my job to get you to the hospital. Yes, I know. It was bad," he said and threw his hands up as if apologizing. "But we sometimes do things like that."

"Is that why I have never become pregnant afterwards?" It was something she had thought about, but never discussed with anybody. Abortions were at the time, if not illegal, in any case taboo. And hers had been a secret.

"I can't imagine that the faked abortion would have such consequences," said Louis, looking her in the eyes the way he always did when he wanted to convince her of something.

She let it pass.

"And Fatima? Did you kill her? Who was she?"

"Are you sure you want to know?"

Oh God, he knows me far too well, Klara thought. He knew that when reality became too painful to bear, she would choose to evade it.

"I need to know the whole story. The truth, once and for all, Louis." The fact that he was ill and the knowledge that if she accepted Lennart's proposal to work for the KSI she wouldn't be seeing him much more, made the need to know imperative. He nodded.

"Fatima was the daughter of a Swedish nurse and a Palestinian activist," he said. "Her parents died in an Israeli attack before she was twelve. She spent four years with her paternal grandfather in different refugee camps. At sixteen she was recruited by Al-Fatah, in part because of her father's affiliation, but also due to her fair complexion."

"So that grandfather Fahrid said 'hello' from is alive?"

"I'm afraid so," answered Louis. "Mossad had promised to take care of him, he should never have left the prison. But that is another story."

"This just gets worse."

"Now is your chance to know. This is most probably the last time we meet, Klara," he said, echoing her own thoughts.

She nodded to him to continue.

"Fatima was trained in the former Soviet Union and Libya. She came across as inhuman, devoid of emotions and programmed to kill. Very good both with knives and firearms. Some time before you and I met she turned up in Madrid. The Spanish intelligence services, CESID, gradually closed in on her and forced her into a corner. When she realized that she had nowhere to go, she came to us. We let her believe that we agreed to a change of identity in return for her becoming a double agent. That was about the same time you and I started working together, at TVE. The two of you were close enough in age and build, Fatima was less than an inch shorter, a little stockier, but she kept fit and the difference was hardly noticeable with the heels you used to wear then. Both of you had green eyes. There was enough for a good cosmetic surgeon to work with. When I found out that you don't have siblings, and had been away from family and friends for more than a year, I knew you were the best we could hope for..."

"Stop right there!" Klara put a hand on his arm, her voice sharp. She wasn't going to let him make her feel that she had brought it on to herself.

"Let me finish, Klara," he said, as if he was eager to get it over with. "We only had to make sure you didn't get to see your parents until after the surgery, for the plan to work. The night guard at the German Hospital was a snitch, so the word that it was you who left the hospital in a body bag that night conveniently reached a few interested parties, among them Al-Fatah, and recently, Mossad."

Louis paused, looking down into his drink, swirling the ice cube around.

It was hard to take in that Fatima had existed, had had a life, been somebody's child, somebody's love. And that he, Louis, long ago had hatched such a devilish plan. He had exploited her naivety and romantic ideas about supporting democratic values and fighting fascism. He had forged a trap, with pregnancy as the bait. Later, when she became aware that she was being manipulated, she had been stuck like an insect on fly paper. She had loved the exciting world of television. He had opened the doors for her to New York University, paid the tuition, and made it possible to advance in her career. From time to time he had pulled strings, and she had reacted precisely as he planned, like a marionette.

The insight was frightening. She needed to be in control. To know she herself made the decisions about her life, not being misled or forced.

She had mixed feelings about Fatima. The only thing they had in common was that they had been at the German Hospital in Madrid that same night. A thought struck her:

"One of us had to disappear for the plan to work. Why not me? She was trained and cold blooded. Just what you needed."

Louis eyes searched her face. Looking uncharacteristically uncomfortable, he stretched out his arm and stroked her cheek.

"My assessment was that we would take a greater risk with Fatima. Her basic convictions and background would most likely make her resume the contact with Al-Fatah when she felt it was safe. With you, there was no such risk."

He kept gazing at her.

"And it was my way of tying you to me," he added. "I have always loved you."

He had said it so softly she wouldn't have heard him if she hadn't seen his lips move. In her heart Klara knew that was true. The fire suddenly crackled in the open fireplace and sent sparkles up the chimney. The air around them tightened. Klara was drawn to him. She wanted to trust him and discarded a furtive thought that he exercised the same power over all his assets. The thing spies call honey-traps, only it was mostly women seducing men.

She broke the silence, trying to be realistic:

"If you had really cared for me, you wouldn't have involved me in such a risky business."

"We were looking for a suitable person, an asset, in Spain. And at the time only the results counted."

"But not anymore?"

"I have always been close to you. I've always known where you were and have kept you safe."

Again, they were balancing on the brink of forbidden feelings, the dangerously intimate zone. He stroked her cheek lightly again, with the back of his hand. Time stood still for a moment while they collected themselves.

"After operation Absinth Angel I turned you into a sleeper. It usually takes years to train a sleeper and create a believable past. And far too often they end up not being used," he said. "You already had the legend, and I was almost sure we would never have to call on you."

They had never talked about it in so many words, but they had discussed her situation when Klara was going to marry Manuel. Louis had asked her not to reveal the truth about their relationship. And for the duration of her marriage, they had occasionally had dinner together, he had visited their home, but she had not reported to him anymore.

"I think I understand. But how are you going to handle the situation with Mossad—and Al-Fatah, from now on?"

"The Mossad situation can be solved as follows: I'll inform a man in Mossad's top brass that you're a valuable double agent and to prove that to be true, I will occasionally pass interesting information that seemingly comes from you. As for Al-Fatah, I will continue to do what I have been doing ever since they got word that it was Fatima who left the clinic in Madrid.

"And that is?"

"Exactly the same: feeding them selected intelligence in Fatima's name. Under such circumstances, neither will take action against you. I can guarantee that. You are simply more valuable to both of them alive than dead."

The plan seemed plausible, but her mind was back in the past; she was not quite ready to discuss the future.

"Couldn't you have told me the truth, right from the start?" she asked.

"You were so young. Would you have accepted that Fatima had to die? Would you have trusted me, if you had known I made that choice? It was unnecessary to expose you to that part of the plan, and it might have influenced you in a way that compromised our objectives. Think about it. I am sure you understand that now."

She nodded, surprised at her absence of emotions. Was it possible that she still was under the influence of the drugs she had been given? That those drugs subdued her reactions? That Louis had chosen this moment to tell her the truth for that reason?

"Klara, it was no big deal back then. Routine work. We got rid of a dangerous opponent at the same time as we prepared an opportunity for the future. That's how we saw it. The Palestinians believed Fatima took your place. And I assure you, that part has been every bit as productive as your own efforts in Spain and Czechoslovakia."

The fire had turned to embers and a cool draft pervaded the room. She remembered that ambulance leaving the German Hospital in the middle of the night with a body bag. Fatima's body.

She started to say something, but Louis interrupted her.

"Once you moved to Sweden, the intensity decreased because Klara was supposed to be Swedish and had to lie low."

"So now I am guilty of having destroyed your setup because I moved to Sweden."

"Don't be childish; it doesn't become you," he scolded her. "We were desperately looking for options for how to get to that very secret and well-funded Saudi terrorist organization. It was extremely delicate, due to our relations with the King and the Prince. When we found out that they were eyeing Karlskrona shipyard, and I contacted SÄPO, they introduced me to Lennart Svensson, and we started to explore how we could cooperate. He commented that the Chileans were visiting, and I immediately knew that was it. Hand in glove. Nobody else could have fitted the operation so perfectly."

"Then you two fixed a job for me there, and set me up to impersonate Fatima for real. You should have told me..."

"Lennart insisted on having Pär vet you first. There was no way I could inform you until after that," He sounded exhausted. "You know that's how it's done."

Need to know only. If Pär had discarded her, she would never have known...

She didn't want to discuss the matter any further. She hadn't yet processed all that he had told her. Despite his betrayal and the lies, he had admittedly kept her safe. She didn't even have the energy to hate him right now. Contrary to all logic, he made her feel safe in a way that nobody else ever had.

CHAPTER FORTY-EIGHT

Brussels, two months later

Klara advanced along the clean blue wall-to-wall carpet in the corridor on the seventh floor of Espace Léopold, balancing two cups of *lait russe* and trying not to spill. Halfway to Anders' office the corridor widened, making a space for a concierge's table.

"*Hola, Pepe.*" She smiled at him. "I brought a cup for you as well."

"*Que detalle!*" How kind of you.

She blessed the EU policy of including people from all member states in the administrative staff. A friendly greeting in Pepe's own language had broken the ice weeks ago. She used to stop and make small talk with him. After some time, he had of course understood that she was having an affair with Anders. Pepe claimed it was part of his job description to keep an eye on who came and went on his floor.

"Is he alone?" she asked.

"No, he isn't here. A couple of men came by and they left together."

Anders hadn't mentioned that he was expecting visitors. "Do you know who they were?" she asked, surprised.

"No, I don't think it was planned. At least they weren't on the list, and he didn't say he was expecting anybody. But, last

278

time they came to see him, they stayed for quite some time. I was off my shift before they left."

"Oh, and we have tickets for the opera tonight," she improvised. "I wouldn't want us to miss that."

"But if he didn't tell you, he'll probably be back soon." Pepe winked conspiratorially.

"You're right," Klara said. She did not want to seem suspicious and changed the subject. "Have you heard from home?"

Pepe's face lit up; he pointed with a big gesture to a drawer in his desk and then opened it. On a piece of aluminum foil were some slices of *jamón serrano* and a baguette that he had obviously started breaking pieces from.

"*Si gustas*, help yourself," he said generously. "It's better with a glass of *tinto*, but in the absence of wine, *café con leche* is not bad at all."

"Thank you, Pepe, but I haven't got the heart to deprive you of your precious jamón."

He insisted and Klara had to accept. She broke off a piece of the baguette to go with the ham. It tasted lovely.

"It's delicious! Thanks again," she said, and then: "Can you believe this weather? Rain, rain and more rain. I wonder how long it can possibly go on like that."

"Oh, it rains all the time in winter here," Pepe answered.

"So, you don't know who they were, the men who came to see him?" she asked, nodding towards Anders' office.

"No idea. But as I said, it's not the first time they come. They were talking to each other, but I didn't recognize the language they spoke."

"How many do you recognize?"

"Well, you know, by now I pick up a word here and there of all the EU languages, even if I don't speak them. And I can tell if somebody's speaking Sephardi."

"Why on earth is that?" Klara was genuinely curious.

"I do come from Toledo, you know." There was pride in his voice.

"But surely that's not a language still spoken?"

"Not in Spain, but there are people who speak Sephardi. Or Ladino, as it's also called. In Israel, for instance. It sounds a bit like old-fashioned Spanish. My father was a teacher and took a special interest in the history of our city, so, I suppose it has stuck with me. Have you been to Toledo?"

"Of course I have. Many times. I love it. I heard that the girls there have beautiful legs because it's so hilly. Is that true?"

"I never thought of that." He chuckled.

"Will you return the cups, please?" She spoke lightly, disguising how much his words had disturbed her. "I have to get going, and please ask Anders to call me if he comes back, will you?"

The coffee cups with the EU Parliament's crest were popular souvenirs and at all the cafés there were signs depicting a padlocked cup and saucer. The text was a threat; if people didn't stop stealing them, the crested cups would be replaced by plain white ones. And that would be a pity.

"*Hasta luego*, Pepe."

The fact that Anders had said nothing about the visitors was strange. They had spoken that morning. She usually knew exactly what his days were going to be like. Why had he not called to tell her the change of plans? She had befriended Pepe without hidden intentions, and had never ever expected to have a reason to spy on Anders. But she couldn't let go of this. The fact that Pepe had mentioned Sephardi was creepy. Maybe the men visiting Anders had spoken Hebrew, and Pepe had subconsciously made the connection. She decided to ask at the front desk about the visitors.

Good God, she thought, please let them just be regular lobbyists.

"Hello," she greeted the guard at the reception and showed him her ID.

He looked at it and nodded. "What can I do for you?"

"I'm meeting with Mr. Källström and his visitors, and I would like to know their names."

The guard read the visitors' list, moving his finger along the names stopping at Anders'. He leafed through some papers and looked at some others further back in the file, from earlier that day, but found nothing.

"According to our records he has no visits today," said the man with a shrug.

He looked at her and must have sensed something, because he suggested an alternative: "Do you know if they were seeing somebody else also?"

Of course. That must be it, she thought. The lobbyists often only stated the name of whoever they were meeting first, and once they passed security, had a badge and were inside the Parliament, they would take the opportunity to try to visit as many MEPs as possible. She felt a little better. It could be an entirely ordinary, unplanned, and, for Anders, unexpected visit.

"Actually, I have no idea. Sorry, could you turn those papers my way? I may be able to recognize the names if I see them. Maybe if you let me read that page...."

The list was handwritten in all different styles of writing. It was difficult to discern the foreign-sounding names.

"I don't know if this is legit," the guard doubted.

"Please," she pleaded, looking him in the eyes and smiling prettily.

Looking at the list, Klara turned ice cold. There was a name she knew far down on the second page. It said Tel Aviv University, Abraham Nathanson X 2. It was the man her colleagues from TV Plus had interviewed about Mossad's terrorist database. Here it said that Nathanson and the other person were meeting a MEP from Ireland. She had to check it out.

"Think I've got it," Klara forced a smile. "Thank you so very much! Do you have Mr. McMillan's extension?"

He didn't, but things were quiet this late in the afternoon, and he looked it up for her.

She felt that she had gone pale, and passed by the restroom to take a few deep breaths and refresh the rouge. Then she went to the nearest telephone and dialed McMillan's extension.

"McMillan speaking," said a deep voice.

"Mr. McMillan, my name is Klara Andersson. I'm an interpreter here at the Parliament and wonder if I may trouble you for a minute."

"Well, that depends. If you can do it in about fifteen seconds, it's all right," said McMillan in his Irish brogue.

"Absolutely. I'm looking for Mr. Nathanson."

"Who's that?"

"A lobbyist, I think."

"I don't know anybody by that name," said McMillan, sounding annoyed.

"He's from the university in Tel Aviv, if that brings him to mind…"

"I've never had anything to do with them."

"Sorry, I must have got it wrong. I thought that he had come to see you."

"No, he has definitely not."

"Thank you very much, and I'm so sorry to have troubled you," said Klara.

"No problem. Sorry I couldn't be of help," answered Mc-Millan, his voice friendlier now.

She hung up. Was McMillan lying? Or was Mossad concealing who they were really meeting?

CHAPTER FORTY-NINE

Fahrid was standing at the corner of Rue Belliard and van Maerlandt when he saw them come. From where he was, he had a good view of both entrances. Before he contacted Klara again, he wanted to know everything about her. Who she socialized with, and as far as possible, the extent of her networks.

This did not look good. Her lover was leaving the building accompanied by two men from Mossad's top brass. Though one of them was officially retired from active service, this could hardly be a coincidence. Fahrid had great respect for Mossad's work and the fact that the three men were meeting openly seemed careless, not common procedure. He withdrew into the shadow of a gate pretending to read nameplates by the door while they walked past him. A completely unnecessary precaution, as none of them had ever seen him before. They stopped and flagged a taxi.

This was something he needed to follow up. A possible connection between Klara and Mossad must be thoroughly investigated. Not in order to protect her, if her lover betrayed her, that was her problem. If she was as good as he thought, she ought to be aware of what was going on.

The sneer on his lips stiffened; this *was* disturbing.

A few days later, Fahrid was outside a single-story bungalow in one of the better suburbs. The house was dark and Fahrid walked around the block to get his bearings. When he was sure that the garden behind the house was shielded from sight from the nearby houses, he crept in and looked for the alarm system and surveillance cameras. As expected, on each window pane a small square box was attached. If a glass was broken or even touched, someone would immediately detect it on a control panel far away from here, at the embassy.

He pulled out a square piece of dark glass from his pocket. Crouching at the corner of the house he scanned the garden through the glass, but could see no signs of any laser-based alarm there. Relieved, he got up, but then, through the side pane of the large bay window overlooking the back yard, he saw a weak red pulsating light inside the room. A motion detector. He quickly bent down again.

Better wait until the owner of the house had deactivated it.

Fahrid heard a car on the driveway. A door slammed shut and there were footsteps on the gravel. Someone walked up the doorsteps whistling a happy tune. Benjamin Gold, Israel's cultural attaché to Brussels, was obviously in a good mood. Fahrid knew that he was returning from a dinner party at the French embassy. Gold had been appointed when Mossad's former agent was exposed helping the Belgian police to locate the perpetrators of the mass killings at Bataclan in Paris.

Fahrid knew that it was a safety measure to keep Gold in the dark about the contents of his diplomatic bag when he traveled to and from Tel Aviv. He would probably also not know about the significance of the messages he received and forwarded on behalf of Mossad, but Fahrid was confident the man would know enough to tell him whether Klara was involved or unaware of her boyfriend's dealings.

He heard the door open and close; shortly after, the faint pulsating red light inside disappeared. The room lit up as

Gold opened the door to the fridge by the far wall. It must be one of those space solutions where the kitchen was open to the living room. Benjamin Gold took out a bottle and, without turning on the lights in the living room, he walked up to the patio window. His bow tie hung untied around his neck, and he had opened the uppermost button of his dress shirt. Drinking right out of the bottle, he seemed to be contemplating the garden.

Fahrid had always marveled at the slightly indecent habit Westerners had of exposing themselves and their homes through those large windows. It often made his life easier. Maybe Gold felt the same way, and that was why he refrained from switching on the lights. He seemed to be looking at a large fruit tree in the middle of the small garden. It still had no foliage, but the way things grew here, seemingly effortlessly, probably amazed Benjamin as much as it did Fahrid. He knew Gold had grown up on a kibbutz.

Soundlessly, with his back flat against the wall, Fahrid moved closer to the patio door, pulling on thick protective gloves. As soon as Gold turned his back, he would smash the glass and get in.

But that turned out not to be necessary. Gold swung open the door and Fahrid heard him taking deep breaths of the muddy, moist aroma from the garden's moldering greenery. He grabbed the door handle on the outside. When Gold stretched out his hand to close the door Fahrid tore it out of his hand. Fear had not had time to settle on his face when the nozzle of Fahrid's handgun with its silencer was shoved at his chest.

Gold stepped back, almost falling into the house, and Fahrid closed the door behind them.

"We're going to have a talk," he said.

"I know nothing that could interest you," answered Gold.

"Let me be the judge of that," snapped Fahrid.

He took a chair by the wall and placed it in the middle of the sparsely furnished living room. With the pistol he waved at Gold to sit. He tied his hands together with silver tape behind the back of the chair. Tight. Once he was sure that the hands were firmly tied, he stuffed his gun into his belt at the small of his back.

A little later Fahrid once more had that vague feeling of disappointment. It had been too easy. No resistance at all. No balls. The man had been frightened out of his mind when he saw the knife. The silver tape over his mouth had muffled his screams until he fainted with fear. But before that, he had been singing like a bird. Fahrid had found out that Mossad knew Klara was an Al-Fatah agent and that her boyfriend was cooperating, spying on her. They wanted to know what she was up to here in Brussels.

Before he left, Fahrid emptied the safe in Gold's bedroom and now carried the contents in two plastic bags.

He stood completely still on the stairs outside the house for a moment, greedily breathing the cold, moist night air. After a few breaths, the smell of blood, faeces, and urine had dissipated to the point that it hardly bothered him anymore. He then walked away quickly, soon swallowed by the dark on the narrow streets of the quiet suburb.

CHAPTER FIFTY

"If you don't get a divorce, we should stop seeing each other," Klara said.

They were sitting on the couch in her living room, each of them with a glass of white wine. Anders rested his on the coffee table, put his hands on her shoulders and turned her towards him.

"Look at me." His voice was trembling a little. "I love you. More than I ever thought I was able to love anybody. You make me feel things I didn't know existed. I don't want to lose you, but I can't break up my marriage."

"Why not?" Klara had already asked that question several times during the course of the evening and got the same answer every time. It was an answer she did not understand. She felt cheated, even though in all truth, he had never said he would divorce his wife. She had just taken for granted he would. A divorce was no big deal anymore; his career wouldn't suffer.

"I have wanted to tell Karin so many times. I've been hoping that she would notice—question me. Confront me. She has found viable excuses to it all, my absences, my lack of commitment and interest in things at home. Her entire world would collapse if I didn't come home any more. That disarms me and makes me incapable of pronouncing the words."

"What about my world? Why is hers more important to you than mine?"

"Klara, you are used to facing the world alone, to doing what you please; you have so many resources. Karin is nothing like that; she has lived for the family ever since we married. I simply can't imagine her on her own."

"Is there anything I haven't yet said or done that would change things?" she asked.

"I don't think so. Please, be patient a little longer."

"I don't know, Anders." Klara got up from the couch. It was late and they were both exhausted, more emotionally than physically.

"Go home or sleep here tonight." He didn't move, so she went to the bedroom and brought back a duvet and a pillow.

After having tossed and turned alone in bed for hours, she gave up. She felt split in two and hated herself for it. She didn't want to lose him. The fact that she didn't really want to get married again had made her accept the situation and not realize that his loyalties were elsewhere.*Maybe things will still work out. Maybe Karin will meet somebody... No happiness is complete,* she debated with herself. *Nobody gets it all. Together we have almost everything.*

It was with a heavy heart she went into the living room.

"You can come sleep in the bed if you promise we'll just sleep."

She lay down on her side, with her back to him and he snuggled up close. Carefully, he lifted her head and inserted his arm, the other around her waist. They soon fell asleep.

After a couple of hours, she woke up because he was stroking her and kissing her neck. She didn't move. Said nothing. His caresses became bolder and she noticed with mixed feelings that he was hard.

Is this all he wants? Exciting sex with a willing woman?

"No, Anders. I don't want to make love. I'm much too sad," she said.

He stopped, but started again after a little while.

"Don't," she repeated.

It was as if he hadn't heard her. Anders had changed. Their relationship had changed. What could possibly hold him back in a marriage that had dried out long before the two of them met? His explanations were incomprehensible. She felt this was a farewell and did not actively resist his embrace. Only when he realized how dry and passive she was, did he react.

"I'm sorry," he said. "Will you please forget that this ever happened? I'm a selfish idiot."

She wasn't angry, just deeply sad, and said nothing.

"I wanted to be close to you again," he said. "I thought it would help mend things. I'm so sorry."

Thoughts were churning in Klara's head. Lately he had hinted that she had got him involved in something he did not want to be a part of. That it was unfortunate that their relationship now was common knowledge in circles he would have preferred not to know. She put one hand under his cheek and pushed her fingers into his thick, coarse hair. She wanted to hold him still and look deep into his soul when she asked the question.

"Who came to see you last Tuesday?"

He looked away, couldn't meet her eyes.

"I can't talk about it," he said after a few seconds, looking back at her now, as if trying to convince her about his candor.

She wouldn't let go of his gaze.

"It's got to do with Sven Åmansson," he continued. "My old friend at the Government Offices."

"The guy you went to see when I was kidnapped?"

Anders stretched out his hand and found his glasses. His habit was to leave them on top of the headboard. He needed them to see her, even this close. Klara didn't let go of his face while he put them on.

"I have trouble believing that it is a coincidence," she said.

"What are you talking about?"

"That you receive visitors from Israel at the request of the person who informed you about where I was."

"What makes you think they were from Israel?"

"I'm not going to tell you, as long as I don't know why you're meeting them."

"Then we won't get any further. I'm not allowed to talk about it."

She looked at him for a long time. He met her gaze. It was hard to believe that the man she loved would be disloyal or betray her.

But it was not impossible...

CHAPTER FIFTY-ONE

The murder of Benjamin Gold was on the front page of all the newspapers, big headlines. Nothing that terrible had happened in Brussels since the pedophilia scandal. The cultural attaché of Israel had been killed in an exceptionally brutal way. Was it a sex murder? When his boyfriend found him early the next morning, he had been dead for less than an hour. Still dressed in a tuxedo, with the bow tie hanging loose around his neck, the trousers cut at the fly, he was sitting on a chair with his hands tied behind his back, and his genitals stuffed into his mouth. So far, no suspicions regarding the perpetrator had been published.

The safe in the apartment had been opened and emptied of its contents. Klara was convinced that the murder victim was tied to the intelligence services. The insignificant embassy job was a typical cover. The MO indicated that he had snitched. And the simple fact that he was an Israeli raised the odds that the perpetrator would be an Arab.

She contacted Lennart to find out if she was right in her assumptions and if there was anything she should follow up on. After a whole lot of being passed from one person to the other, she got him on the line.

"Hello Lennart. What do you know about this business with the Israeli?"

"Not much, actually. Maybe others who know more will share. Can you check with Louis?"

"Yes, I'll do that, if it's okay with you."

"Of course, but I appreciate your asking. It is us you are working for now, don't forget that."

"I never forget that."

"Your reports are excellent. You're doing a great job."

She wasn't used to receiving praise for her reports. Louis had never hinted that they were good or bad, not until they talked about it up north in Sweden. This was yet another skill with a very limited range of uses. Reporting to intelligence organizations... Not something she could do for a living except for her present employer. Or include in her CV. But now, earning a living was no longer that important. The money from the CIA for the Karlskrona job would last a long time. And the Swedish Armed Forces were paying her enough to not need to touch any of it for the time being.

Her work as an interpreter was icing on the cake, providing her with a cover and an excellent vantage point. Her main task was to observe who displayed a special interest in decisions regarding military cooperation and the defense industry in the EU. But she was ambitious and wrote about whatever else she thought could be relevant and interesting, and that was obviously being appreciated.

"Good," said Klara. "Bye, then..."

"Wait," said Lennart. "There is something you should know... We've just confirmed what it is that Mossad is investigating about you..."

She startled.

"What?"

"They have a hard time letting go of the idea that Fatima assisted Atef Bseiso in escaping from Madrid to Paris, when he was on his way to see the family in Tripoli."

"I suspected that was it. But was Bseiso involved in the events at the Olympics in Munich?" she asked.

"I don't think they have any evidence to that effect."

"Please keep them away from me, Lennart. That is a condition."

"You don't have to worry. You are untouchable. Louis has made sure of that."

CHAPTER FIFTY-TWO

Fahrid was enjoying the drive and stayed on the highway for as long as possible. As he approached Amsterdam, he kept an eye out for the right exit. He was headed for the city center, Hotel de l'Europe on Nieuwe Doelenstraat, one of the oldest and most elegant hotels in Amsterdam. He had never stayed there before and had to concentrate to find the way. Pretending to be an assistant, he had called in advance and made a reservation, hissing orders about discretion he had hinted that the guest was traveling incognito, and that he would come alone, without his usual security detail. That usually worked to make the hotel staff try a little harder to be of service..

The passport from the United Arab Emirates was the most travel-friendly passport of the Arab World, visa waived in 165 countries. It had both Zayed and Mansour as part of the names, hinting at family ties to the president of the Emirates for anyone who knew. The job stated on his calling cards made him advisor to a little-known association of powerful oil companies. If someone bothered to check, they would find a web page for the organization, and among its employees, a blurry picture of a man that could be Fahrid. He had grown a beard from the day he left Brussels: by now it was thick and well-tended.

A young man in uniform took care of the car keys as he entered. "Just call, and the car will be ready for you right here whenever you need it."

When he put his passport on the counter at the front desk, the receptionist immediately asked:

"May I suggest a suite? It provides a lot more comfort than the rooms..."

"Yes, why not? I don't know what my secretary booked." He hadn't thought of booking a suite, but realized that would be convenient. There he could receive visitors and wouldn't need to rent one of the smaller meeting rooms for the purpose.

"Ah, and a package arrived for you this morning," the receptionist told him. "The bell boy will bring it to your suite together with your luggage."

"Good. Thank you. My suitcases are in the trunk."

Fahrid was surprised, he hadn't expected the traditional clothing to arrive ahead of him, but the back-up organization was in place and well oiled. This time he could count on support, if he needed it. He had asked for a couple of white kanduras and ghutras to be delivered, because he was aware of the intimidating effect the white garb and head cloth had on most Europeans. In this case, dressing up traditionally could contribute to the success of his mission.

The suite was beautifully furnished. It had a coffee table with a couch and an armchair in blue. Behind wide sliding doors, the bedroom picked up the same shade of blue in bedspread and curtains. The walls in the bathroom were covered in pink marble and the bathtub was a kind of jacuzzi. In one corner there was also a fantastic glass booth with a shower. Fahrid couldn't resist the temptation to take a bath. This was a long-term project. He was planning to stay a week or two, and eventually come back again in a month, if necessary.

Researchers and experts in the home country were gathering data on NGOs that would suit this mission, but it might take a few days. And before he accessed the high security virtual private network to retrieve that information, he needed to establish an unthreatening identity as a citizen of the UAE, tied to the petrol business. A pattern of internet access on the hotel network browsing the typical news sites, looking at some NGOs on his own, and the normal communications with "his" company were necessary to avoid triggering the interest of anyone keeping an eye on him. He knew that any Arab, even a rich one, would be scrutinized before being discarded as inoffensive. Only when that was accomplished would he connect to the secure secret Virtual Private Network.

He was in no hurry and enjoyed playing this part. This time the legend drew on his own; that always worked best. Studies in the U.S., combined, for the occasion, with a documented interest in environmental issues. The hackers in his organization had prepared this. Searching hard enough for the name in his passport you would find fake articles that showed his deep concern regarding what the oil that made his country rich and powerful had done to the planet. And he would pretend he was trying to do something about it... In order to add to the credibility, he was considering hinting at a certain understanding for the views and goals of the jihadists, though not for their means and methods, when he met with the people that would work with him.

In a way he owed Klara. She had shone the torch. It was while he monitored her lover's doings that he came across this opportunity. At first he had intended to simply hand over the material from the Israeli diplomat's safe, but when the man explained what it was intended for, he had changed his mind. He had spent time preparing a plan, the when and the where... and exploring the means necessary to carry it out. His superiors had not needed much time to consider his proposition. He had got the green light then and there, in St. Petersburg. Not only the order to go ahead, but also a six-digit sum to spend for the purpose. Untraceably transferred through a network of banks to an account in his new name.

Money can buy everything, they were well aware of that. Sure, it hurt to see such a large sum disappear into other people's pockets, but it was worth it.

He had lunch by the water, in the hotel restaurant. Really pleasant, the food was not halal, but he was on a mission, after all. Wanting to make the best of the "downtime", he spent the afternoon at a particularly famous diamond retailer's. He found the expensive stones fascinating, and hoped to add a few to the small but precious collection he kept in a bank deposit in Paris. *Just in case...*

After a couple of lazy days including numerous visits to different diamond dealers—and on the way back from a boat cruise on the canals, he entered an internet café. There was an email in the draft folder of his fake email account, which meant it had never been sent over the internet and was untraceable. His colleagues in the home country had gathered substantial information. He didn't take the time to read any of it, just copied it all to a thumb drive and then erased the mail.

Once back in his room, he disconnected the computer from the hotel's courtesy internet connection and opened the files on the USB memory. The research staff had been fast and thorough. There was a list of Amsterdam based NGOs members of SFP, the umbrella organization Smoke Free Partnership. Fahrid studied them all carefully.

He learned that a little over a year ago, a number of organizations had coordinated an effort requesting a rise in tax on tobacco. The aim was, apart from encouraging people to quit smoking, that the extra tax money would go to finance the NGOs' activities. The government had in fact increased the tax, but the money never filtered down. This suited him perfectly.

Anxious to shortlist a few candidates, Fahrid read up on their background. Dawn was breaking when he finished. He entered the VPN and sent a short, encrypted email, requesting live feed, audio, and video from three of the NGOs' headquarters.

CHAPTER FIFTY-THREE

Two days later Fahrid got word that the NGO headquarters were bugged. He could watch and hear all three of them live at any time. To test the set-up, they had agreed that someone should call, announcing that they were short-listed for a possible financial contribution from an organization in the Emirates, and that Shahib Mansour would get in touch with them in a day or two. Now he had received the video feed recorded when those calls took place and was eager to see them. The first was from the office of YSFW, Youth for a Smoke-Free World. Fahrid pulled up the background material on the organization to refresh his memory before starting the video.

Hans Meier and Eva Spengler were the founders and the only full-time employees. During the six previous years YSFW had received public funds, but last year they had missed the goal-qualifications. The NGO was in dire straits and just about to have to file for bankruptcy. The only income was a small grant from the municipality providing them with less than the minimum wage. They lived in the same squat, but were not a couple.

The video started rolling and Fahrid saw an intense man in his early 30s and a woman of about the same age, sitting at a very worn desk strewn with papers. He deduced that they must be Hans and Eva. His first impression was that the NGO had outgrown its name. Youth for a Smoke Free World didn't seem appropriate any more. Neither of them would qualify as "youth" any longer.

Before listening—he knew enough Dutch to follow a simple conversation—he paused the video to study the premises. The lack of funding was obvious. Everything within sight was recycled. The one-room office had two windows situated just under the roof, and from the background check he knew it was in a storehouse close to Amsterdam's Schiphol airport.

Fahrid had been informed that as not many smoke any more, these people had been forced to find some other cause to support in order to apply for funding. The idea that land should only be used for cultivating food crops had been adopted as their new focus area, but they had not yet started to produce propaganda to that effect. The walls remained covered with buttons, stickers and posters from former campaigns, demonstrations, and actions. The words "anti-tobacco", "non-smoking", and "quit smoking NOW" were written in all kinds of typeface everywhere.

He pressed play again.

The old table surface showed more rings from glasses and cups than un-marred surface. Their cups held a steaming drink. Green tea, he guessed.

"Take it from the beginning," said Eva said as she put the cup down and rubbed her hands together. "I want to know exactly what he said."

"Yes, well, at about twenty to ten when the phone rang I picked up."

"I know that, go on..." she urged him.

"First he asked if he had reached the Amsterdam branch of YSFW..."

"Did he actually use the acronym?"

"Yes, and that was a little strange because I answered the phone with that name. Why do you ask?"

"I think it indicates something, but go on," Eva said.

Fahrid could see that she was excited, and made a mental note of her comment.

"Then he introduced himself. Mustafa something, I couldn't pronounce it even if I tried," Hans continued. "I didn't focus on the name, because I thought it was just somebody applying for a job or a traineeship or something. I asked what he wanted, and then he said that he was calling to let us know that his boss, Shahib Mansour, from the Emirates is looking into non-profit organizations with a view to discuss a possible sponsorship, and that he would soon call us himself."

"Incredible! Do you think somebody is having us on? Are you sure he was legit?"

"I have no idea. But we'll find out if he calls. At any rate, he added that this Shahib, on certain conditions, would consider donating a lump sum to sponsor an eco-friendly purpose."

"Did you ask him how he had heard of us?"

"No, I never asked that."

"What do you think he meant? What kind of conditions? What language did he speak?"

"English. With an accent. But he didn't go into detail, he only asked who had the authority to discuss the matter with him. So I told him that that would be you and I, together."

Hans paused, then added:

"That's when this guy said something about his boss not being used to discussing business with women..."

"Pig! If he doesn't even want to speak with us just because I'm a woman, we can't accept money from him. Surely you understand that?"

Fahrid could see Hans react to Eva's words.

"Eva, we have discussed this every single day since we lost public funding. It is only a matter of time until we will have to fold. There is no money in the bank and it's been two months since we last paid the rent. If we can't fix the copy machine or *get a new one, we can't even make flyers. And in that case, we will have to give up. I think we need to hear him out, see what it's about."*

Eva shrugged. *"We can only hope that he calls back, then,"* she said. *"A financial contribution would mean the world, I know that. Things would happen, we'd get an opportunity to prove that the time we've spent struggling has not been in vain."*

"It would be an 'up-yours' to market liberalism, turbo capitalism, and environmental crime, too..." Hans added.

Fahrid detected a certain bitterness in their voices. He could tell that their idealism was frayed. The possibility of a major economic contribution had re-ignited the spark, the hope that they could still become the heroes they had dreamed of being.

Fahrid would let them sweat for another couple of days.

He saw the other two videos, but as those organizations were in better shape financially, he judged them to be less inclined to follow his lead. More questioning and demanding. YSFW was his choice for now.

He would call them himself, and ask Hans and Eva to prepare a couple of draft projects in line with his own ideas, then schedule a personal meeting a few days later. If it didn't work out the way he expected, he would continue to search for the right organization.

Three days later a stern and serious Shahib, dressed in a simple floor-length white tunic, dark trousers and a keffiyeh opened the door to his suite for Hans and Eva. He didn't smile, just said: "Welcome. Come in."

He nodded to a couple of chairs with armrests in front of a beautiful table, in the same Louis XIV style, with a slim laptop and a smartphone. He sat down behind the table. Not a single scrap of paper disturbed the neat impression.

"Well, my friends," Fahrid said. "I know that you are a serious organization and have been in business for over five years. You must understand that I can't decide until I know that the money will be used in a way that I feel is right. I am willing to be convinced, so please explain why your project, and no other, is what we should invest in."

"We have prepared two different proposals, just as you asked us," said Hans and waited for Fahrid's go-ahead.

Hans presented his project and Fahrid asked intelligent questions from time to time, while behind his mask of composure he was growing more and more impatient. What a lot of nonsense, he thought. The idea was to buy a truck in order to collect old furniture and other bulky recycle items from the city and surroundings, then rent a storage space where the salvage was to be sold again. In that way, Hans explained, the organization was going to generate an income and survive at the same time as they contributed to caring for the environment by recycling useful stuff that otherwise would end up in the landfill.

Fahrid thanked Hans for his presentation, and saw him make a gesture to Eva, to start with hers.

"Why don't you explain it?" Fahrid asked Hans, well aware that this would make Eva bristle up. Amused to tease her, he ignored her hard stare.

"She prepared it," protested Hans meekly.

"Never mind, you are working together, aren't you?" Fahrid insisted.

Eva shoved the binder in Hans' lap and leaned back, sulking.

This project was about launching a campaign demanding a new rise in the tax on tobacco, and that this time some of the revenue would be earmarked to support NGOs like theirs.

Now we are on track, Fahrid thought. This project could be steered towards the desired end.

"The campaign should be carried out in connection with a political meeting with a lot of media attention, like a summit of some kind," Fahrid suggested. He was going to make sure they were ready for the one he was targeting. "This way you will kill two birds with one stone, that is, reaching politicians as well as the media," he said, smiling for the first time.

Hans and Eva loved the idea of media attention.

"But it won't work just to march," Hans said. "The Amsterdam police would never allow us to march when there are major international meetings. We will have to find some other way."

Fahrid paused, thinking. "I will make sure you will have access to part of the money already in the next few days, so that you can prepare for this." Then he turned serious. "I expect to see you again before the week is over with a more elaborate plan. I would be pleased if we can decide the date fairly soon, because I would like to be here then and see for myself how it works."

After they left, he ordered a meal from room service. Then he switched on the live feed from their office. He wanted to hear them talk, if they returned there. A good three quarters of an hour later he heard them entering, and went back to his computer to observe them.

"I never thought he'd go for my suggestion," Eva said. "I mean him, a towelhead who refused to even talk to a woman in the first place. We have to get in touch with all the volunteers as soon as we get the money. We won't be able to do this between the two of us."

"Right, and we need to buy a new printer."

"Incidentally, he's gay."

"I don't know. But so what?"

"No well, I mean... He was so cool and collected and businesslike... I have never ever met a heterosexual man who hasn't looked at my cleavage!"

Fahrid remembered that Eva's blouse had been sliding off one of her shoulders all the time.

"So that makes him gay, does it?" laughed Hans. "I got all excited when he hinted that this was maybe not a one-time thing, if it works out to his satisfaction."

Eva was no "looker", Fahrid thought. It was true that she had a large bust, and he could tell that she was used to capturing men's attention that way. *What a slut.* He smiled. His indifference had annoyed her.

"And what made you think he hinted that?" she asked. "I didn't hear anything like that."

"It's a long stretch, and I may be wrong, but when he said that he wanted to see for himself how it worked out, I got that impression."

Fahrid let out a long sigh and turned off the video feed. Hans' wishful thinking was an unintended bonus. It would make them try harder.

CHAPTER FIFTY-FOUR

In the middle of a work shift, the concierge stuck his head into the booth and left a note for Klara. Eva-Karin summoned her to the office, urgently. Klara checked the speakers on the list. No Spanish. She showed the note to her colleague, got a thumbs up in response, and left.

She cast a glance through the window at the unusual sculpture on the ceiling of the Bridge of Sighs, a naked woman who looks like she is running towards the spectator, with outstretched arms, surrounded by ribbons adorned with shiny stars blowing in the wind. It's made of dark, matte metal. Only the stars are bright and shining. It is a beautiful work of art. From the street you can hardly see it, just the woman's profile.

It was the only statue Klara knew of depicting a naked elderly woman. At first glance, you don't really see it, but if you look closely there is no doubt. The woman's curves are less firm and her breasts less full, but she is still very beautiful. Klara had always loved that sculpture and wished that she herself would look like that when the time came.

She forced herself not to walk too fast through the long corridors towards the Interpreting Services offices. A little nervous, she knocked on the doorframe, as the door was open.

"Come in," Eva-Karin said, sounding a little rushed.

She was an attractive woman in her forties who knew how to use her tendency to freckles and her strawberry blonde hair to her advantage. She looked a little exotic, her curvy figure enhanced by a black tailor-made dress with a perfect neckline showing off her charming freckles. Over the dress, she wore a jacket with a black and burgundy pattern and a shawl collar. She looked very smart.

Klara had for some time hoped that they could get to know each other and become friends, but that had not happened. Eva-Karin's agenda was probably constantly full, and maybe not only with things she herself had chosen.

"Hello," Klara said, trying not to show that she was nervous. "You asked me to come?"

Eva-Karin was not particularly diplomatic when it came to holding her interpreters responsible for their errors.

"Good of you to come so fast," she said with a thin smile. "But I do hope you didn't leave your colleagues in the lurch?"

Typical, thought Klara. *She would find a reason to reproach me no matter what I do.*

"There were no Spanish speakers on the list when I left. The German and the English interpreters also have good Spanish, so if necessary, my colleague can take an eventual intervention from them, on relay."

Eva-Karin studied her for a while without saying anything. Klara managed to sit still and look her in the eyes. She prayed she looked more self-confident than she felt.

"NATO is short of interpreters for a meeting and they've asked for help. Two of our regulars are on maternity leave, and now Serge has got a bad back and is on indefinite sick leave, so I was thinking of you. How do you feel about that?"

"What?" Klara exclaimed.

It was very unusual for freelancers to interpret at NATO meetings. Klara's immediate reaction was that there were others that were better qualified for the job.

"How about Harald and Pär?" she asked loyally, her tone of voice neutral.

Both of them had the same language combination as Klara, and a lot more experience.

"Neither of them can make it. The Swedish International Development Cooperation Agency has something large-scale going on in Stockholm the same days, with a lot of Latin-American participants and both of them are already booked for that. Moreover, they've been here longer than you, and work more, so I thought I'd give you the chance."

The free market paid better than the institutions, including NATO. Part of the truth was probably that Eva-Karin wouldn't lend the two other interpreters to anybody and later risk having to compete for them.

Klara had mixed feelings about the offer. The thought of interpreting at a NATO summit was exciting, but it was not all good news.

"How about material? I know nothing about military stuff, or weapons or defense and such matters, not even in Swedish...."

"Count on it being as usual. You google articles, find terms and make your own glossary. I hardly think you'll get any documents in advance. I don't even know what the summit is about. But it's not just the NATO members. Non-member states will also be participating, hence the need for Swedish."

"May I think about it?" NATO would obviously do a security check on her. She had no idea what a check like that would come up with.

"Take a coffee, have a quick think and come back with your answer in a quarter of an hour," said Eva-Karin and turned back to the computer.

"I'll do that."

The time to think about it was just a formality.

I need to get hold of Lennart and ask if it's all right, she thought.

She hurried back to the Bridge of Sighs. There she would be able to spot anyone approaching while she talked to Lennart. On the way she pressed the digits for his direct line.

"Speak to me Klara," he answered, almost at once. He could see who was calling.

"Hi, Klara here. Listen, I've been offered an assignment at a NATO summit. Can I accept?"

"I'll be darned. Of course you can."

"They'll surely do a background check. I don't know what might surface about me and I don't want to be embarrassed if they come back with a 'no thank you.'"

"You will turn up as innocent as the Virgin Mary herself. We're no morons. Officially there's nothing on you, you ought to know that."

There was total silence apart from the clicking of keys on the keyboard in Eva-Karin's office. This time Klara walked in without knocking.

"I'll be happy to do it. Thank you very much!"

"Thought so," smiled Eva-Karin.

There was a flash of warmth, perhaps appreciation, in Eva-Karin's gaze when their eyes met.

Klara was proud, but quite nervous when she returned to her shift. The nightmare of an interpreting error with major political consequences was going to make her spend a lot more time than usual studying.

CHAPTER FIFTY-FIVE

The hotel was fully booked and there was almost no free table at seven a.m. when Klara came down for breakfast. She was tense and nervous. It was the first day of the NATO meeting, and she wanted to start with a proper, unrushed morning meal. She had invested in a light laptop, with subscriptions to several state-of-the-art on-line dictionaries and had added lists of military terminology that she had prepared herself. It was helpful to be able to link her own comments and notes to the technical jargon and incomprehensible acronyms she had found browsing articles on the web. She was as prepared as she would ever be.

When Lennart confirmed that NATO had requested information about her and she had been cleared, he had been particularly helpful advising her on what to read up on to prepare for the job. His enthusiasm about her new assignment made her wonder how much communication there actually was between the different departments of the Swedish armed forces. It was obvious that he was happy to see her work for NATO.

Eva-Karin had recommended a hotel close to the event venue and she guessed that most of the people staying there were, in some way or another, connected to the meeting. In the lobby a young man in a neon pink t-shirt blurting out *YSFW de-*

mands raise in tobacco tax was handing out blister packs with nicotine chewing gum.

Why not? Klara thought and accepted one on her way back to her room after breakfast. She would find someone to give it to, there were still enough smokers around. The hand-out must have been a success, because the young man and his supply had disappeared by the time she left.

The air was fresh, the sun hadn't starting warming yet, but it was going to be a nice day. Klara walked the stretch between her hotel and the meeting venue in less than ten minutes. The first security check was done by the police on the street by the riot fences. She had her pass and her summons ready, and the police officer checked both against a list. The young uniformed police officer looked at the photograph in the passport and back at Klara.

"Not a bad picture," he said, smiling while he pushed the fence open to let her in. The security guards in the entrance hall also had lists of interpreters and participants and were ticking them off as they came in. She had to pass her handbag, briefcase, and computer through the metal detector and walk through the portal machine. In spite of having made sure she was not wearing metal buttons or buckles and that she did not carry any metal object, the machine beeped loudly.

"Step over here, please."

The man was middle-aged and wore a blue uniform. He was not military, probably a security guard, maybe a NATO employee. Klara obediently emptied her pockets onto a small tray while the man screened her with a hand-held device. It stayed silent.

"Must be something you had in your pockets," he said and started poking among the things on the tray.

"Here's the culprit! Nothing gets past our equipment! Not even the metal foil in a cigarette pack," he said proudly.

The blister package with nicotine gum blinked in his hand as he handed it back to her.

"You can keep it," Klara said. "I don't need them."

"By all means, take it. Lots of people seem to be using that stuff. Does it actually work?"

"I don't know, never tried."

"There's a smoker's balcony at the end of the corridor by the toilets, should you need it. Have a nice day!"

The venue was on the first floor, a spacious conference hall with the wall towards the street all in glass. On the other end wall hung a banner showing the flags of all the countries participating. The delegates were to sit at tables forming an inner oval, with a grand flower arrangement in the center. There was another ring of tables surrounding the main oval, for the advisers and consultants. Nicely designed carafes with water and glasses were placed on all the tables, as well as in the interpreter booths.

I hope the Swedish booth is well placed, thought Klara. She did a better job if she was able to see the speaker.

She found the Swedish booth empty, it was the last one on the left-hand side. The same set-up as at the Parliament's plenary meetings, three interpreters per booth. As she always drank a lot of water during a work shift, she wanted to check out where the restrooms were. Right behind the booth there was a door. She peeked in and there they were, plus the balcony for smokers the guard had mentioned.

She plugged in her computer, started it and got online. It was only 8:25 and the meeting was scheduled for 9:00. People kept dropping in. She assumed that the military staff would be super-punctual, but that might just be prejudice. Nothing very specific about the objective of the meeting had been made public, as Klara had scrutinized absolutely everything published, gathering as much background information as possible.

The media had speculated about whether sanctions against Iran were going to be an issue, but that had not been confirmed. She was genuinely curious aobut the reasons for this extra-ordinary meeting, and also rather nervous.

The other booths were filling up and Klara nodded greetings to several colleagues. She saw Elsa Martinez from the EU Parliament sitting in the Spanish booth, but Klara didn't feel like making small talk, so she pretended to be busy with her computer, and just waved to her.

Maria and Ulla, the other two Swedish interpreters, came together. They all did English-Swedish-English, but Maria also did Dutch-Swedish and Portuguese-Swedish, whereas Ulla had French and German as working languages.

"It's going to be tough with Italian on relay all the time," said Ulla. "But the Greeks are generally not that active. Unless it's going to be about their economy..."

"Do we have any Swedish interpreters who do Greek?" wondered Klara.

"Of course we do, but it is impossible to cover all spoken languages on a meeting like this. Think about it: each booth with three of us will in average cover nine to twelve source languages, out of the twenty-some spoken, so for some speakers, we will always have to rely on our colleagues in other booths," Maria said.

Of course I knew, I just never did the math, Klara thought.

"I have always suspected that they have a secret pecking order for the interpreters they call," Ulla said.

They agreed on which order they would be working, Maria and Ulla starting out, except if a speaker in their own source languages would take the floor. She was grateful for the chance to listen to them, and check words and expressions she ought to keep in mind. Both of them had done NATO conferences before and seemed totally at ease.

Assuming that no one spoke Spanish during the first hour, she wouldn't be on until ten

"You're lucky, the Spanish guy hardly ever speaks except when asked a specific question," Ulla said as if reading her thoughts. "It's not like when Javier Solana was Secretary General, he often spoke Spanish."

Javier Solana had been Minister of Education when Klara was at university. His nomination as General Secretary of NATO came as a surprise, but he had done a great job. She couldn't help feeling a little proud.

"Will it disturb you if I use this?" Klara asked, nodding towards her computer.

"No, but make sure that the sound is off and keep it far enough from the microphone to avoid the clicking keys to be heard over the headsets. Some delegates find that very annoying."

Maria wound a handkerchief around a number of bracelets that she couldn't or wouldn't take off, so they wouldn't rattle.

"Here," Ulla said and handed Klara a package of nicotine chewing gum. "You smoke, don't you? There was a girl handing them out in the hotel lobby."

"I quit a long time ago. I got one too. It was a guy that handed them out at our hotel. It made the metal detector react so I left it with the security guard."

"Rather cool, this initiative, and good timing. This place is practically teeming with journalists, everybody wondering what it's about. They were taking pictures and interviewing that girl at our hotel," Maria said. "Good PR for them if the press buys it."

"The chewing gum makes sense here where you can't buy snuff," Ulla said. As if reminded, she took a round box of snuff from her purse, opened the lid and put away the used little pillow of tobacco from her mouth in the special compartment for used portions. Then she put in a fresh one, deep back in between the cheek and her molars. "I missed the nicotine kick too much to quit totally, and turned to smoke-free tobacco," she excused herself, looking guilty. "At least I don't poison anybody else. Though it is becoming a problem, because you can only buy it in Scandinavia now, so I always have to remember to stock up when I go home."

Klara was glad to end the small talk. Everyone was in place and the meeting was about to start. The Italians wore the flashiest uniforms and the French had the largest number of security guards, so many that some had to go back out. The delegate from Sweden was around thirty-five years old, with glasses, and dressed as a civilian in a gray suit. A typical bureaucrat. The Norwegian Secretary General, whom the Norwegians, almost two decades ago, had proudly pronounced "the most handsome prime minister in Europe", walked in, nodding politely to the people present.

The Spanish delegate was a tough-looking, sinewy little man with a moustache and a gray-brown uniform with four blinking stars on his shoulder. Too old to speak English, Klara noted. Mostly only Spaniards under forty spoke English. Languages used to be badly taught in Spain, both in elementary school and at higher levels of education, and just a decade ago only those who had the opportunity to study abroad mastered another language. The fact that languages had been considered of minor importance during the Franco dictatorship had actually contributed to Klara's career, and once he was gone, it had taken some time for the country to get up to speed.

When the opening speech finished, it was not yet quite 9:30. The meeting was going to be about Syria and the different actors intervening in the conflict. Klara decided to go to the bathroom before it was time to take her turn. Maria was interpreting and she didn't dare risk a whisper being caught by the microphone, so she wrote "loo" on the steno pad between her and Ulla.

She seemed to sense Klara's nervousness. She smiled and nodded.

A handful of people were talking in the corridor, and on the balcony, a few were smoking. She was happy not to share the craving any more. Not knowing any of the people present very well, she just nodded at them in greeting and went into the restroom.

She entered the stall and closed the door behind her. As she was about to hang her handbag on a hook on the wall, a blast blew the door open and slammed her violently in the back. She fell forward, her head hitting the tiled wall.

CHAPTER FIFTY-SIX

People had already gathered by the cordons. Disoriented, Klara sat down on the stairs outside the hotel. She had double vision and her ears were ringing so loudly that she could hear nothing else. Her eyes would not keep up with the movements of her head and the dizziness made her nauseous.

She just sat there, completely numb, still unable to grasp what had happened. Her brain did not seem to be working and her head felt like it would explode.

Someone put a jacket over her shoulders, took hold of her arm and pulled her to her feet. "Glad you made it, Klara," a remotely familiar voice said. She slowly lifted her eyes and managed to focus.

The relief of seeing someone she knew alive made her cry. He led her away. No one stopped them. Everyone seemed to move like robots, programmed, not thinking by themselves.

He had held her arm like that before, been there, at her left side, she knew. They walked a couple of blocks, to his silver BMW. After throwing something in a wastepaper basket on the sidewalk, he unlocked the doors with the remote and helped her into the passenger seat.

"Sorry, I didn't trust you enough to prevent you from coming," he said while he peeled off a pair of thin latex gloves.

Starting the car, he continued: "Couldn't take any risks. You would have done the same, wouldn't you?"

He turned on the radio. Klara's ears were still ringing and she had trouble hearing, but made out a shaky voice reporting from some bomb-site.

A bomb-site? Why is he here? She struggled to clear her head. *Why am I shaking so bad?*

"We have to get out of town before the police cordon off the highways," he said and then drove in silence for a beat. The city seemed deserted; there was almost no traffic at all. A smile formed on his lips and then he laughed a little. Klara stared at him.

"It's strange," Fahrid said, "that you, of all people, should survive. How come you got away with just scratches?"

A trace of reality clicked in Klara's brain and it dawned on her that she should have died too. How come she was alive? She searched laboriously for the answer.

"The bathroom," she whispered. "I was in the loo."

They passed a sign indicating the highway.

"Wipe your face Klara, there are wet wipes in the glove compartment. You look awful." he said handing her his sunglasses. "And put these on. Your eyes are starting to bruise."

In a while I will be able to think... she thought. As if on autopilot she lowered the sunblock mirror and looked at herself. Her mascara had smeared and she had been bleeding from her left ear. She rubbed the dry patches of blood, but they wouldn't go away.

Fahrid took a fresh moist tissue from the pack.

"Try this," he said handing it to her.

She was struggling to clear her head. Then she felt that they were losing speed and changed focus to the road ahead. A patrol car half blocked the exit to the highway. Two policemen were working on getting the cordon ready. Fahrid pulled out a handgun from under the seat and slid it under his thigh.

"Don't do anything stupid now, or you will be accessory to a double cop kill," he said patting the gun.

Their vehicle crept slowly towards the policemen. Fahrid made an inquiring gesture. One of the policemen looked at them through the windshield, seemed to check out the car and then waved to them to go on. As they entered the highway Klara let out her breath.

"Just what I thought." He touched his clean-shaven chin with his knuckles. "You came in handy. They're not looking for a smart couple in a nice sports car." Though visibly relaxed, he did not put the gun back under the seat.

Now the reporter on the radio was saying that almost all of the high-ranking military officers were injured or dead. The number of fatalities was still unknown.

"I'm going to be the hero of the caliphate," he exclaimed. "How many survivors do you reckon there will be? You were in there. What did it look like?"

Finally reality registered: *Fahrid had done this... this massacre. He was guilty of the unspeakable thing that had happened...*

"What have you done?" she shouted, white-hot fury building up inside her. "Bastard. Inhuman son of a bitch." She turned on him with her fists, punching as hard as she could but he just laughed, blocking her blows with his right arm, without even looking. Realizing that there was no point in trying to hurt him she returned to clutching the handbag in her lap.

They were driving through a sparsely populated area and there was almost no one else on the road, in either direction.

"Did you know your fuck-buddy was spying on you? On Mossad's behalf?"   he asked.

Klara stared at him in silence.

"In a way I owe this to you. When I discovered that connection between your lover and Mossad I had to follow up.

319

That led me to Benjamin Gold, the Israeli diplomat. He sang like a bird before I cut his dick off. Apart from all this," Fahrid said with a gesture encompassing everything, "he confirmed that you are an Al-Fatah agent. Such a jerk... Deserved to die."

She tried to put order in her head. Anders ... Mossad... the assassinated diplomat, nothing made sense.

"So, tell me, how were you involved in the protection of Atef Bseiso? Mossad must have been so frustrated when you blew their plans to kill him in Madrid."

The name triggered her memory. For how long is that lie going to mark my life? she wondered, but remained silent.

Used to her lack of response he suddenly changed the subject: "Now it's going to be really interesting to see how Mossad explains that their bomb blew up the NATO meeting."

He seemed to need to boast about his achievements and pretended not to notice how appalled Klara was. "What a victory!"

If I can only get a minute to myself, maybe I can think of a way to get out of here.

"I need to go to the loo," she said. "I never did my business there."

"You'll have to use the ditch, so I can keep an eye on you," he said.

"But I need to change tampons...."

"I don't give a shit, you're not going anywhere on your own."

"In that case I'll wait," she said, as dignified as she could manage.

Shortly after crossing the border to Germany, he did stop at a petrol station. The toilets were at the back, out of view from the till. He went in with her. There, he grabbed her around the waist and pressed her to him. When he kissed her and forced his tongue into her mouth, she almost threw up.

He must have noticed, because his immediate reaction was to bite her lower lip hard. Her hand flew up, but he reacted with lightning speed and caught her wrist before she could hit him.

"There's some life in you again." he said. He was excited, high on his deed.

As soon as he loosened his grip on her waist, she took a step back, away from him.

"It's kind of special that you are a part of my two most remarkable achievements ever."

The words hit Klara like a blow in midriff. She steadied herself against the sink.

"Lucky I didn't kill you once I got the documents," he went on. "We haven't got the time now, but tonight I'm going to fuck you. Kinky, as you ought to be dead..."

"You sick bastard," she hissed.

"But don't get your hopes up..." He said it with a mean sneer. "Nothing personal, no hard feelings." He laughed, pretending to shoot her with his index finger. The meaning was crystal clear. She was only going to live as long as she was useful to him.

There was only cold water in the faucet. She washed her face several times and bathed her neck. She cupped her hands and drank thirstily. The water tasted of blood from her mangled lip. There were no paper towels and she searched for a tissue in her handbag. Her fingertips touched the knife. It felt hot and cold at the same time. She carefully pushed the stiletto up the sleeve of her blouse. It took too long and he got suspicious.

"Let me see what you've got there," he barked and snatched her handbag.

While he was going through the contents of her purse and checking that her cell phone was still switched off, she let the stiletto handle glide down into her palm.

When he had made sure that there was nothing else of interest in the bag, he didn't return it to her but put it on the shelf above the sink. Then he opened his fly and started urinating right there, not bothering to use the toilet. Klara didn't think at all. With one step she was behind him. She grabbed hold of his hair with her left hand and forced his head back as she slid the knife over his throat with all her strength.

Blood sprayed, covering the mirror above the sink. A first gush, then it drained and covered again, the blood pumping out in spurts. His arms flailed out, trying to grab her. Hypnotized, she stared at him in the mirror. There was astonishment, not pain, in his face. He was moving his lips, but no sound came out. When his knees gave way, his body grew heavy and he slipped out of her grip. He was drooling a little as he sank down onto the floor. The gun at the back of his waistband clattered as it hit the floor.

She was still wearing his jacket and wiped the knife on a sleeve without taking her eyes off him. The blood was spurting with less force each time. His eyes became glassy. Urine was still leaking out of his lifeless body and made a growing dark stain on his blue Calvin Klein jeans. Klara turned around and vomited into the sink. She couldn't stand the sight of his exposed penis and pulled his shirt out of the trousers to cover it. Then, with trembling fingers, she searched for the car keys in his trouser pocket. She took off his jacket and covered him with it.

It was a little after eleven thirty. Only one hour ago she would have finished her first interpreting shift at a NATO meeting. Instead, she had murdered a man.

She closed the door and walked out into the sunshine.

As soon as she was on the highway again, she turned on her cellphone. It beeped and showed messages. Klara thanked her lucky stars that the Germans despised speed limits and drove as fast as she dared. She had to find somewhere to turn and go back. Return to Amsterdam. To report what had happened.

An anonymous voice announced nine new messages.

The first one was from Anders.

"Klara, this is terrible," he said. "Call me as soon as you can."

Not if you can, she thought.

His voice was like the umbilical cord to a normal life, a cord that now had to be severed, a life that she would never again have access to.

The insight was devastating. She had crossed the line when she killed Fahrid.

Next message was from Lennart, speaking in a very everyday tone of voice. "Please contact me as soon as you get this message, the usual number."

The third was from Louis. His voice sounded broken and tired, but his message was clear: "Run, Klara, run for your life. I saw you on the tape from the surveillance camera outside the venue. If the guy you're with is the perpetrator they will believe you're an accomplice and I won't be able to protect you."

The phone slipped from her hand and fell down to the floor. Tears welled up in her eyes and made it difficult to see. Mechanically she reduced the speed. She didn't register that she had passed the first exit.

I survived and therefore I am a traitor. Will the truth convince anyone? Will I even get a chance to explain?

Klara jumped when a passing car honked at her. The speedometer showed thirty, way too slow for the autobahn.

What shall I do...? Is there anything I can do? she asked herself. *Or should I just step on the gas and crash into the nearest road shoulder?*

She pulled up at a service area with a café. It was practically empty and she parked close to the entrance. A cold and uninviting place, the lighting neon. It had just been cleaned and smelled of disinfectant. The coffee was bitter and black.

Minutes later, she had made her decision and was studying the map on her cell.

Zürich was within reach...

EPILOGUE

When authorities from the Emirates confirmed that the man found dead in the toilet at the petrol station just outside Enschede, near the border to Germany, had a fake passport, both the CIA and the Swedish security services became interested. With their help, the man's identity was established. He was the Saudi-born spy that the Swedes had been trying to track down because of his illicit activities in Sweden. The suspicion that he was behind the terrorist attack on the NATO meeting was confirmed when the hotel staff at l'Europe identified him, and his connection to the environmental organization was uncovered.

Mossad never surfaced in the investigation; instead several minor jihadist groups claimed responsibility for the deed.

YS 2000, the silent undetectable ship also known as the Visby, got major media attention in connection with the events and the stories about the terrorist involved.

Klara was officially declared missing. She was she not among the injured and no body was found.

When Anders' taxi halted outside the villa in Malmö the following weekend, Karin was waiting for him on the stairs. She held a red frame with photographs.

The frame had been sent from the credit card company with a letter from an elegant hotel in Scheveningen, The Netherlands, alleging that Mr. and Mrs. Källström had left the frame in the hotel room when they spent a weekend there about a month ago. The hotel staff had not succeeded in retrieving a correct home address and had therefore turned to the credit card company, which now had the pleasure of returning the frame with the photographs to its owners.

Karin, however, had never been to Scheveningen. The frame held pictures of a couple of persons unknown to her: a young man squinting at the camera from a sunbed on a beach, and a young woman straddling an antique chair by a window with beautiful curtains. A photograph of Anders that she had never seen before was wedged between them. He was wearing a white shirt open at the neck and the navy cardigan Karin had given him for his birthday. Smiling at the camera, he was leaning against a balcony parapet and beyond him, there was an amazing winter-view of Stockholm.

Thank you!

I am deeply grateful to many people for their contributions to this book:

Line Valen, who translated Den vidunderliga utsikten (An Amazing View) into English, thank you from the bottom of my heart. This would not have happened without you.

Elin Barnes, my daughter, thank you for reading it all, including the deleted parts, debating with me and helping me see where the story was halting. Thanks to you, it is much better than the original.

Mischa LLuch, my son, thank you for always believing in me and supporting me, and Virginia, thank you for the beautiful logo.

Lyle Krewson, thank you for reading innumerable versions of the text and bearing with me during the (long) process of modifying and trying to improve this book.

And **Lynn Knowles**, thank you, for reading, correcting and improving my manuscript. The changes were substantial and you were my best editor.

Yoga is alchemy.
If you are willing to stick with it, yoga changes you.

What if you could use the time on your yoga mat as a sport specific training for the game of life? Yoga teaches how to connect to your body and mind in a more intentional, conscious way. It shifts and shapes you in subtle, yet profound ways. Even if you may have a wonderful yoga teacher, the asanas in conjunction with your own inner wisdom becomes the ultimate teacher.

The Alchemy of Yoga: Living yoga off the mat will change you in a way you might find surprising. It will teach you much about yourself and how to engage flexibility, strength, balance, and surrender in your daily life. It takes you on a deeper exploration of the larger questions yoga always inspires- who am I and why am I here?

This is the ideal book for everyday people who simply want to enjoy life to the fullest and make a difference to the world around them. Yoga is not just for the young, beautiful, healthy people of this world. It is for all, including you.

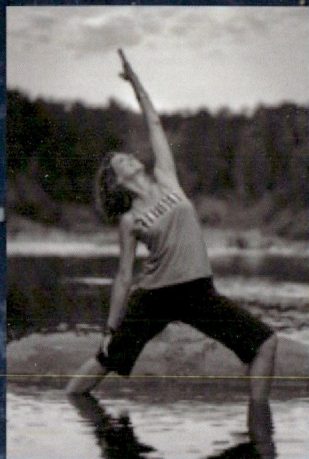

Wendy Reese Hartmann is a 500 hour certified yoga teacher, Holistic Personal Trainer, Mindful Living Mentor, author, and speaker.

ISBN 9780692784433

90000

9 780692 784433